The Random Walk Path of Pál Révész in Probability

The Random Walk Path of Pál Révész in Probability

Guest Editors

Antónia Földes
Endre Csáki

MDPI

Basel • Beijing • Wuhan • Barcelona • Belgrade • Novi Sad • Cluj • Manchester

Guest Editors
Antónia Földes
Department of Mathematics,
College of Staten Island
The City University of New York
New York
USA

Endre Csáki
Department of Probability Theory
Alfréd Rényi Institute of Mathematics
Budapest
Hungary

Editorial Office
MDPI AG
Grosspeteranlage 5
4052 Basel, Switzerland

This is a reprint of the Special Issue, published open access by the journal *Entropy* (ISSN 1099-4300), freely accessible at: https://www.mdpi.com/journal/entropy/special_issues/X5EJCO3JQ0.

For citation purposes, cite each article independently as indicated on the article page online and as indicated below:

Lastname, A.A.; Lastname, B.B. Article Title. *Journal Name* **Year**, *Volume Number*, Page Range.

ISBN 978-3-7258-4555-2 (Hbk)
ISBN 978-3-7258-4556-9 (PDF)
https://doi.org/10.3390/books978-3-7258-4556-9

Contents

Preface

With the passing of Pál Révész in 2022, the world of probability theory suffered a great loss. His trailblazing contributions are reflected in his influential books on a range of important topics: *Laws of Large Numbers* (1968), *Strong Approximations in Probability and Statistics* (1981, written together with Miklós Csörgo), *Random Walks of Infinitely Many Particles* (1990), and *Random Walk in Random and Non-Random Environments* (1994, 2005, 2013). He had many collaborators and devoted students around the world, and he is deeply missed. We (the guest editors of this volume) had the privilege of working with him and his closest collaborator, Miklós Csörgo, for many decades. We now present this volume of scientific papers by his friends, collaborators, students, and fellow probabilists, who wish to honor his memory. Each paper is closely related to Pál Révész's work and groundbreaking ideas. We hope these papers will inspire a new generation of probabilists, who, though they will not have the opportunity to meet him, will surely build upon his remarkable legacy.

Antónia Földes and Endre Csáki
Guest Editors

entropy

MDPI

erspective

Some Open Questions About the Anisotropic Random Walks

ndre Csáki [1] and Antónia Földes [2,*]

1 Alfréd Rényi Institute of Mathematics, P.O. Box 127, H-1364 Budapest, Hungary; csaki.endre@renyi.hu
2 Department of Mathematics, College of Staten Island, The City University of New York, 2800 Victory Blvd., Staten Island, NY 10314, USA
* Correspondence: antonia.foldes@csi.cuny.edu

Abstract: Between 2007 and 2018, we collaborated extensively with Pál Révész and Miklós Csörgő on many of the problems discussed in this paper. Over the past six years, we have continued to explore these issues, and here, we present some of the most intriguing open questions in these areas. This paper compiles key results from a dozen of our previous works, providing the necessary background to frame these compelling unresolved questions.

Keywords: anisotropic random walk; strong approximation; two-dimensional Wiener process; local time

MSC: 60F17; 60G50; 60J65; 60F15; 60J10

1. Introduction

The investigation of the two-dimensional anisotropic random walk goes back almost fifty years. The first papers were written by Silver, Shuler and Lindenberg [1]; Shuler [2]; Seshadri, Lindenberg and Shuler [3] and Westcott [4] followed by Heyde [5,6]; Roerdink and Shuler [7]; and den Hollander [8]. Let us begin with the definition. We consider a symmetric nearest-neighbor random walk on $\mathbb{Z}^2$, such that its transition probabilities only depend on the vertical coordinate. To be precise, here is the formal definition: the anisotropic random walk $\{\mathbf{C}(N) = (C_1(N), C_2(N)),\ N = 0,1,2,\ldots\}$ on $\mathbb{Z}^2$ has the following transition probabilities:

$$\begin{aligned}
\mathbf{P}(\mathbf{C}(N+1) &= (k+1,j)|\mathbf{C}(N)=(k,j)) = \\
\mathbf{P}(\mathbf{C}(N+1) &= (k-1,j)|\mathbf{C}(N)=(k,j)) = \frac{1}{2}-p_j, \\
\mathbf{P}(\mathbf{C}(N+1) &= (k,j+1)|\mathbf{C}(N)=(k,j)) = \\
\mathbf{P}(\mathbf{C}(N+1) &= (k,j-1)|\mathbf{C}(N)=(k,j)) = p_j, \qquad (1)
\end{aligned}$$

for $(k,j) \in \mathbb{Z}^2$, $N = 0,1,2,\ldots$ We will suppose that $0 < p_j \le 1/2$ and $\min_{j\in\mathbb{Z}} p_j < 1/2$ and that $\mathbf{C}(0) = (0,0)$.

Obviously, this model contains the simple symmetric walk, when $p_i = 1/4$ for all $i = 0, \pm 1, \pm 2, \ldots$ The simple symmetric walk has been discussed extensively, so we just mention a few important works here: Erdős and Taylor [9], Dvoretzky and Erdős [10] and Révész [11]. The condition $\min_{j\in\mathbb{Z}} p_j < 1/2$ excludes the case where the walk is one-dimensional. However, the case when all $p_i = 1/2$ except one is a particularly famous case. More precisely, if $p_0 = 1/4$ and all the other $p_i = 1/2$, we have the **two-dimensional comb** model, which has been investigated by Weiss and Havlin [12]; Bertacchi [13]; Bertacchi and Zucca [14]; and us [15,16]. We will mention some other special cases later on.

2. Recurrence and Transience

One of the most important issues is whether a particular random walk is transient or recurrent. We investigated this question for the anisotropic random walk in [17]. It turned out that to obtain criteria for recurrence, only the simple application of the famous

Nash–Williams theorem is required [18]. For completeness, we recall this theorem here. To do so, we need some notations and definitions. Let $(\mathbf{X}, \mathbf{Y}, p)$ be a Markov chain with a countable state space $\mathbf{X}$ and a process $\mathbf{Y}$ with transition probabilities $p(\mathbf{u}, \mathbf{v})$. The chain is called *reversible* if there exist strictly positive weights $\pi_{\mathbf{u}}$ for all $\mathbf{u} \in \mathbf{X}$ such that

$$\pi_{\mathbf{u}} p(\mathbf{u}, \mathbf{v}) = \pi_{\mathbf{v}} p(\mathbf{v}, \mathbf{u}). \tag{2}$$

For reversible chains, it is convenient to introduce the notation

$$a(\mathbf{u}, \mathbf{v}) := \pi_{\mathbf{u}} p(\mathbf{u}, \mathbf{v}).$$

Our anisotropic walk introduced above is a Markov chain on the state space $\mathbf{X} = \mathbb{Z}^2$, with the transition probabilities defined in (1), and it is reversible with the strictly positive weights

$$\pi(k, j) = \frac{1}{p_j},$$

with $p_j, j = 0, \pm 1, \pm 2, \ldots$ defined in (1). Thus, we have, for neighboring sites,

$$\begin{aligned} a((k,j),(k,j+1)) &= a((k,j),(k,j-1)) = 1 \\ a((k,j),(k+1,j)) &= a((k,j),(k-1,j)) = \frac{1}{2p_j} - 1 \end{aligned} \tag{3}$$

(and for non-nearest-neighbor sites $a(\cdot, \cdot) = 0$). Our Markov chain is also time-homogeneous and irreducible (it is possible to get to any state from any state with positive probability). The invariant measure is defined by

$$\mu(\mathbf{u}) = \sum_{\mathbf{v}} \mu(\mathbf{v}) p(\mathbf{v}, \mathbf{u}),$$

where the summation goes over the four nearest neighbors of $\mathbf{u}$. For $\mathbf{u} = (k, j)$, we obtain

$$\mu(\mathbf{u}) = \mu(k, j) = \pi(k, j) = \frac{1}{p_j}, \quad (k, j) \in \mathbb{Z}^2. \tag{4}$$

Now we recall the Nash–Williams theorem:

Theorem 1 ([18]). *Suppose that $(\mathbf{X}, \mathbf{Y}, p)$ is a reversible Markov chain and that $\mathbf{X} = \bigcup_{k=0}^{\infty} \Lambda^k$ where Λ^k are disjoint. Suppose further that $\mathbf{u} \in \Lambda^k$ and $a(\mathbf{u}, \mathbf{v}) > 0$ together imply that $\mathbf{v} \in \Lambda^{k-1} \bigcup \Lambda^k \bigcup \Lambda^{k+1}$, and that for each k, the sum $\sum_{\mathbf{u} \in \Lambda^k, \mathbf{v} \in \mathbf{X}} a(\mathbf{u}, \mathbf{v}) < \infty$. Let $[\Lambda^k, \Lambda^{k+1}]$ denote the set of pairs $(\mathbf{u}, \mathbf{v})$ such that $\mathbf{u} \in \Lambda^k$ and $\mathbf{v} \in \Lambda^{k+1}$. The Markov chain is recurrent if*

$$\sum_{k=0}^{\infty} \left(\sum_{(\mathbf{u},\mathbf{v}) \in [\Lambda^k, \Lambda^{k+1}]} a(\mathbf{u}, \mathbf{v}) \right)^{-1} = \infty. \tag{5}$$

To apply this theorem, let Λ^k be the set of the $8k$ lattice points on a square of width $2k$, centered at the origin. Furthermore, let $[\Lambda^k, \Lambda^{k+1}]$ be the set of the $8k + 4$ nearest-neighbor pairs (edges) between Λ^k and Λ^{k+1}.

It is easy to see from (3) that the sum in (5) is equal to

$$\sum_{k=0}^{\infty} \left(2 \left(\sum_{j=-k}^{k} \left(\frac{1}{2p_j} - 1 \right) + \sum_{j=-k}^{k} 1 \right) \right)^{-1} = \sum_{k=0}^{\infty} \left(\sum_{j=-k}^{k} \frac{1}{p_j} \right)^{-1}.$$

Consequently, we have

Theorem 2. *The anisotropic walk is recurrent if*

$$\sum_{k=0}^{\infty}\left(\sum_{j=-k}^{k}\frac{1}{p_j}\right)^{-1}=\infty. \tag{6}$$

This implies the following.

Corollary 1. *If* $\min_{j\in\mathbb{Z}} p_j > 0$, *then the anisotropic walk is recurrent.*

Of course, it is very tempting to believe that the converse of this statement is true as well. Unfortunately, *we cannot prove* that if

$$\sum_{k=0}^{\infty}\left(\sum_{j=-k}^{k}\frac{1}{p_j}\right)^{-1}<\infty, \tag{7}$$

then the anisotropic walk is transient, but we managed to show a somewhat weaker result:

Theorem 3 ([17]). *Assume that*

$$\sum_{j=-k}^{k}\frac{1}{p_j}=Ck^{1+A}+O(k^{1+A-\delta}),\quad k\to\infty \tag{8}$$

for some $C>0$, $A>0$ *and* $0<\delta\le 1$. *Then, the anisotropic random walk is transient.*

So, our first open question is

Question 1. *Find an if and only if criterion for the recurrence of the anisotropic walk .*

3. Strong Approximation

Let us start with some history. After the early works given in [1,2], Heyde [5] proved an almost sure approximation for $C_2(N)$, the second coordinate of the anisotropic walk, under the following conditions:

$$n^{-1}\sum_{j=1}^{n}p_j^{-1}=2\gamma+o(n^{-\eta}),\qquad n^{-1}\sum_{j=1}^{n}p_{-j}^{-1}=2\gamma+o(n^{-\eta}) \tag{9}$$

as $n\to\infty$ for some constants γ, $1<\gamma<\infty$ and $1/2<\eta<\infty$.

In our paper [19], we proved for $\{\mathbf{C}(N),\ N=0,1,2,\ldots\}$ the following joint strong approximation theorem:

Theorem 4. *Under condition* (9), *with* $1/2<\eta\le 1$ *on an appropriate probability space for the random walk* $\{\mathbf{C}(N)=(C_1(N),C_2(N)),\ N=0,1,2,\ldots\}$, *one can construct two independent standard Wiener processes* $\{W_1(t);\,t\ge 0\}$, $\{W_2(t);\,t\ge 0\}$ *so that, as* $N\to\infty$, *we have, with any* $\varepsilon>0$,

$$\left|C_1(N)-W_1\left(\frac{\gamma-1}{\gamma}N\right)\right|+\left|C_2(N)-W_2\left(\frac{1}{\gamma}N\right)\right|=O(N^{5/8-\eta/4+\varepsilon})\quad a.s.$$

We also considered a special case of this result which dealt with the so-called periodic case. The anisotropic walk is called **periodic** if $p_i=p_{i+L}$ for each $i\in\mathbb{Z}$ with some positive integer $L\ge 1$. By indicating this periodicity with the superscript P, we obtained a somewhat better approximation, as the next theorem shows.

- **Periodic walk**

Theorem 5. *On an appropriate probability space for the periodic anisotropic random walk,*

$$\{\mathbf{C^P}(N) = (C_1^P(N), C_2^P(N));\ N = 0,1,2,\ldots\},$$

one can construct two independent standard Wiener processes, $\{W_1(t);\ t \geq 0\}$ *and* $\{W_2(t);\ t \geq 0\}$*, so that, as* $N \to \infty$*, we have, with any* $\varepsilon > 0$*,*

$$\left|C_1^P(N) - W_1\left(\frac{\gamma - 1}{\gamma} N\right)\right| + \left|C_2^P(N) - W_2\left(\frac{1}{\gamma} N\right)\right| = O(N^{1/4+\varepsilon}) \quad a.s., \tag{10}$$

where

$$\gamma = \frac{\sum_{j=1}^{L} p_j^{-1}}{2L}. \tag{11}$$

Remark 1. *In what follows, we will talk about the different important classes of anisotropic random walks, like the two-dimensional comb anisotropic random walk, the periodic anisotropic random walk and many others. To simplify the language from now on, we will often call these the (two-dimensional) comb walk and periodic walk, thus avoiding the use of anisotropic random expression.*

It is a natural question to ask whether Theorem 4 can be generalized for the case where, in the two conditions of (9), one permits different γ values. The first such result was achieved by Heyde et al. [20]. (see also Horvath [21]). To formulate their result, we need some notations and definitions.

Let

$$n^{-1} \sum_{j=1}^{n} p_j^{-1} = 2\gamma_1 + \epsilon_n, \qquad n^{-1} \sum_{j=-n}^{-1} p_j^{-1} = 2\gamma_2 + \epsilon_n^*, \tag{12}$$

and define the function $\sigma^2(y)$ as

$$\sigma^2(y) = \begin{cases} \frac{1}{\gamma_1} & \text{for} \quad y \geq 0, \\ \frac{1}{\gamma_2} & \text{for} \quad y < 0. \end{cases}$$

Let $\{Y(t), t \geq 0\}$ be a diffusion process on the same probability space as $\{C_2(N)\}$ defined by

$$Y(t) = W(A^{-1}(t)), \quad t \geq 0,$$

where $\{W(t), t \geq 0\}$ is a Wiener process,

$$A(t) = \int_0^t \sigma^{-2}(W(s))\, ds,$$

and $A^{-1}(\cdot)$ is the inverse of $A(\cdot)$. If $\gamma_1 \neq \gamma_2$, then $Y(t)$ is a so-called oscillating Brownian motion, namely, a diffusion with the speed measure $m(dy) = 2\sigma^{-2}(y)dy$ (see, e.g., Keilson and Wellner [22]).

Now, we are ready to formulate Heyde et al.'s result:

Theorem 6 ([20]). *Suppose that in* (12), ϵ_k *and* ϵ_k^* *are* $o(1)$ *as* $k \to \infty$*. Then, for* $C_2(\cdot)$*, we obtain the second coordinate of the anisotropic walk as* $N \to \infty$*:*

$$\sup_{0 \leq t \leq N} |N^{-1/2} C_2([Nt]) - Y(t)| \to 0 \quad a.s.$$

Our aim was to have a general enough strong approximation for both coordinates with rates. This was partially achieved as follows.

Theorem 7 ([23]). *Suppose that*

$$n^{-1}\sum_{j=1}^{n} p_j^{-1} = 2\gamma_1 + o(n^{-\eta}), \qquad n^{-1}\sum_{j=1}^{n} p_{-j}^{-1} = 2\gamma_2 + o(n^{-\eta}) \tag{13}$$

as $n \to \infty$ for some constants $1 < \max(\gamma_1, \gamma_2) < \infty$ and $1/2 < \eta \leq 1$. Under the conditions given in (13), on an appropriate probability space for the anisotropic random walk $\{\mathbf{C}(N) = (C_1(N), C_2(N));\ N = 0,1,2,\ldots\}$, one can construct two independent standard Wiener processes, $\{W_1(t);\, t \geq 0\}$ and $\{W_2(t);\, t \geq 0\}$, so that, as $N \to \infty$, we have, with any $\varepsilon > 0$,

$$\left|C_1(N) - W_1\left(N - A_2^{-1}(N)\right)\right| + \left|C_2(N) - W_2\left(A_2^{-1}(N)\right)\right| = O(N^{5/8-\eta/4+\varepsilon}) \quad a.s., \tag{14}$$

where $A_2(t) = \gamma_1 \int_0^t I(W_2(s) \geq 0)\, ds + \gamma_2 \int_0^t I(W_2(s) < 0)\, ds$ and $A_2^{-1}(\cdot)$ is its inverse.

Remark 2. *We have to say that our goal was only partially achieved, as the $\gamma_1 = \gamma_2 = 1$ case is not contained in the theorem.*

Remark 3. *Observe that in the case that $\gamma_1 = \gamma_2 = \gamma > 1$, $A(t) = \gamma t$, $A^{-1}(t) = t/\gamma$ and $Y(t) = W(t/\gamma)$ is a time-changed Wiener process, and we recover Theorem 4.*

To shed some light on the extent of this result, we mention some important classes of anisotropic random walks.

- **Comb-Type walk:** We begin by defining an arbitrary subset $B \in \mathbb{Z}$ such that

$$p_i = 1/4 \quad \text{if} \quad i \in B \quad \text{and} \quad p_i = 1/2 \quad \text{if} \quad i \in \mathbb{Z} \setminus B. \tag{15}$$

So, in a comb-type walk, we remove from the two-dimensional integer lattice all the horizontal edges that do not belong to the i-levels in B, and in the remaining lattice, the walker takes each possible edge with equal probability.

In investigating this comb-type walk, we get rid of a lot of technicalities and still obtain interesting results.

- **Infinitely many horizontal lines:** Consider the case now where

$$|B_n| := |B \cap \{-n, n\}| \sim c\, n^{\beta} \quad \text{with} \quad 0 < \beta \leq 1, \quad c > 0. \tag{16}$$

The $\beta = 1$ case turns out to be a special case of Theorem 7; that is to say that under the conditions of Theorem 7, we obtain the same statement.

In order to be able to formulate our next result we need to say a few words about the method which we used here and in many of the other strong approximation results. Namely, we redefined the anisotropic walk in terms of two independent simple symmetric random walks, $S_1(\cdot)$ and $S_2(\cdot)$, and a sequence of independent geometric random variables $\{G_i, i = 1, 2\ldots\}$ defined in the same probability space. Using these random variables, we define the anisotropic walk as taking G_i horizontal steps and one vertical step for each i. The whole construction is given, e.g., in [24]. Now, we define

$$V_N = V_N(B) = \#\{k : 1 < k \leq N,\ C_2(k) \neq C_2(k-1)\},$$

which is the number of vertical steps, and denote by $H_N = N - V_N$ the number of horizontal steps in the first N steps. Then, as a result of the above-mentioned construction, we have

$$\begin{aligned} \{\mathbf{C}(N);\ N = 0,1,2,\ldots\} &= \{(C_1(N), C_2(N));\ N = 0,1,2,\ldots\} \\ &\stackrel{d}{=} \{(S_1(H_N), S_2(V_N));\ N = 0,1,2,\ldots\}, \end{aligned} \tag{17}$$

where $\stackrel{d}{=}$ stands for equality in the distribution. Now, we are ready to formulate our next result. Let

$$\sum_{j \in B} \xi_2(j, V_N)$$

be the occupation time of B by $S_2(\cdot)$ in the first N steps of $\mathbf{C}(\cdot)$, where $\{\xi_2(j,\cdot), j = 0, \pm 1, \pm 2 \ldots\}$ denotes the local time process of $S_2(\cdot)$.

Theorem 8 ([24]). *Under the conditions* (15) *and* (16) *with* $0 < \beta < 1$, *on an appropriate probability space for the comb-type walk* $\{\mathbf{C}(N) = (C_1(N), C_2(N)); N = 0, 1, 2, \ldots\}$, *one can construct two independent standard Wiener processes,* $\{W_1(t);\ t \geq 0\}$ *and* $\{W_2(t); t \geq 0\}$ *so that, as* $N \to \infty$, *we have, with any* $\varepsilon > 0$,

$$\left| C_1(N) - W_1\left(\sum_{j \in B} \xi_2(j, V_N) \right) \right| = O(N^{1/8+\beta/8+\varepsilon}) \quad a.s.$$

$$|C_2(N) - W_2(N)| = O(N^{1/4+\beta/4+\varepsilon}) \quad a.s.$$

It is not hard to check that with the notation $L_2(V_N) := \sum_{j \in B} \eta_2(j, V_N)$, where $\eta_2(j, \cdot)$ denotes the local time of $W_2(\cdot)$, we also have

$$|C_1(N) - W_1(L_2(V_N))| = O(N^{1/8+\beta/4+\varepsilon}) \quad a.s.$$

Thus, we can replace the random walk local time with the corresponding Wiener local time. Furthermore, we can replace V_N with N while obtaining a somewhat weaker rate:

$$|C_1(N) - W(L_2(N))| = O(N^{1/8+3\beta/8+\varepsilon}) \quad a.s.$$

- **Half-plane, half-comb walk (HPHC)** is the case where we have $B = \{0, 1, 2, \ldots\}$; thus, under the x-axis, all horizontal lines are deleted. This model was discussed by us in [25,26]. In this case, Theorem 7 is true with $\gamma_1 = 2$ and $\gamma_2 = 1$ and the rate is somewhat better, as follows:

Theorem 9. *On an appropriate probability space for the HPHC walk, one can construct two independent standard Wiener processes,* $\{W_1(t);\ t \geq 0\}$ *and* $\{W_2(t);\ t \geq 0\}$, *such that, as* $N \to \infty$, *we have, with any* $\epsilon > 0$,

$$\left| C_1(N) - W_1\left(N - A_2^{-1}(N)\right) \right| + \left| C_2(N) - W_2\left(A_2^{-1}(N)\right) \right| = O(N^{3/8+\epsilon}) \quad a.s.,$$

with $A_2(t) = 2\int_0^t I(W_2(s) \geq 0)\, ds + \int_0^t I(W_2(s) < 0)\, ds$.

- **Two-dimensional comb walk** (walk on $\mathbb{C}^2$): This is one of the most important examples, where the set B only contains one element, $B = \{0\}$; thus, we keep only the x-axis, and all the other horizontal lines are deleted. For this case, $\gamma_1 = \gamma_2 = 1$, so Theorem 7 is not applicable. After Bertacchi's remarkably weak convergence result [13], we proved the following.

Theorem 10 ([15]). *On an appropriate probability space for the comb walk* $\{\mathbf{C}(N) = (C_1(N), C_2(N));\ N = 0, 1, 2, \ldots\}$ *on* $\mathbb{C}^2$, *one can construct two independent standard Wiener processes,* $\{W_1(t);\ t \geq 0\}$ *and* $\{W_2(t);\ t \geq 0\}$, *such that, as* $N \to \infty$, *we have, with any* $\epsilon > 0$,

$$N^{-1/4}|C_1(N) - W_1(\eta_2(0, N))| + N^{-1/2}|C_2(N) - W_2(N)| = O(N^{-1/8+\epsilon}) \quad a.s.,$$

where $\eta_2(0, \cdot)$ *is the local time process at the zero of* $W_2(\cdot)$.

- **K-comb walk** (walk on $\mathbb{C}_K^2$): In this model, we relax the conditions of (15), replacing them with

$$p_i < 1/2 \quad \text{if} \quad i \in B \quad \text{and} \quad p_i = 1/2 \quad \text{if} \quad i \in \mathbb{Z} \setminus B, \tag{18}$$

but we require that $|B|$ should be finite. In this case, by denoting $|B| = K$, the corresponding lattice by $\mathbb{C}_K^2$ and introducing the notation

$$A_K = \sum_{i \in B} \left(\frac{1}{2p_i} - 1 \right) \tag{19}$$

we proved the following theorem:

Theorem 11 ([27]). *On an appropriate probability space for the K-comb walk* $\{\mathbf{C}(N) = (C_1(N), C_2(N));\ N = 0,1,2,\ldots\}$ *on* $\mathbb{C}_K^2$, *one can construct two independent standard Wiener processes,* $\{W_1(t); t \geq 0\}$ *and* $\{W_2(t); t \geq 0\}$, *such that, as* $N \to \infty$, *we have, with any* $\epsilon > 0$,

$$N^{-1/4}|C_1(N) - W_1(A_K \eta_2(0,N))| + N^{-1/2}|C_2(N) - W_2(N)| = O(N^{-1/8+\epsilon}) \quad \text{a.s.},$$

where $\eta_2(0,\cdot)$ *is the local time process at the zero of* $W_2(\cdot)$.

Remark 4. *Clearly, Theorem 11 is a generalization of Theorem 10. One of the interesting features of this result is that the positions of the K-horizontal lines are irrelevant.*

For the comb and the K-comb $\gamma_1 = \gamma_2 = 1$, so they do not meet the conditions of Theorem 7, they need separate proofs. Our second open question is

Question 2. *Find a generalization of Theorem 7 without the condition* $1 < \max(\gamma_1, \gamma_2) < \infty$. *It would be very nice to have only the condition of* $\max(\gamma_1, \gamma_2) < \infty$, *and the most ambitious version would be if we only needed to assume the recurrence of the anisotropic walk.*

4. Local Time

We spent a lot of time investigating this topic, and we proved many results for the different important special models, but there are many interesting questions which are still unanswered.

- **Periodic walk:** We managed to give a complete answer using some results from [7], which are known for this case only.

Theorem 12 ([19]). *For the 2N-step return probability of the periodic walk for any* $L \geq 1$,

$$\mathbf{P}(\mathbf{C^P}(2N) = (0,0)) \sim \frac{1}{4\pi N p_0 \sqrt{\gamma - 1}}, \quad \textit{as} \quad N \to \infty \tag{20}$$

with γ *given in* (11).

Observe that in the case where $L = 1$ and $p_0 = 1/4$, $\gamma = 2$ and we recover the well-known result for the simple symmetric two-dimensional walk. We remark that in the periodic case, γ is always bigger than 1.

From (20), we immediately obtain the truncated Green function

$$g(N) = \sum_{k=0}^{N} \mathbf{P}(\mathbf{C^P}(k) = (0,0)) \sim \frac{\log N}{4p_0 \pi \sqrt{\gamma - 1}}, \quad \textit{as} \quad N \to \infty. \tag{21}$$

Now, define the local time as

$$\Xi^P((k,j),N) =: \sum_{r=1}^{N} I\{\mathbf{C}^{\mathbf{P}}(r) = (k,j)\},$$

where $I\{\cdot\}$ is the indicator function. Taking into account that our periodic walk is Harris-recurrent with the invariant measure given in (4), we obtain, using, e.g., Chen's work [28], that

$$\lim_{N\to\infty} \frac{\Xi^P((0,0),N)}{\Xi^P((k,j),N)} = \frac{p_j}{p_0} \quad a.s.$$

for fixed (k,j). Using $g(N)$, we deduced many other results for the local time of the periodic walk, which we will mention later.

- **Two-dimensional comb walk:** In [16], we proved many results about local time on a generalized comb. Instead of introducing this general version, we want to recall here some of these results only in the context of the two-dimensional comb walk as it was given in [29].

Theorem 13. *On the probability space of our Theorem 10, as $N \to \infty$, we have for the comb walk that*

$$\sup_{x\in\mathbb{Z}} |\Xi((x,0),N) - 2\eta_1(x,\eta_2(0,N))| = O(N^{1/8+\delta}) \quad a.s.,$$

with any $\delta > 0$, where $\eta_i(x,.)$, $i = 1,2$ are the local times of the corresponding independent Wiener processes in Theorem 10. Furthermore, we have, for any $0 < \varepsilon < 1/4$,

$$\max_{|x|\le N^{1/4-\varepsilon}} |\Xi((x,0),N) - \Xi((0,0),N)| = O(N^{1/4-\delta}) \quad a.s. \tag{22}$$

and

$$\max_{0<|y|\le N^{1/4-\varepsilon}} \max_{|x|\le N^{1/4-\varepsilon}} |\Xi((x,y),N) - \frac{1}{2}\Xi((0,0),N)| = O(N^{1/4-\delta}) \quad a.s.,$$

for any $0 < \delta < \varepsilon/2$, where the maximum is taken at integers.

Here, the first statement of the theorem describes the behavior of the local time of the sites on the x-axis. The second statement claims that on the x-axis, up to $|x| \le N^{1/4-\varepsilon}$, all sites have approximately the same local time, while the last statement explains that away from the x-axis, the local time is approximately half of the local time at the origin. Theorem 13 has many nice consequences, which are given in [16]. These results were obtained using strong approximation methods. However, we did not calculate the $2N$-step return probability to the origin. This was achieved much earlier by Gerl [30]. He even proved it for higher-dimensional combs. He obtained the following result:

Theorem 14 ([30]). *For the two-dimensional comb walk, as $N \to \infty$,*

$$\mathbf{P}(\mathbf{C}(2N) = (0,0)) \sim \frac{1}{\sqrt{2}\,\Gamma(1/4)N^{3/4}}. \tag{23}$$

His proof strongly relies on the fact that the comb lattice is a tree. So, here is our next question:

Question 3. *Find a probabilistic proof of* (23) *and generalize it for the K-comb.*

- **Periodic-like walk:**
  In our paper, we proved the following:

Theorem 15 ([31]). *Consider the anisotropic walk defined in* (1). *Suppose that*

(i) *Conditions (9) hold with some* $1 < \gamma < \infty$ *and* $1/2 < \eta < \infty$.
(ii) *There is an* $\omega > 0$ *such that* $p_j \geq \omega, \quad j = 0, \pm 1, \pm 2, \ldots$
(iii) $\sup_{n\geq 0} \sqrt{n} \sup_{N\geq n} \sum_{m=n}^{N} (\mathbf{P}(C_2(2m+2) = 0) - \mathbf{P}(C_2(2m+1) = 0)) < \infty$.
Then,

$$\mathbf{P}(\mathbf{C}(2N) = (0,0)) \sim \frac{1}{4Np_0\pi\sqrt{\gamma - 1}}, \quad as \quad N \to \infty. \tag{24}$$

It is very interesting that the limiting $2N$-step return probability in this theorem is identical to the result that we obtained in the case of the periodic walk. This is the only reason that we call the anisotropic walks which satisfy the three conditions listed in Theorem 15 **periodic-like**.

As before, this theorem immediately implies that the truncated Green function is

$$g(N) = \sum_{k=0}^{N} \mathbf{P}(\mathbf{C}(k) = (0,0)) \sim \frac{\log N}{4p_0\pi\sqrt{\gamma - 1}}, \quad as \quad N \to \infty,$$

from which, using Chen's work [28] again, we can conclude that for any fixed (x, y),

$$\lim_{N\to\infty} \frac{\Xi((0,0), N)}{\Xi((x,y), N)} = \frac{p_y}{p_0} \quad a.s.$$

In the proof of the above theorem, we used a local limit theorem for a certain type of Markov chain introduced by Stenlund [32]. The Markov chain he deals with goes from state i to states $i+1$ and $i-1$ with the same probability p_i and remains in state i with a probability of $1 - 2p_i$. This is exactly what the second coordinate, $C_2(\cdot)$, of our anisotropic walk does.

Remark 5. *In Theorem 15, condition* (iii) *is difficult to check. This condition comes from Stenlund's paper, where he made the following comment on this: if the walk is lazy, i.e., all* $p_j \leq 1/4$, *then* (iii) *is trivially satisfied. His simulation suggests that, generally, under the other conditions of Theorem 15, condition* (iii) *holds if* $p_k \neq 1/2$ *for at least one* $k \in \mathbb{Z}$. *So* (iii) *could well turn out to be equivalent to the Markov chain being aperiodic.*

Question 4. *Find a class of anisotropic random walks for which condition* (iii) *above holds (besides being lazy).*

Question 5. *Find some conditions which are equivalent to condition* (iii) *but simpler to check.*

This theorem brings up the most puzzling questions. In Theorems 12 and 15, we obtained identical results. The first one was for the periodic walk (see the definition of periodic walk in Section 3, which is very different from periodic Markov chains), and the second was for periodic-like walks, that is, under the three conditions listed above. Clearly, the periodic walk satisfies (i) and (ii) above. So, either every periodic walk satisfies condition (iii) in Theorem 15, which we cannot prove or disprove, or there is a common generalization of Theorems 12 and 15.

Question 6. *Find a common generalization of Theorems 12 and 15.*

Clearly, (24) does not make sense when $\gamma = 1$. So, we would like to have a result which contains the K-comb given in (24) and, if possible, all anisotropic walks with $\gamma = 1$.

The only case where we managed to find local time results for the anisotropic walk, when $\gamma_1 \neq \gamma_2$, was the following:

- **The half-plane, half-comb walk.**

Theorem 16 ([26]). *For the 2N-step return probability of the HPHC walk, starting at* $(0,0)$, *we have*

$$\mathbf{P}(\mathbf{C}(2N) = (0,0)) \sim \frac{2}{\pi N}, \quad as \quad N \to \infty. \tag{25}$$

Of course, this result allows us to calculate the truncated Green function and proceed similarly to the way we described above in the case of the periodic walk. In this particular case, $\gamma_1 = 2$ and $\gamma_2 = 1$.

Question 7. *What is the reason that the asymptotic return probability of the HPHC walk is twice as much as that of the simple symmetric walk on the plane? Even a heuristic explanation would be nice.*

Question 8. *Find a general result for the asymptotic 2N-step return probability in the case of* $\gamma_1 = \gamma_2$, *under weaker conditions than the periodicity.*

Question 9. *Find a general result for the asymptotic 2N-step return probability in the case of* $\gamma_1 \neq \gamma_2$.

5. Range

The range is defined as the number of sites visited by the walk during the first N steps. Formally, it is defined as

$$R(N) = \sum_{\mathbf{u} \in \mathbb{Z}^2} I\{\Xi(\mathbf{u}, N) > 0\},$$

where $I\{\cdot\}$ is the indicator function. In the case of the simple symmetric walk in two dimensions, we know from Dvoretzky and Erdős [10] that

$$\mathbf{E}(R(N)) = \frac{\pi N}{\log N} + O\left(\frac{N \log\log N}{(\log N)^2}\right)$$

and that the following law of large numbers holds:

$$\lim_{N\to\infty} \frac{R(N)}{\mathbf{E}(R(N))} = 1 \quad a.s.$$

As for the anisotropic walk, we know very little.

- **Periodic walk**

Roerdink and Shuler [7] proved that

$$\mathbf{E}(R(N)) \sim \frac{2\pi\sqrt{\gamma - 1}}{\gamma} \frac{N}{\log N}, \quad as \quad N \to \infty.$$

Furthermore, from Nándori's work [33], one can conclude the following laws of large numbers:

$$\lim_{N\to\infty} \frac{R(N)}{\mathbf{E}(R(N))} = \lim_{N\to\infty} \frac{\gamma\, R(N) \log N}{2\pi\sqrt{\gamma - 1}\, N} = 1 \qquad a.s.$$

Question 10. *How to generalize these results for the anisotropic walk, without the restriction of periodicity, requesting only that* $\gamma > 1$.

- **Two-dimensional comb walk**

Pach and Tardos [34] proved for the expected value of the range of the comb that

$$\mathbf{E}(R(N)) = \left(\frac{1}{2\sqrt{2\pi}} + o(1)\right)\sqrt{N}\log N, \quad \text{as} \quad N \to \infty.$$

As to the almost sure behavior of the range of the comb walk, we just have some crude estimates. We can create a lower bound by observing that the range of the vertical walk, $C_2(\cdot)$, is the lower bound of the range of the comb. We proved in [15] that

$$\liminf_{n\to\infty}\left(\frac{8\log\log n}{\pi^2 n}\right)^{1/2} \max_{1\le k\le n} |C_2(k)| = 1 \quad a.s.,$$

so

$$\liminf_{n\to\infty} \frac{\sqrt{8\log\log n}}{\pi\sqrt{n}} R_n \ge 1 \quad a.s.$$

In order to obtain an upper bound for the range of the comb, we prove that

$$\limsup_{n\to\infty} \frac{R_n}{n^{1/2}\log n(\log\log n)^{5/2+\epsilon}} \le c \quad a.s., \tag{26}$$

with some $c > 0$. To see this, first, we recall a few facts.
We proved in [15] that

$$\limsup_{n\to\infty} \frac{C_1(n)}{n^{1/4}(\log\log n)^{3/4}} = \frac{2^{5/4}}{3^{3/4}} \quad a.s., \tag{27}$$

which means that if n is big enough, then in n steps, we do not have more than $const\; n^{1/4}(\log\log n)^{3/4}$ sites occupied on the x-axis. From (34) (see later), we also know that from none of these sites can we have more than $const\, n^{1/4}(\log\log n)^{3/4}$ excursions if n is big enough.
If κ is an excursion away from the x-axis, then for its height H, we have that $P(H \ge k) = 1/k$. So, we fix a site $(x,0)$ on the x-axis. If $\{\kappa_i\; i = 1,2,\ldots\}$ is the i-th excursion away from $(x,0)$ and its height is $\{H_i\; i = 1,2,\ldots\}$, then for the probability that if in the first n step m_n excursions start from $(x,0)$, at least one of them is higher than ℓ_n, we have

$$\mathbf{P}\left(\max_{i\le m_n} \kappa_i > \ell_n\right) = 1 - \left(1 - \frac{1}{\ell_n}\right)^{m_n} \le 1 - e^{-\frac{m_n}{\ell_n}} \le \frac{m_n}{\ell_n}.$$

Select $m_n = \alpha n^{1/4}(\log\log n)^{3/4}$ and $\ell_n = \beta n^{1/4}\log n(\log\log n)^{7/4+\epsilon}$ with some $\alpha > 0$ and $\beta > 0$. Let $n_k = e^k$. Then,

$$\begin{aligned}\mathbf{P}\left(\max_{i\le m_{n_{k+1}}} \kappa_i > \ell_{n_k}\right) &\le \frac{m_{n_{k+1}}}{\ell_{n_k}} = \frac{\alpha}{\beta}\left(\frac{n_{k+1}}{n_k}\right)^{1/4}\left(\frac{\log\log n_{k+1}}{\log\log n_k}\right)^{3/4} \frac{1}{k(\log k)^{1+\epsilon}} \\ &\le const\left(\frac{\log(k+1)}{\log k}\right)^{3/4} \frac{1}{k(\log k)^{1+\epsilon}}.\end{aligned} \tag{28}$$

So,

$$\sum_k \mathbf{P}(\max_{i\le m_{n_{k+1}}} \kappa_i > \ell_{n_k})$$

is finite. Hence, for a big enough k,

$$\max_{i\le m_{n_{k+1}}} \kappa_i \le \ell_{n_k}.$$

So, for $n_k \leq n \leq n_{k+1}$, we have

$$\max_{i \leq m_n} \kappa_i \leq \max_{i \leq m_{n_{k+1}}} \kappa_i \leq \ell_{n_k} \leq \ell_n \quad a.s.$$

if k is big enough. Thus, in n steps in each tooth, we have, at most, $\beta n^{1/4} \log n (\log\log n)^{7/4+\epsilon}$ points visited. Now, using the fact that according to (27) at most $const\, n^{1/4} (\log\log n)^{3/4}$ sites are visited on the x-axis, we obtain

$$R_n \leq const\, n^{1/4} (\log\log n)^{3/4}) \beta n^{1/4} \log n (\log\log n)^{7/4+\epsilon} = const\, n^{1/2} \log n (\log\log n)^{5/2+\epsilon},$$

proving (26).

Question 11. *Find some exact result about the range of the comb walk.*

Question 12. *What is the range of the K-comb walk and the HPHC walk.*

6. Strassen Theorems and Strong Laws for the Coordinates of the Anisotropic Walks

In this section, we want to mention some of the consequences of the strong approximation results discussed in Section 3. In order to mention our Strassen theorems, we need some definitions.

Let $\mathcal{S}$ be the Strassen class of functions, i.e., $\mathcal{S} \subset C([0,1], \mathbb{R})$ is the class of absolutely continuous functions (with respect to the Lebesgue measure) on $[0,1]$ for which

$$f(0) = 0 \qquad \text{and} \qquad \int_0^1 \dot{f}^2(x) dx \leq 1. \tag{29}$$

Remark 6. *In this topic, instead of the usual $f'(\cdot)$ for the derivative, we use the traditional $\dot{f}(\cdot)$ notation; see, e.g.,* [35].

Define the Strassen class $\mathcal{S}^2$ as the set of $\mathbb{R}^2$-valued, absolutely continuous functions

$$\{(f(x), g(x));\, 0 \leq x \leq 1\} \tag{30}$$

for which $f(0) = g(0) = 0$ and

$$\int_0^1 (\dot{f}^2(x) + \dot{g}^2(x)) dx \leq 1. \tag{31}$$

At first, we mention the general case

Theorem 17 ([19]). *Under the conditions of Theorem 4 for the anisotropic walk $\mathbf{C}(\cdot)$, we have that the sequence of random vector-valued functions*

$$\left(\sqrt{\frac{\gamma}{\gamma - 1}} \frac{C_1(xN)}{(2N \log\log N)^{1/2}}, \sqrt{\gamma} \frac{C_2(xN)}{(2N \log\log N)^{1/2}},\quad 0 \leq x \leq 1 \right)_{N \geq 3}$$

is almost surely relatively compact in the space $C([0,1], \mathbb{R}^2)$ and its limit points are the set of functions $\mathcal{S}^2$. In particular, the vector sequence

$$\left(\frac{C_1(N)}{(2N \log\log N)^{1/2}}, \frac{C_2(N)}{(2N \log\log N)^{1/2}} \right)_{N \geq 3}$$

is almost surely relatively compact in the rectangle

$$\left[-\frac{\sqrt{\gamma - 1}}{\sqrt{\gamma}}, \frac{\sqrt{\gamma - 1}}{\sqrt{\gamma}} \right] \times \left[-\frac{1}{\sqrt{\gamma}}, \frac{1}{\sqrt{\gamma}} \right],$$

and the set of its limit points is the ellipse

$$\left\{(x,y) : \frac{\gamma}{\gamma-1}x^2 + \gamma y^2 \leq 1\right\}. \tag{32}$$

We do not have any Strassen-type results if $\gamma_1 \neq \gamma_2$, so we ask the following:

Question 13. *How can we generalize Theorem 17 for the case where* $\gamma_1 \neq \gamma_2$.

The only other case where we managed to prove a Strassen theorem was the two-dimensional comb walk.

Theorem 18 ([15]). *For the random walk* $\{\mathbf{C}(n) = (C_1(n), C_2(n));\ n = 1, 2, \ldots\}$ *on the* two-*dimensional comb lattice* $\mathbb{C}^2$, *we have that the sequence of random vector-valued functions*

$$\left(\frac{C_1(xn)}{2^{3/4}n^{1/4}(\log\log n)^{3/4}}, \frac{C_2(xn)}{(2n\log\log n)^{1/2}},\quad 0 \leq x \leq 1\right)_{n\geq 3}$$

is almost surely compact in the space $C([0,1], \mathbb{R}^2)$, *and its limit points are the set of functions*

$$\begin{aligned} \mathcal{S}^{(2)} :\ =\ & \{(k(x), g(x)) : k(0) = g(0) = 0,\ k, g \in \dot{C}([0,1], \mathbb{R})\} \\ & \int_0^1 (|3^{3/4}2^{-1/2}\dot{k}(x)|^{4/3} + \dot{g}^2(x))\, dx \leq 1,\ \dot{k}(x)g(x) = 0 \ a.e., \end{aligned} \tag{33}$$

where $\dot{C}([0,1], \mathbb{R})$ *stands for the space of absolutely continuous functions in* $C([0,1], \mathbb{R})$. *The sequence*

$$\left(\frac{C_1(n)}{n^{1/4}(\log\log n)^{3/4}}, \frac{C_2(n)}{(2n\log\log n)^{1/2}}\right)_{n\geq 3}$$

is almost surely compact in the rectangle

$$R = \left[-\frac{2^{5/4}}{3^{3/4}}, \frac{2^{5/4}}{3^{3/4}}\right] \times [-1, 1],$$

and the set of its limit points is the domain

$$D = \{(u,v) : k(1) = u,\ g(1) = v,\ (k(\cdot), g(\cdot)) \in \mathcal{S}^{(2)}\}.$$

In fact, in [15], we established some other important consequences of this theorem as well.

Question 14. *How to generalize Theorem 18 for the K-comb walk.*

In what follows, we present some LIL-type theorems.

Theorem 19 ([23]). *Under the conditions of Theorem 7, we have the following LIL-type results for the anisotropic walk:*

- $\limsup_{t\to\infty} \frac{W_1(t - A_2^{-1}(t))}{\sqrt{t\log\log t}} = \limsup_{N\to\infty} \frac{C_1(N)}{\sqrt{N\log\log N}} = \sqrt{2\left(1 - \frac{1}{\gamma_1}\right)}$ *a.s.;*
- $\liminf_{t\to\infty} \frac{W_1(t - A_2^{-1}(t))}{\sqrt{t\log\log t}} = \liminf_{N\to\infty} \frac{C_1(N)}{\sqrt{N\log\log N}} = -\sqrt{2\left(1 - \frac{1}{\gamma_1}\right)}$ *a.s.;*
- $\limsup_{t\to\infty} \frac{W_2(A_2^{-1}(t))}{\sqrt{t\log\log t}} = \limsup_{N\to\infty} \frac{C_2(N)}{\sqrt{N\log\log N}} = \sqrt{\frac{2}{\gamma_1}}$ *a.s.;*
- $\liminf_{t\to\infty} \frac{W_2(A_2^{-1}(t))}{\sqrt{t\log\log t}} = \liminf_{N\to\infty} \frac{C_2(N)}{\sqrt{N\log\log N}} = -\sqrt{\frac{2}{\gamma_2}}$ *a.s.*

where $A_2(t) = \gamma_1 \int_0^t I(W_2(s) \geq 0)\, ds + \gamma_2 \int_0^t I(W_2(s) < 0)\, ds$*, and* $A_2^{-1}(\cdot)$ *is its inverse.*

This theorem contains almost all the special cases which we discussed earlier. For instance, in the **HPHC walk** case, where we have $\gamma_1 = 2$ and $\gamma_2 = 1$, we obtain

- $\limsup_{N\to\infty} \frac{C_1(N)}{\sqrt{N\log\log N}} = 1$ *a.s.;*
- $\liminf_{N\to\infty} \frac{C_1(N)}{\sqrt{N\log\log N}} = -1$ *a.s.;*
- $\limsup_{N\to\infty} \frac{C_2(N)}{\sqrt{N\log\log N}} = 1$ *a.s.;*
- $\liminf_{N\to\infty} \frac{C_2(N)}{\sqrt{N\log\log N}} = -\sqrt{2}$ *a.s.*

However, again, the $\gamma_1 = \gamma_2 = 1$ case in general is unknown, but we have some LIL for the **K-comb walk**.

Theorem 20 ([27]). *For the K-comb walk, we have*

- $\limsup_{N\to\infty} \frac{C_1(N)}{\sqrt{A_K} N^{1/4} (\log\log N)^{3/4}} = \frac{2^{5/4}}{3^{3/4}}$ *a.s.,*
- $\limsup_{N\to\infty} \frac{C_2(N)}{(2N\log\log N)^{1/2}} = 1$ *a.s.,*

where A_K *was defined in* (19).
Furthermore, let $\rho(n), n = 1, 2 \ldots$*, be a non-increasing sequence of positive numbers such that* $n^{1/4}\rho(n)$ *is non-decreasing. Then, we have almost surely that*

- $\liminf_{N\to\infty} \frac{max_{0\leq k\leq N} C_1(k)}{N^{1/4}\rho(N)} = 0$ *or* ∞
- $\liminf_{N\to\infty} \frac{max_{0\leq k\leq N} C_2(k)}{N^{1/2}\rho(N)} = 0$ *or* ∞

according to whether the series $\sum_{i=1}^{\infty} \rho(n)/n$ *diverges or converges.*
Furthermore, for $|C_2(\cdot)|$ *and* $|C_1(\cdot)|$*, we have*

- $\liminf_{N\to\infty} \left(\frac{8\log\log N}{\pi^2 N}\right)^{1/2} \max_{0\leq k\leq N} |C_2(k)| = 1$ *a.s.*
- $\liminf_{N\to\infty} \frac{\max_{0\leq k\leq N} |C_1(k)|}{N^{1/4}\rho(N)} = 0$ *or* ∞*,* *a.s.*

as to whether the series $\sum_{n=1}^{\infty} \rho^2(n)/n$ *diverges or converges.*

7. Some Limit Distributions and Strong Laws for the Local Time of the Anisotropic Walk

- **Periodic and periodic-like walk**

From (11), using the work of Darling and Kac [36], we concluded in [19] that for the periodic walk,

- $$\lim_{N\to\infty} \mathbf{P}\left(\frac{4p_0\pi\sqrt{\gamma-1}\,\Xi((0,0),n)}{\log n} \geq x\right) = e^{-x}, \quad x \geq 0.$$

As for the lim sup result, we have, using Chen's work [28], that

- $$\limsup_{n\to\infty} \frac{\Xi((0,0),n)}{\log n \log\log\log n} = \frac{1}{4p_0\pi\sqrt{\gamma-1}} \quad a.s.$$

Naturally, the above two statements are also valid for the periodic-like walk as well. A functional limit theorem was also proved in [37].

- **Two-dimensional comb walk**

Based on an old Strassen theorem [38], which we proved for the iterated Wiener local time process $\{\eta_1(0, \eta_2(0, xt)),\ 0 \leq x \leq 1\}$, where $\eta_1(\cdot)$ and $\eta_2(\cdot)$ are the local times of two independent standard Wiener processes, we concluded in [16] that for the local time of the comb, we have

- $$\limsup_{n\to\infty} \frac{\Xi((x,0),n)}{n^{1/4}(\log\log n)^{3/4}} = \frac{2^{9/4}}{3^{3/4}} \quad \text{a.s.,} \tag{34}$$

- $$\limsup_{n\to\infty} \frac{\Xi((x,y),n)}{n^{1/4}(\log\log n)^{3/4}} = \frac{2^{5/4}}{3^{3/4}} \quad y \neq 0 \text{ a.s.}$$

Furthermore, we would like to mention a couple of integral tests for $\sup_{x\in\mathbb{Z}} \Xi((x,0),n)$ [17].

Theorem 21 ([17]). *Let $a(n)$ be a non-decreasing sequence. Then, as $n \to \infty$,*

$$\mathbf{P}(\sup_{x\in\mathbb{Z}} \Xi((x,0),n) > n^{1/4}a(n) \ i.o.) = 0 \ \ or \ \ 1$$

according to

$$\sum_{n=1}^{\infty} \frac{a^2(n)}{n} \exp\left(-\frac{3a^{4/3}(n)}{2^{5/3}}\right) < \infty \ \ or \ \ = \infty.$$

Theorem 22 ([17]). *Let $b(n)$ be a non-increasing sequence. Then, as $n \to \infty$,*

$$\mathbf{P}(\sup_{x\in\mathbb{Z}} \Xi((x,0),n) < n^{1/4}b(n) \ i.o.) = 0 \ \ or \ \ 1$$

according to

$$\sum_{n=1}^{\infty} \frac{b^2(n)}{n} < \infty \ \ or \ \ = \infty.$$

- **HPHC walk**

As a consequence of Theorem 16, we have for the HPHC walk that $g(N) \sim \frac{2}{\pi}\log N$. In [26], we obtained again from Darling and Kac [36] and Chen [28] that

- $$\lim_{N\to\infty} \mathbb{P}\left(\frac{\pi\,\Xi((0,0),N)}{2\log N} \geq x\right) = e^{-x}.$$

and

$$\bullet \quad \limsup_{N\to\infty} \frac{\Xi((0,0),N)}{\log N \log\log\log N} = \frac{2}{\pi} \quad a.s.$$

Author Contributions: Writing—original draft, E.C. and A.F.; Writing—review and editing, E.C. and A.F. All authors have read and agreed to the published version of the manuscript.

Funding: This research received no external funding.

Institutional Review Board Statement: Not applicable.

Data Availability Statement: No new data were created or analyzed in this study.

Conflicts of Interest: The authors declare no conflicts of interest.

References

1. Silver, H.; Shuler, K.E.; Lindenberg, K. Two-dimensional anisotropic random walks. In *Statistical Mechanics and Statistical Metho in Theory and Application (Proc. Sympos., Univ. Rochester, Rochester, N.Y., 1976)*; Plenum: New York, NY, USA, 1977; pp. 463–505
2. Shuler, K.E. Random walks on sparsely periodic and random lattices I. *Phys. A* **1979**, *95*, 12–34. [CrossRef]
3. Seshadri, V.; Lindenberg, K.; Shuler, K.E. Random Walks on Periodic and Random Lattices. II. Random Walk Properties v Generating Function Techniques. *J. Stat. Phys.* **1979**, *21*, 517–548. [CrossRef]
4. Westcott, M. Random walks on a lattice. *J. Stat. Phys.* **1982**, *27*, 75–82. [CrossRef]
5. Heyde, C.C. On the asymptotic behavior of random walks on an anisotropic lattice. *J. Stat. Phys.* **1982**, *27*, 721–730. [CrossRef
6. Heyde, C.C. Asymptotics for two-dimensional anisotropic random walks. In *Stochastic Processes;* Springer: New York, NY, US 1993; pp. 125–130.
7. Roerdink, J.; Shuler, K.E. Asymptotic properties of multistate random walks. I. Theory. *J. Stat. Phys.* **1985**, *40*, 205–240. [CrossRe
8. den Hollander, F. On three conjectures by K. Shuler. *J. Stat. Phys.* **1994**, *75*, 891–918. [CrossRef]
9. Erdős, P.; Taylor, S.J. Some problems concerning the structure of random walk paths. *Acta Math. Acad. Sci. Hung.* **1960**, *11*, 137–1 [CrossRef]
10. Dvoretzky, A.; Erdős, P. Some problems on random walk in space. In Proceedings of the Second Berkeley Symposium, Berkel CA, USA, 31 July–12 August 1951; pp. 353–367.
11. Révész, P. *Random Walk in Random and Non-Random Environments*, 2nd ed.; World Scientific: Singapore, 2005.
12. Weiss, G.H.; Havlin, S. Some properties of a random walk on a comb structure. *Phys. A* **1986**, *134*, 474–482. [CrossRef]
13. Bertacchi, D. Asymptotic behaviour of the simple random walk on the 2-dimensional comb. *Electron. J. Probab.* **2006**, *11*, 1184–12 [CrossRef]
14. Bertacchi, D.; Zucca, F. Uniform asymptotic estimates of transition probabilities on combs. *J. Aust. Math. Soc.* **2003**, *75*, 325–3 [CrossRef]
15. Csáki, E.; Csörgő, M.; Földes, A.; Révész, P. Strong limit theorems for a simple random walk on the 2-dimensional comb. *Electr J. Probab.* **2009**, *14*, 2371–2390. [CrossRef]
16. Csáki, E.; Csörgő, M.; Földes, A.; Révész, P. On the local time of random walk on the 2-dimensional comb. *Stoch. Process. Ap* **2011**, *121*, 1290–1314. [CrossRef]
17. Csáki, E.; Földes, A.; Révész, P. Some results and problems for anisotropic random walk on the plane. *Fields Inst. Commun.* **20** *76*, 55–76.
18. Nash-Williams, C.S.T.A. Random walks and electric currents in networks. *Proc. Camb. Phil. Soc.* **1959**, *55*, 181–194. [CrossRef]
19. Csáki, E.; Csörgő, M.; Földes, A.; Révész, P. Strong limit theorems for anisotropic random walks on Z^2. *Periodica Math. Hun* **2013**, *67*, 71–94. [CrossRef]
20. Heyde, C.C.; Westcott, M.; Williams, E.R. The asymptotic behavior of a random walk on a dual-medium lattice. *J. Stat. Phys.* **19** *28*, 375–380. [CrossRef]
21. Horváth, L. Diffusion approximation for random walks on anisotropic lattices. *J. Appl. Probab.* **1998**, *35*, 206–212. [CrossRef]
22. Keilson, J.; Wellner, J.A. Oscillating Brownian motion. *J. Appl. Probab.* **1978**, *15*, 300–310. [CrossRef]
23. Csáki, E.; Földes, A. Strong approximation of the anisotropic random walk revisited. *J. Theor. Probab.* **2022**, *35*, 2879–28 [CrossRef]
24. Csáki, E.; Földes, A. Random walks on comb-type subsets of $\mathbb{Z}^2$. *J. Theor. Probab.* **2020**, *33*, 2233–2257. [CrossRef]
25. Csáki, E.; Csörgő, M.; Földes, A.; Révész, P. Random walk on half-plane half-comb structure. *Ann. Math. Inform.* **2012**, *39*, 29–
26. Csáki, E.; Földes, A. On the local time of the Half-Plane Half-Comb walk. *J. Theor. Probab.* **2022**, *35*, 1247–1261. [CrossRef]
27. Csáki, E.; Földes, A. Random walks on the two-dimensional K-comb lattice. *Math. Pannonica* **2023**, *29*, 29–36. [CrossRef]
28. Chen, X. Moderate deviations for Markovian occupation time. *Stoch. Process. Appl.* **2001**, *94*, 51–70. [CrossRef]
29. Földes, A. We like to walk on the comb. *Period. Math. Hung.* **2010**, *61*, 165–181. [CrossRef]
30. Gerl, P. Natural spanning trees of $\mathbb{Z}^d$ are recurrent. *Discret. Math.* **1986**, *61*, 333–336. [CrossRef]
31. Csáki, E.; Földes, A. On the local time of the anisotropic walk on $\mathbf{Z}^2$. *J. Theor. Probab.* **2024**, *37*, 1654–1673. [CrossRef]

Stenlund, M. A local limit theorem for random walks in balanced environments. *Electron. Commun. Probab.* **2013**, *18*, 19. [CrossRef]

Nándori, P. Number of distinct sites visited by a random walk with internal states. *Probab. Theory Relat. Fields* **2010**, *150*, 373–403. [CrossRef]

Pach, J.; Tardos, G. The range of a random walk on a comb. *Electron. J. Comb.* **2013**, *20*, 1–7. [CrossRef]

Strassen, V. An invariance principle for the law of iterated logarithm. *Z. Wahrscheinlichkeitstheorie Verw. Geb.* **1964**, *4*, 265–268. [CrossRef]

Darling, D.A.; Kac, M. On occupation times for Markoff processes. *Trans. Amer. Math. Soc.* **1957**, *84*, 444–458. [CrossRef]

Csáki, E.; Révész, P.; Rosen, J. Functional laws of the iterated logarithm for local times of recurrent random walks on $\mathbb{Z}^2$. *Ann. Inst. Henri Poincaré Probab. Stat.* **1998**, *34*, 545–563. [CrossRef]

Csáki, E.; Földes, A.; Révész, P. Strassen theorems for a class of iterated processes. *Trans. Amer. Math. Soc.* **1997**, *349*, 1153–1167 . [CrossRef]

entropy

MDPI

Article

Lacunary Series and Strong Approximation †

István Berkes

Rényi Mathematical Institute, Reáltanoda u. 13-15, 1053 Budapest, Hungary; berkes@renyi.hu

† Dedicated to the memory of Pál Révész.

Abstract: Strong approximation, introduced by Strassen (1964), is one of the most powerful methods to prove limit theorems in probability and statistics. In this paper we use strong approximation of lacunary series with conditionally independent sequences to prove uniform and permutation-invariant limit theorems for such series.

Keywords: lacunary series; limit theorems; exchangeability; subsequence principle; conditional independence

MSC: 60F05; 60F15; 60G09

1. Introduction

It is known that sufficiently thin subsequences of any (dependent) sequence of random variables behave like independent random variables. Révész [1] proved that if $(X_n)_{n\geq 1}$ is a sequence of random variables satisfying $\sup_n \mathbb{E}(X_n^2) < \infty$, then there exists a subsequence $(X_{n_k})_{k\geq 1}$ and a random variable $X \in L_2$ such that the series $\sum_{k=1}^{\infty} a_k(X_{n_k} - X)$ converges a.s. for any coefficient sequence $(a_k)_{k\geq 1}$ with $\sum_{k=1}^{\infty} a_k^2 < \infty$. Komlós [2] proved that from any sequence $(X_n)_{n\geq 1}$ of random variables satisfying $\sup_n \mathbb{E}|X_n| < \infty$, one can select a subsequence $(X_{n_k})_{k\geq 1}$ such that

$$\lim_{N\to\infty} \frac{1}{N} \sum_{k\leq N} X_{n_k} = X \qquad \text{a.s.} \tag{1}$$

for some $X \in L_1$. Gaposhkin [3] and Chatterji [4,5] proved that if $(X_n)_{n\geq 1}$ is a sequence of random variables satisfying $\sup_n \mathbb{E}X_n^2 < \infty$, then there exist a subsequence $(X_{n_k})_{k\geq 1}$ and random variables $X \in L_2$, $Y \in L_1$, $Y \geq 0$ such that

$$\frac{1}{\sqrt{N}} \sum_{k\leq N} (X_{n_k} - X) \xrightarrow{d} N(0, Y) \tag{2}$$

and

$$\limsup_{N\to\infty} \frac{1}{\sqrt{2N\log\log N}} \sum_{k\leq N} (X_{n_k} - X) = Y^{1/2} \qquad \text{a.s.,} \tag{3}$$

where $N(0, Y)$ denotes the distribution of $\sqrt{Y}g$; here g is an $N(0, 1)$ variable independent of Y. Chatterji [6] formulated the following heuristic principle:

Subsequence Principle. *Let T be a probability limit theorem valid for all sequences of i.i.d. random variables belonging to an integrability class L defined by the finiteness of a norm* $\|\cdot\|_L$*. Then, if* $(X_n)_{n\geq 1}$ *is an arbitrary (dependent) sequence of random variables satisfying* $\sup_n \|X_n\|_L < \infty$*, then there exists a subsequence* $(X_{n_k})_{k\geq 1}$ *satisfying T in a mixed form.*

In a profound study, Aldous [7] proved the validity of the subsequence principle for all distributional and almost sure limit theorems subject to minor technical conditions. Dacunha-Castelle [8] showed that every tight sequence $(X_n)_{n\geq 1}$ has a subsequence $(X_{n_k})_{k\geq 1}$ whose finite dimensional distributions are close to those of an exchangeable sequence $(Y_k)_{k\geq 1}$, defined on a possibly different probability space. However, the closeness of the finite dimensional distributions of $(X_{n_k})_{k\geq 1}$ and $(Y_k)_{k\geq 1}$ is not enough to transfer limit theorems from $(X_{n_k})_{k\geq 1}$ to $(Y_k)_{k\geq 1}$ and Aldous [7] used a delicate subsequence extraction technique tailored to the individual limit theorem we want to establish for (X_{n_k}).

An alternative way to prove Aldous' theorem would be to use strong approximation and to show that every tight sequence $(X_n)_{n\geq 1}$ has a subsequence $(X_{n_k})_{k\geq 1}$ which is close to an exchangeable sequence $(Y_k)_{k\geq 1}$ defined on the same probability space in the sense that

$$\sum_{k=1}^{\infty} |X_{n_k} - Y_k| < \infty \qquad \text{a.s.} \tag{4}$$

Clearly, by passing to a further subsequence, one can make the speed of a.s. convergence of $X_{n_k} - Y_k$ to 0 as rapid as one wishes; then, transferring limit theorems from $(Y_k)_{k\geq 1}$ to $(X_{n_k})_{k\geq 1}$ becomes easy. Unfortunately, however, the approximation (4) is not valid in general, as is shown by the examples in [7,9]. For a necessary and sufficient condition on (X_n) to have a subsequence $(X_{n_k})_{k\geq 1}$ satisfying (4) with an exchangeable $(Y_k)_{k\geq 1}$, see [9]. However, in [10] we showed that a slightly weaker version of (4) is nevertheless true, namely we have

Theorem 1. *Let $(X_n)_{n\geq 1}$ be an arbitrary (not necessarily tight) sequence of random variables with tail σ-field $\mathcal{T}$. Then, after suitably enlarging the probability space, there exists a subsequence $(X_{n_k})_{k\geq 1}$ and a sequence $(Y_k)_{k\geq 1}$ of random variables such that Y_k are conditionally independent with respect to $\mathcal{T}$ and (4) holds.*

Theorem 1 is an almost sure invariance principle in the sense of Strassen [11], but it yields a.s. approximation of the individual r.v's X_{n_k}, instead of their partial sums.

By De Finetti's theorem, the exchangeability of a sequence $(Y_k)_{k\geq 1}$ can be "split" into two properties, namely, to the conditional independence of $(Y_k)_{k\geq 1}$ relative to its tail σ-field $\mathcal{T}$ and the conditional identical distribution of $(Y_k)_{k\geq 1}$ relative to $\mathcal{T}$. As Theorem 1 shows, the conditional independence of $(Y_k)_{k\geq 1}$ can always be guaranteed in (4) and the difficulties are caused by the second, seemingly much simpler property, the conditional identical distribution of the Y_k's. In [10] we gave an example showing that even in the case when the sequence $(X_n)_{n\geq 1}$ is uniformly bounded, the behavior of the conditional distribution functions $\mathcal{F}_k(t) = \mathbb{P}(Y_k < t|\mathcal{T})$ of Y_k can be extremely irregular, with no subsequence $\mathcal{F}_{m_k}$ converging in any useful sense. However, even without the conditional identical distribution of the Y_k's, the approximation (4) has many useful consequences. As the examples in the next section will show, Theorem 1 provides important information for nonstationary lacunary series, e.g., for the a.s. convergence and asymptotic properties of series $\sum a_k X_{n_k}$. For example, while the Aldous–Chatterji subsequence theory yields the Hartman–Wintner-type LIL (3) for sufficiently thin subsequences $(X_{n_k})_{k\geq 1}$ of L_2-bounded sequences $(X_n)_{n\geq 1}$, Theorem 1 yields the Kolmogorov-type LIL

$$\limsup_{N\to\infty} \frac{\sum_{k=1}^{N} a_k (X_{n_k} - X)}{\sqrt{2A_N^2 \log\log A_N}} = Y^{1/2} \ \text{a.s.} \tag{5}$$

for suitable subsequences $(X_{n_k})_{k\geq 1}$ of uniformly bounded sequences $(X_n)_{n\geq 1}$, where $(a_n)_{n\geq 1}$ is a weight sequence satisfying

$$A_N = \left(\sum_{k=1}^{N} a_k^2\right)^{1/2} \longrightarrow \infty, \quad \max_{k\leq N} |a_k| = o\left(\frac{A_N}{\sqrt{\log\log A_n}}\right). \tag{6}$$

In conclusion we note that in [12] it is proved that for any tight sequence $(X_n)_{n\geq 1}$, there is a subsequence $(X_{n_k})_{k\geq 1}$ and a sequence $(Y_k)_{k\geq 1}$ of random variables which is 'strongly exchangeable at infinity' in a certain technical sense and (4) holds. Thus, we have an a.s. approximation theorem even in the context of the Chatterji–Aldous subsequence theory, but it applies only for limit theorems for i.i.d. or near-i.i.d. sequences.

2. Applications

By the result of Révész [1] cited in the Introduction, if $(X_n)_{n\geq 1}$ is a sequence of r.v.'s with $\sup_n \mathbb{E}(X_n^2) < \infty$, then there exist a subsequence $(X_{n_k})_{k\geq 1}$ and a random variable $X \in L_2$ such that $(X_{n_k} - X)_{k\geq 1}$ is a convergence system, i.e., for any numerical sequence $(c_k)_{k\geq 1}$ with $\sum_{k=1}^{\infty} c_k^2 < \infty$, the series $\sum_{k=1}^{\infty} c_k(X_{n_k} - X)$ converges almost surely. Komlós [13] proved that with a suitable choice of (n_k) and X, $(X_{n_k} - X)_{k\geq 1}$ will actually be an unconditional convergence system (i.e., it will be a convergence system after any permutation of its terms), settling a long-standing open problem in the theory of orthogonal series, see [14], p. 54. Another, equally elaborate proof of Komlós' theorem was given by Aldous [7]. Since conditional independence is a permutation-invariant property, the two-series version of the Kolmogorov three-series criterion and Beppo Levi's theorem imply that a conditionally independent sequence with conditional mean 0 and bounded second moments is an unconditional convergence system. Thus, observing that (4) and $\sum_{k=1}^{\infty} c_k^2 < \infty$ imply

$$\sum_{k=1}^{\infty} |c_k||X_{n_k} - Y_k| \leq \left(\sum_{k=1}^{\infty} c_k^2\right)^{1/2} \left(\sum_{k=1}^{\infty} |X_{n_k} - Y_k|^2\right)^{1/2} < \infty \text{ a.s.,}$$

the following version of Komlós' theorem follows immediately from Theorem 1:

Theorem 2. *Let $(X_n)_{n\geq 1}$ be a sequence of r.v.'s with tail σ-algebra $\mathcal{T}$ such that $\sup_n \mathbb{E}(X_n^2) < \infty$. Then $(X_n - \mathbb{E}(X_n|\mathcal{T}))_{n\geq 1}$ contains an unconditional convergence system.*

By passing to a further subsequence and using a weak compactness theorem, the centering sequence $\mathbb{E}(X_n|\mathcal{T})$ can be replaced by a single random variable $X \in L_2$.

Proving the unconditionality of a convergence system is a difficult problem of analysis, with a number of famous results and open problems. By Carleson's theorem, $(\cos nx)_{n\geq 1}$ is a convergence system, but, as Kolmogorov pointed out in [15], this property breaks down after a suitable permutation of the sequence. In the opposite direction, Garsia [16] showed that if $(f_n)_{n\geq 1}$ is an orthonormal system and $\sum_{n=1}^{\infty} c_n^2 < \infty$, then the sum $\sum_{n=1}^{\infty} c_n f_n$ is a.e. convergent after a suitable permutation of its terms. But whether there is a universal permutation $\sigma : \mathbb{N} \to \mathbb{N}$ of the positive integers such that $\sum_{n=1}^{\infty} c_n f_{\sigma(n)}$ is a.e. convergent for any coefficient sequence $(c_n)_{n\geq 1}$ with $\sum_{n=1}^{\infty} c_n^2 < \infty$ (i.e., $(f_{\sigma(n)})_{n\geq 1}$ is a convergence system) is still an open question.

As mentioned above, the subsequence $(n_k)_{k\geq 1}$ constructed in the proof of Aldous' theorem depends on the limit theorem we want to verify and different limit theorems require different subsequences. For example, Aldous' theorem implies that if (X_n) is a sequence of r.v.'s with $\sup_n \mathbb{E}(X_n^2) < \infty$, then for any fixed numerical sequence $(c_k)_{k\geq 1}$ with $\sum_{k=1}^{\infty} c_k^2 < \infty$, there exist a subsequence $(X_{n_k})_{k\geq 1}$ and $X \in L_2$ such that $\sum_{k=1}^{\infty} c_k(X_{n_k} - X)$

converges a.e., but the theorem does not yield a universal subsequence $(X_{n_k})_{k\geq 1}$ working for all square summable sequences $(c_k)_{k\geq 1}$ simultaneously, and thus Révész' theorem mentioned in the Introduction does not follow from Aldous' theorem. The same applies for the weighted CLT and LIL for lacunary sequences proved by Gaposhkin (see [17], Theorem 1.5.1 and Theorem 1.6.1). However, both results are immediate consequences of Theorem 1 and since conditional independence is a permutation-invariant property, we automatically get their permutation-invariance as well:

Theorem 3. *Let $(X_n)_{n\geq 1}$ be a uniformly bounded sequence of random variables with $\|X_n\|_2 = 1$ $(n = 1, 2, \ldots)$. Then, there exists a subsequence $(X_{n_k})_{k\geq 1}$ and bounded random variables X and $Y \geq 0$ such that*

$$\lim_{N\to\infty} A_N^{-1} \sum_{k=1}^{N} a_k (X_{n_k} - X) \xrightarrow{d} N(0, Y) \tag{7}$$

for any positive numerical sequence $(a_n)_{n\geq 1}$ satisfying

$$A_N = \left(\sum_{k=1}^{N} a_k^2\right)^{1/2} \longrightarrow \infty, \quad \max_{k\leq N} |a_k| = o(A_N).$$

Moreover, relation (7) remains valid after any permutation of the sequence $(X_{n_k})_{k\geq 1}$.

Theorem 4. *Let $(X_n)_{n\geq 1}$ be a uniformly bounded sequence of random variables with $\|X_n\|_2 = 1$ $(n = 1, 2, \ldots)$. Then, there exist a subsequence $(X_{n_k})_{k\geq 1}$ and bounded random variables X and $Y \geq 0$ such that (5) holds for any positive numerical sequence $(a_n)_{n\geq 1}$ satisfying (6). Moreover, relation (5) remains valid after any permutation of the sequence $(X_{n_k})_{k\geq 1}$.*

The unpermuted forms of Theorems 3 and 4 are due to Gaposhkin [17]. To deduce the permutation-invariant forms from Theorem 1, it suffices to use the version of the CLT and LIL for independent random variables due to Kolmogorov [18] and Lévy ([19], p. 105), the permutation-invariance of conditional independence and the observation that by (4) we have

$$\sum_{k=1}^{N} |a_k||X_{n_k} - Y_k| \leq (\max_{k\leq N} |a_k|) \sum_{k=1}^{N} |X_{n_k} - Y_k| = o(A_N).$$

Next, we formulate a version of the Kolmogorov–Erdős–Feller–Petrowski upper–lower class test for lacunary series.

Theorem 5. *Let $(X_n)_{n\geq 1}$ be a uniformly bounded sequence of random variables with $\|X_n\|_2 = 1$ $(n = 1, 2, \ldots)$. Then there exists a subsequence $(X_{n_k})_{k\geq 1}$ and bounded random variables X and $Y \geq 0$ such that for any numerical sequence $(a_n)_{n\geq 1}$ satisfying*

$$A_N = \left(\sum_{k=1}^{N} a_k^2\right)^{1/2} \longrightarrow \infty, \quad \max_{k\leq N} |a_k| = o\left(\frac{A_N}{(\log\log A_n)^{3/2}}\right) \tag{8}$$

we have

$$\mathbb{P}\left(\sum_{k=1}^{n} a_k X_{n_k} > Y^{1/2} A_n \varphi(A_n) \text{ i.o.}\right) = 1 \text{ or } 0 \tag{9}$$

according as

$$\sum_{n=1}^{\infty} \frac{\varphi(n)}{n} e^{-\varphi(n)^2/2} = \infty \text{ or } < \infty. \tag{10}$$

Moreover, the result remains valid after any permutation of the sequence $(X_{n_k})_{k\geq 1}$.

Again, the result follows from the corresponding result for independent random variables in [20], Theorem 1, and the observation that

$$\sum_{k=1}^{N} |a_k||X_{n_k} - Y_k| \le (\max_{k\le N} |a_k|) \sum_{k=1}^{N} |X_{n_k} - Y_k| = o(A_N/(\log\log A_N)^{3/2}).$$

Replacing the exponent $3/2$ in (8) by $1/2 < \rho < 3/2$, the upper–lower class test (9)–(10) will continue to hold with new terms appearing gradually in the exponent of $e^{-\varphi(n)^2/2}$ as ρ approaches $1/2$, according to the hierarchy of results described in [20].

In conclusion, we formulate a weighted strong law for lacunary sequences.

Theorem 6. *Let $(X_n)_{n\ge1}$ be a sequence of random variables, let $p, q > 1$ satisfying $1/p + 1/q = 1$, and assume that there exists a random variable $X \in L_p$ such that*

$$\mathbb{P}(|X_n| > t) \le C\mathbb{P}(|X| > t) \text{ for some constant } C > 0 \text{ and } n = 1, 2, \ldots. \tag{11}$$

Then there exist a subsequence $(X_{n_k})_{k\ge1}$ and a random variable $X \in L_p$ such that for any array $(a_{N,i})_{N\ge1, 1\le i\le N}$ satisfying

$$\sup_N \left(\frac{1}{N}\sum_{i=1}^{N} |a_{N,i}|^q\right)^{1/q} < \infty \tag{12}$$

we have

$$\lim_{N\to\infty} \frac{1}{N}\sum_{i=1}^{N} a_{N,i}(X_{n_i} - X) = 0 \text{ a.s.}$$

Moreover, the result remains valid after any permutation of the sequence $(X_{n_k})_{k\ge1}$.

This follows immediately from Theorem 1 and the conditional version of Theorem 1.1 of [21] upon observing that (4) and (12) imply

$$\frac{1}{N}\sum_{i=1}^{N} a_{N,i}|X_{n_i} - Y_i| \le \left(\frac{1}{N}\sum_{i=1}^{N} |a_{N,i}|^q\right)^{1/q} \left(\sum_{i=1}^{N} |X_{n_i} - Y_i|^p\right)^{1/p} N^{-(q-1)/q}$$

and noting that the identical distribution of r.v.'s in Theorem 1.1 of [21] can be replaced by the stochastic domination condition (11). Finally, the permutation-invariance statement follows from the permutation-invariance of conditional independence.

Note that the the assumption (11) and $X \in L_p$ made on X_n in Theorem 6 are stronger than the moment boundedness condition $\sup_n \mathbb{E}|X_n|^p < \infty$, typically assumed in the theory of lacunary series. Whether Theorem 6 remains valid under $\sup_n \mathbb{E}|X_n|^p < \infty$ remains open.

In conclusion we mention an interesting recent paper of Karatzas and Schachermayer [22] on the weak law of large numbers for lacunary series. The main result of [22] can also be deduced by using Theorem 1 and the classical criteria for the weak law of large numbers for independent random variables, but since such a proof would not be simpler than the original proof in [22], we do not discuss this problem here.

Funding: This research received no external funding.

Data Availability Statement: Data is contained within the article.

Acknowledgments: The author wishes to express his gratitude to two anonymous referees for their useful comments on the paper.

Conflicts of Interest: The authors declare no conflicts of interest.

eferences

Révész, P. On a problem of Steinhaus. *Acta Math. Acad. Sci. Hung.* **1965**, *16*, 311–318. [CrossRef]

Komlós, J. A generalisation of a problem of Steinhaus. *Acta Math. Acad. Sci. Hung.* **1967**, *18*, 217–229. [CrossRef]

Gaposhkin, V.F. Convergence and limit theorems for subsequences of random variables. *Teor. Verojatnost. Primenen.* **1972**, *17*, 401–423. (In Russian)

Chatterji, S.D. A principle of subsequences in probability theory: The central limit theorem. *Adv. Math.* **1974**, *13*, 31–54; Erratum in *Adv. Math.* **1974**, *14*, 266–269. [CrossRef]

Chatterji, S.D. A subsequence principle in probability theory II. The law of the iterated logarithm. *Invent. Math.* **1974**, *25*, 241–251. [CrossRef]

Chatterji, S.D. Un principe de sous-suites dans la théorie des probabilités. In *Séminaire de Probabilités VI, Université de Strasbourg*; Lecture Notes in Mathematics; Springer: Berlin/Heidelberg, Germany, 1972; Volume 258, pp. 72–89.

Aldous, D.J. Limit theorems for subsequences of arbitrarily dependent sequences of random variables. *Z. Wahrscheinlichkeitstheorie Verw. Geb.* **1977**, *40*, 59–82. [CrossRef]

Dacunha-Castelle, D. Indiscernability and exchangeability in L^p-spaces. In Proceedings of the Seminar on Random Series, Convex Sets and Geometry of Banach Spaces, Aarhus, Denmark, 14–20 October 1974; Aarhus Universitet: Aarhus, Denmark, 1975; Volume 25, pp. 50–56.

Berkes, I.; Rosenthal, H.P. Almost exchangeable sequences of random variables. *Z. Wahrscheinlichkeitstheorie Verw. Geb.* **1985**, *70*, 473–507. [CrossRef]

Berkes, I. Lacunary sequences and conditional independence. *Acta Math. Hung.* **1995**, *67*, 253–259. [CrossRef]

Strassen, V. An invariance principle for the law of the iterated logarithm. *Z. Wahrscheinlichkeitstheorie Verw. Geb.* **1964**, *3*, 211–226. [CrossRef]

Berkes, I.; Péter, E. Exchangeable random variables and the subsequence principle. *Prob. Theory Rel. Fields* **1986**, *73*, 395–413. [CrossRef]

Komlós, J. Every sequence converging to 0 weakly in L_2 contains an unconditional convergence sequence. *Ark. Mat.* **1974**, *12*, 41–49. [CrossRef]

Uljanov, P.L. Solved and unsolved problems in the theory of trigonometric and orthonormal series. *Uspehi Mat. Nauk* **1964**, *19*, 3–69. (In Russian)

Kolmogorov, A.; Menshov, D. Sur la convergence des séries des fonctions orthogonales. *Math. Z.* **1927**, *26*, 432–441. [CrossRef]

Garsia, A. Existence of almost everywhere convergent rearrangements for Fourier series of L_2 functions. *Ann. Math.* **1964**, *79*, 623–629. [CrossRef]

Gaposhkin, V.F. Lacunary series and independence. *Uspehi Mat. Nauk* **1966**, *21*, 3–82. (In Russian)

Kolmogorov, A. Über das Gesetz des iterierten Logarithmus. *Math. Ann.* **1929**, *101*, 126–135. [CrossRef]

Lévy, P. *Théorie de L'Addition Des Variables Aléatoires*; Gauthier-Villars: Paris, France, 1954.

Feller, W. The general form of the so called law of the iterated logarithm. *Trans. Amer. Math. Soc.* **1943**, *54*, 373–402. [CrossRef]

Cuzick, J. A strong law for weighted sums of i.i.d. random variables. *J. Theor. Probab.* **1995**, *8*, 625–641. [CrossRef]

Karatzas, I.; Schachermayer, W. A weak law of large numbers for dependent random variables. *Theory Probab. Appl.* **2023**, *68*, 501–509. [CrossRef]

entropy

MDPI

Article

Limit Laws for Sums of Logarithms of *k*-Spacings

Paul Deheuvels

Laboratoire de Statistique Théorique et Appliquée, Université Paris VI, 7 Avenue du Château, F 92340 Bourg-la-Reine, France; pd@ccr.jussieu.fr

Abstract: Let $Z = Z_1, \ldots, Z_n$ be an i.i.d. sample from the absolutely continuous distribution function $F(z) := P(Z \leq z)$, with density $f(z) := \frac{\mathrm{d}}{\mathrm{d}z}F(z)$. Let $Z_{1,n} < \ldots < Z_{n,n}$ be the order statistics generated by $Z_1, \ldots, Z_n$. Let $Z_{0,n} = a := \inf\{z : F(z) > 0\}$ and $Z_{n+1,n} = b := \sup\{z : F(z) < 1\}$ denote the end-points of the common distribution of these observations, and assume that the density f is Riemann integrable and bounded away from 0 over each interval $[a', b'] \subset (a, b)$. For a specified $k \geq 1$, we establish the asymptotic normality of the sum of logarithms of the k-spacings $Z_{i+k,n} - Z_{i-1,n}$ for $i = 1, \ldots, n-k+2$. Our results complete previous investigations in the literature conducted by Blumenthal, Cressie, Shao and Hahn, and the references therein.

Keywords: order statistics; parametric hypothesis testing; hypergeometric functions

1. Introduction and Results

Let $X_1, X_2, \ldots$ be a sequence of independent replicæ of a non-degenerate random variable X, with distribution function $F(x) := \mathbb{P}(X \leq x)$, defined for $x \in \overline{\mathbb{R}} := \mathbb{R} \cup \{-\infty\} \cup \{-\infty\}$. We denote by $a := \inf\{x : F(x) > 0\}$, and $b := \sup\{x : F(x) < 1\}$, the distribution end-points, and we assume that a version of the the density $f(x) = \frac{\mathrm{d}}{\mathrm{d}x}F(x)$ of X exists for $x \in \mathbb{R}$ and is Riemann integrable and bounded away from 0 over each interval $[a', b'] \subset (a, b)$. For each $n \geq 0$, we set $X_{0,n} := a$ and $X_{n+1,n} := b$, and for each $n \geq 1$, we denote the order statistics of $X_1, \ldots, X_n$ by $X_{1,n}, \ldots, X_{n,n}$, which fulfill almost surely the strict inequalities

$$-\infty \leq a = X_{0,n} < X_{1,n} < \ldots < X_{n,n} < b = X_{n+1,n} \leq \infty. \tag{1}$$

Given a specified integer $k \geq 1$, we are concerned with the limiting behavior as $n \to \infty$ of the sums of the logarithms of the k-spacings $\{D_{i,n}^{(k)} : 1 \leq i \leq n-k+2\}$, defined for $n \geq k-1$ by

$$D_{i,n}^{(k)} := X_{i+k-1,n} - X_{i-1,n} \quad \text{for} \quad i = 1, \ldots, n-k+2. \tag{2}$$

Since the first and last among the k-spacings in (2), namely, $D_{1,n}^{(k)}$ and $D_{n-k+2,n}^{(k)}$, are possibly infinite, we set

$$p_0 := \begin{cases} 1 & \text{when} \quad a > -\infty, \\ 2 & \text{when} \quad a = -\infty, \end{cases} \tag{3}$$

$$q_0 := \begin{cases} 1 & \text{when} \quad b < \infty, \\ 2 & \text{when} \quad b = \infty, \end{cases} \tag{4}$$

and consider only the finite k-spacings $\{D_{i,n}^{(k)} : p_0 \leq i \leq n-k+3-q_0\}$.

Our goal is to investigate the limiting behavior, as $n \to \infty$, of the statistic

$$T_n(k;p,q) := \sum_{i=p}^{n-k+3-q} \Big\{ -\log\Big(\frac{n}{k} D_{i,n}^{(k)}\Big)\Big\}, \tag{5}$$

defined for each set of integers $k \geq 1$, $p \geq p_0$, $q \geq q_0$, and $n \geq k+p+q-3$. In the present paper, we establish the asymptotic normality of $T_n(k;p,q)$ when k, p, and q are fixed, and $n \to \infty$. The motivation of these statistics is to provide tests of the goodness of fit of the null hypothesis $(H.0)$ that X is uniformly distributed on $(0,1)$ with $f(x) = \mathbb{I}_{(0,1)}(x)$, against the alternative. Darling [1] introduced the statistic $T_n := T_n(1;2,2)$, and, later, Blumenthal [2] showed that, under the assumption that f is continuous on $(a,b) \subset (-\infty,\infty)$ and bounded away from 0 on this interval, we have, as $n \to \infty$

$$n^{1/2}\{T_n - n\gamma - n\mathbb{E}(\log f(X))\} \xrightarrow{d} N(0, \zeta(2) + 1 + \text{Var}(\log f(X))). \tag{6}$$

Here, and in the sequel, we write "$\xrightarrow{d}$" to denote weak convergence and "$\stackrel{d}{=}$" to denote equality in distribution. We let $N(\mu,\sigma^2)$ stand for the Gaussian distribution with mean μ and variance σ^2. Throughout, we use the convention that $\sum_{\varnothing}(\cdot) := 0$ and $\prod_{\varnothing}(\cdot) := 1$. We denote by $\gamma = 0.577215\ldots$ *Euler's constant* (see, e.g., (14) below) and set $\zeta(2) = \frac{\pi^2}{6}$ for the value taken by the *Riemann zeta function* $\zeta(z)$ for $z = 2$ (we refer to Remark 2 in the sequel for some basic facts concerning these mathematical objects).

Under the null hypothesis $(H.0)$ that X is uniformly distributed on $(0,1)$, which implies that $f(X) = 1$ a.s., (6) reduces to

$$n^{1/2}\{T_n - n\gamma\} \xrightarrow{d} N(0, \zeta(2) + 1). \tag{7}$$

For $0 < \alpha < 1$, denote by ν_α the upper α quantile of the $N(0,1)$ distribution. It follows from (6) that the test rejecting $(H.0)$ when $n^{1/2}\{T_n - n\gamma\} \geq \nu_\alpha\sqrt{\zeta(2)+1}$ is asymptotically consistent with size α when $n \to \infty$. This result may be refined by using the exact distribution of $n^{1/2}\{T_n - n\gamma\}$, which was obtained in tractable form by Deheuvels and Derzko [3]. The corresponding results allow for the practical use of the so-called Darling–Blumenthal test of uniformity.

Some practical problems arise for the use of the above-described test in the presence of *ties* (see, e.g., pp. 118–124 in Hájek and Šidák [4]) when some of the observed spacings in the sequence $\{D_{i;n}^{(1)} : 2 \leq i \leq n\}$ are null, in which case T_n is not properly defined. In practice, the use of the k-spacings $\{D_{i;n}^{(k)} : 2 \leq i \leq n-k+1\}$ for the choice of $k \geq 1$ that is sufficiently large allows us to overcome this difficulty. This motivates the study of the limiting behavior $T_n(k;p,q)$ for a specified choice of the integer $k \geq 1$.

We work under the assumptions listed in $(F.1–3)$ below:

$(F.1)$ $\text{Var}(\log f(X)) < \infty$;

$(F.2)$ Either $a > -\infty$ and f is Riemann integrable and bounded away from 0 in a right neighborhood of a, or
$a \geq -\infty$ and f is monotone in a right neighborhood of a;

$(F.3)$ Either $b < \infty$ and f is Riemann integrable and bounded away from 0 in a left neighborhood of b, or
$b \leq \infty$ and f is monotone in a left neighborhood of b.

Our main result is stated in Theorem 1 below. We set $\psi(z) := \psi^{(1)}(z) = \frac{d}{dz}\log\Gamma(z)$ for the *digamma function* (see Remark 2 in the sequel for details on Euler's constant γ,

Riemann's $\zeta(\cdot)$ function, the *Gamma function* $\Gamma(\cdot)$, and the *polygamma functions* $\psi^{(m)}(\cdot)$ for $m = 0, 1, \ldots$).

Theorem 1. *Under* $(F.1\text{–}2\text{–}3)$, *for each specified set of integers* $k \geq 1$, $p \geq p_0$, *and* $q \geq p_0$, *we have, as* $n \to \infty$,

$$n^{-1/2}\Big[T_n(k;p,q) - n\Big\{ -\psi(k) + \log k + \mathbb{E}\big(\log f(X)\big)\Big\}\Big] \stackrel{d}{\to} N\Big(0, \psi'(k) + 1 + \mathrm{Var}\big(\log f(X)\big)\Big). \tag{8}$$

Remark 1. *Under the assumptions above, for any specified set of integers* $k \geq 1$, $p', p'' \geq p_0$, *and* $q', q'' \geq p_0$, *we have*

$$|T_n(k;p',q') - T_n(k;p'',q'')| = O_{\mathbb{P}}(1) \quad \textit{as} \quad n \to \infty. \tag{9}$$

Therefore, when the conclusion of Theorem 1 holds for some specified pairs of integers (p,q) *with* $p \geq p_0$ *and* $q \geq q_0$, *it holds for all other pairs of integers* p, q, *fulfilling this condition. Because of this, we set* $T_n(k) := T_n(k;p_0,q_0)$ *and give a proof of the theorem for* $p = p_0$ *and* $q = q_0$.

The proof of Theorem 1 is given in the next section, together with additional results of interest. We mention at this point some historical details about the sums of the logarithms of spacings and related topics. The study of spacings has received considerable attention in the literature, ever since the pioneering work of Darling [1] (see, e.g., Pyke [5,6], Deheuvels [7], and the references therein). To the best of our knowledge, the best result coming close to Theorem 1 was obtained by Cressie [8,9] for $p = q = 2$ and $k \geq 1$. Cressie established a variant of (8) under the assumption that the density f of X is a bounded step function (see Theorem 5.1, p. 352 in [8]). For $p = q = 2$ and $k = 1$, a version of Theorem 1 was given by Blumenthal [2] under rather strenuous conditions on f, assumed to be, at least, twice differentiable. Shao and Hahn [10] largely improved Blumenthal's theorem by showing that (8) holds for $p = q = 1$, $k = 1$, and when $-\infty < a < b < \infty$ under the assumption that f is Riemann integrable and bounded away from 0 on (a,b). Recently, Deheuvels and Derzko [11] (see also [3]) relaxed the assumptions of Blumenthal and Shao and Hahn by giving a version of Theorem 1 for $k = 1$, allowing a and b to be possibly infinite. The present paper improves these results by covering the case of an arbitrary $k \geq 1$ under less strenuous conditions on f. We refer to Shao and Hahn [10], del Pino [12,13], Czekała [14], and the references therein for discussions and further references on the statistical applications of this theorem.

Remark 2. (1°) *The following relations and definitions hold, relating Euler's constant* $\gamma = 0.577215\ldots$ *to the Riemann zeta function* $\zeta(\cdot)$ *in (6) (see, e.g., Spanier and Oldham [15] and Gradshteyn and Ryzhik [16], p. xxix). We have, for each* $r > 1$ *and* $m = 1, 2, \ldots$,

$$\zeta(r) := \frac{1}{\Gamma(r)} \int_0^\infty \frac{t^{r-1}\mathrm{d}t}{e^t - 1} = \sum_{j=1}^\infty \frac{1}{j^r} \quad \textit{for} \quad r > 1, \tag{10}$$

$$\zeta(2m) := \frac{2^{2m}\pi^{2m}B_{2m}}{(2m)!}, \tag{11}$$

where B_n *is the n-th Bernoulli number. In particular, for* $r = 2$ *and* $m = 1$,

$$\zeta(2) = \frac{\pi^2}{6} = \frac{1}{\Gamma(2)} \int_0^\infty \frac{t\mathrm{d}t}{e^t - 1} = \sum_{j=1}^\infty \frac{1}{j^2}. \tag{12}$$

The Bernoulli numbers $\{B_n : n \geq 0\}$ *are defined as the constants in the expansion*

$$\frac{t}{e^t-1}=\sum_{n=0}^{\infty}B_n\frac{t^n}{n!}\quad \text{which converges for}\quad |t|<2\pi. \tag{13}$$

The Euler constant γ may be defined by either one of the relations

$$\gamma:=\int_0^{\infty}(-\log t)e^{-t}\mathrm{d}t=\lim_{r\downarrow 1}\left\{\zeta(r)-\frac{1}{r-1}\right\}$$
$$=\lim_{n\to\infty}\left\{\sum_{j=1}^{n-1}\frac{1}{j}-\log n\right\}. \tag{14}$$

(2°) *The Euler Gamma function $\Gamma(\cdot)$, digamma function $\psi(\cdot)$, and polygamma function $\psi^{(m)}(\cdot)$ are respectively defined via the relations (see, e.g., §§6.3–6.4 in Abramowitz and Stegun [17]) for $z>0$ and $m\geq 1$,*

$$\Gamma(z):=\int_0^{\infty}t^{z-1}e^{-t}\mathrm{d}t, \tag{15}$$
$$\psi(z):=\frac{\mathrm{d}}{\mathrm{d}z}\log\Gamma(z)=-\gamma+\int_0^{\infty}\frac{e^{-t}-e^{-zt}}{1-e^{-t}}\,\mathrm{d}t, \tag{16}$$

which fulfills

$$\lim_{z\to\infty}\left\{\psi(z)-\log z\right\}=0,$$
$$\psi^{(m)}(z):=\frac{\mathrm{d}^{m+1}}{\mathrm{d}z^{m+1}}\log\Gamma(z)=(-1)^{m+1}\int_0^{\infty}\frac{t^m e^{-zt}}{1-e^{-t}}\,\mathrm{d}t. \tag{17}$$

In particular, when $z=n\geq 1$ is an integer, we obtain (see, e.g., Formulas 6.3.2 and 6.4.2 in [17])

$$\Gamma(n)=(n-1)!=\prod_{j=1}^{n-1}j,$$
$$\psi(n):=-\gamma+\sum_{j=1}^{n-1}\frac{1}{j},\quad \psi(1)=-\gamma, \tag{18}$$

which fulfills

$$\lim_{n\to\infty}\left\{\psi(n)-\log n\right\}=0,$$
$$\psi^{(m)}(n):=(-1)^{m+1}m!\left\{\zeta(m+1)-\sum_{j=1}^{n-1}\frac{1}{j^{m+1}}\right\}, \tag{19}$$
$$\psi'(n):=\zeta(2)-\sum_{j=1}^{n-1}\frac{1}{j^2}=\sum_{j=n}^{\infty}\frac{1}{j^2}$$
$$=\int_0^{\infty}\frac{te^{-nt}}{1-e^{-t}}\,\mathrm{d}t=\int_0^1\frac{u^{n-1}\{-\log u\}}{1-u}\,\mathrm{d}u. \tag{20}$$

(3°) *Routine computations show that, as $n\to\infty$,*

$$\left\{\psi(n+1)-\log(n+1)\right\}-\left\{\psi(n)-\log n\right\}=\frac{1+o(1)}{2n^2},$$

whence, as $n\to\infty$,

$$n\left\{\psi(n)-\log n\right\}\quad\to\quad -\frac{1}{2}. \tag{21}$$

(4°) *In view of (12) and (20), we readily obtain that, for* $k = 1, 2, \ldots$,

$$\begin{aligned}\psi'(k) &= \zeta(2) - \sum_{j=1}^{k-1} \frac{1}{j^2} = \sum_{j=k}^{\infty} \frac{1}{j^2} = \sum_{j=k}^{\infty} \frac{1}{j(j+1)} + \sum_{j=k}^{\infty} \left\{ \frac{1}{j^2} - \frac{1}{j(j+1)} \right\} \\ &= \frac{1}{k} + \sum_{j=k}^{\infty} \left\{ \frac{1}{j^2} - \frac{1}{j(j+1)} \right\} = \frac{1}{k} + \sum_{j=k}^{\infty} \left\{ \frac{1}{j^2(j+1)} \right\}\end{aligned}$$

$$\begin{aligned}&= \frac{1}{k} + \sum_{j=k}^{\infty} \left\{ \frac{1}{j^2(j+1)} \right\} + \frac{1}{2k^2} - \frac{1}{2} \sum_{j=k}^{\infty} \left\{ \frac{1}{j^2} - \frac{1}{(j+1)^2} \right\} \\ &= \frac{1}{k} + \frac{1}{2k^2} + \sum_{j=k}^{\infty} \left\{ \frac{1}{j^2(j+1)} - \frac{j + \frac{1}{2}}{j^2(j+1)^2} \right\} = \frac{1}{k} + \frac{1}{2k^2} + \frac{1}{2} \sum_{j=k}^{\infty} \left\{ \frac{1}{j^2(j+1)^2} \right\} \\ &= \frac{1}{k} + \frac{1}{2k^2} + \frac{1}{6k^3} - \frac{1}{6} \sum_{j=k}^{\infty} \left\{ \left\{ \frac{1}{j^3} - \frac{1}{(j+1)^3} \right\} - \left\{ \frac{3j^2 + 3j}{j^3(j+1)^3} \right\} \right\} \\ &= \frac{1}{k} + \frac{1}{2k^2} + \frac{1}{6k^3} - \frac{1}{6} \sum_{j=k}^{\infty} \frac{1}{j^3(j+1)^3}.\end{aligned}$$

This, in turn, implies that, as $k \to \infty$,

$$\begin{aligned}(2k^2 - 2k + 1)\psi'(n) - 2k + 1 &= (2k^2 - 2k + 1)\Big\{\zeta(2) - \sum_{j=1}^{k-1} \frac{1}{j^2}\Big\} - 2k + 1 \\ &= \frac{1}{3k} + \frac{1}{6k^2} + \frac{1 + o(1)}{6k^3} \to 0.\end{aligned} \tag{22}$$

so that the limiting variance of $n^{-1/2}T_n(k; p, q)$ *in (8) equals*

$$\mathrm{Var}\big(\log f(X)\big) + \frac{1 + o(1)}{3k} \to \quad \mathrm{Var}\big(\log f(X)\big),$$

as $k \to \infty$.

(5°) *Likewise, we infer from (14) that, as* $k \to \infty$,

$$\psi(k) = \gamma - \sum_{j=1}^{k-1} \frac{1}{j} + \log k = \sum_{j=k}^{\infty} \Big\{ \log\Big(1 + \frac{1}{j}\Big) - \frac{1}{j} \Big\} = -\frac{1 + o(1)}{k},$$

so that the limiting centering factor of $n^{-1}T_n(k; p, q)$ *in (8) equals*

$$\mathbb{E}\big(\log f(X)\big) - \frac{1 + o(1)}{k} \to \mathbb{E}\big(\log f(X)\big),$$

as $k \to \infty$. *By all this, for large specified values of k,* $n^{-1}T_n(k; p, q)$ *follows approximatively, as* $n \to \infty$, *a normal distribution, with expectation* $\mathbb{E}\big(\log f(X)\big)$ *and variance* $n^{-1/2}Var\big(\log f(X)\big)$. *This gives a heuristical motivation for the use of the statistic* $n^{-1}T_n(k; p, q)$ *(taken with specified large values of k) to estimate the factor* $\mathbb{E}\big(\log f(X)\big)$.

2. Proofs

2.1. Properties of the Gauss Hypergeometric Function

In our proofs, we make use of a series of identities related to hypergeometric functions, which are of independent interest. For any $x \in \mathbb{R}$ and $n \in \mathbb{N}$, define the *Pochhammer function* by

$$(x)_n := x(x+1)\dots(x+n-1) \text{ for } n = 1,2,\dots, \text{ and } (x)_0 := 1. \tag{23}$$

We note that, whenever $x > 0$ and $n \in \mathbb{N} := \{0,1,\dots\}$,

$$(x)_n = \frac{\Gamma(x+n)}{\Gamma(x)}. \tag{24}$$

In particular, we have $(1)_n = n!$ for each $n \in \mathbb{N}$. We refer to 18:3:1; 18:3:2, and 18:10:1 in Spanier and Oldham [15] for additional properties of the Pochhammer function. Recalling (16), (23) and (24), we obtain readily that, for $-x \notin \{0,1,\dots,n-1\}$, $(x)_n \neq 0$ and

$$\frac{\mathrm{d}}{\mathrm{d}x}(x)_n = (x)_n \sum_{j=0}^{n-1} \frac{1}{x+j} = (x)_n\{\psi(x+n) - \psi(x)\}, \tag{25}$$

$$\frac{\mathrm{d}^2}{\mathrm{d}x^2}(x)_n = (x)_n\Big\{\psi'(x+n) - \psi'(x) + \{\psi(x+n) - \psi(x)\}^2\Big\}. \tag{26}$$

The usual Gauss hypergeometric function is defined for $c \notin -\mathbb{N}$ and $z \in \mathbb{C}$ with $|z| < 1$ by

$$F(a,b;c;z) \quad := \quad {}_2F_1(a,b;c;z) := \sum_{m=0}^{\infty} \frac{(a)_m(b)_m}{(c)_m} \frac{z^m}{m!}. \tag{27}$$

The function $F(a,b;c;z)$ is defined for $|z| = 1$ when $\mathrm{Re}(c-a-b) > 0$ (see, e.g., Ch.4 in Rainville). In particular (see, e.g., 60:7:2 in [15]), when this condition holds,

$$F(a,b;c;1) = \frac{\Gamma(c)\Gamma(c-b-a)}{\Gamma(c-a)\Gamma(c-b)}. \tag{28}$$

In particular, we have

$$F(1,b;c;1) = \sum_{m=1}^{\infty} \frac{(b)_m}{m(c)_m} = \frac{\Gamma(c)\Gamma(c-b-1)}{\Gamma(c-1)\Gamma(c-b)} = \frac{c-1}{c-b-1}. \tag{29}$$

The general hypergeometric function of order (p,q) is defined for integer $p \leq q+1$ by

$${}_pF_q(a_1,\dots,a_p;b_1,\dots,b_q;z) \quad := \quad \sum_{m=0}^{\infty} \frac{(a_1)_m \dots (a_p)_m}{(b_1)_m \dots (b_q)_m} \frac{z^m}{m!}. \tag{30}$$

The following identity relates higher-order hypergeometric functions to lower-order ones. We have

$$\begin{aligned} &{}_{p+1}F_{q+1}(a_1,\dots,a_p,r;b_1,\dots,b_q,s;z) \\ = \; &\frac{\Gamma(r)}{\Gamma(s)\Gamma(s-r)} \int_0^1 t^{r-1}(1-t)^{s-r-1}{}_pF_q(a_1,\dots,a_p;b_1,\dots,b_q;tz)\mathrm{d}t. \end{aligned}$$

In particular,

$$\begin{aligned}
{}_3F_2(1,b,r;c,s;1) &= \sum_{m=1}^{\infty} \frac{(b)_m (r)_m}{m(c)_m (s)_m} \\
&= \frac{\Gamma(s)}{\Gamma(r)\Gamma(r-s)} \int_0^1 t^{r-1}(1-t)^{s-r-1} F(1,b;c,t)\mathrm{d}t \\
&= \frac{\Gamma(s)}{\Gamma(r)\Gamma(s-r)} \int_0^1 t^{r-1}(1-t)^{s-r-1} \sum_{m=1}^{\infty} \frac{(b)_m}{m(c)_m} t^m.
\end{aligned}$$

For $a > 1, b > 1, c > 1$, and $0 \le x < 1$, we have (see, e.g., 60:10:3 in [15])

$$\int_0^x F(a,b;c;t)\mathrm{d}t = \frac{c-1}{(a-1)(b-1)} \Big\{ F(a-1,b-1;c-1;x) - 1 \Big\}. \tag{31}$$

Proposition 1. *We have, for $c > b+1$, $c \notin -\mathbb{N}$,*

$$\sum_{m=0}^{\infty} \frac{(b)_m}{(c)_m} = \frac{c-1}{c-b-1}, \tag{32}$$

$$\sum_{m=0}^{\infty} \frac{(b)_m}{(c)_m} \{\psi(c+m) - \psi(c)\} = \frac{b}{(c-b-1)^2}, \tag{33}$$

and

$$\sum_{m=0}^{\infty} \frac{(b)_m}{(c)_m} \{\psi(b+m) - \psi(b)\} = \frac{c-1}{(c-b-1)^2}. \tag{34}$$

Proof. By combining (27) with (28), taken with $a = 1$, so that $(1)_m = m!$ and $z = 1$, we obtain

$$\sum_{m=0}^{\infty} \frac{(b)_m}{(c)_m} = F(1,b;c;1) = \frac{\Gamma(c)\Gamma(c-b-1)}{\Gamma(c-1)\Gamma(c-b)} = \frac{c-1}{c-b-1},$$

which is (32). By combining (25) with (32), we obtain, in turn, that

$$\begin{aligned}
&\frac{\partial}{\partial c}\Big\{ \sum_{m=0}^{\infty} \frac{(b)_m}{(c)_m} \Big\} = \sum_{m=0}^{\infty} \frac{\partial}{\partial c}\Big\{ \frac{(b)_m}{(c)_m} \Big\} = -\sum_{m=0}^{\infty} \frac{(b)_m}{(c)_m} \{\psi(c+m) - \psi(c)\} \\
&= \frac{\partial}{\partial c}\Big\{ \frac{c-1}{c-b-1} \Big\} = \frac{-b}{(c-b-1)^2},
\end{aligned}$$

which is (33). The proof of (34) follows along the same lines with the formal replacement of $\frac{\partial}{\partial c}$ by $\frac{\partial}{\partial b}$. Namely, we obtain

$$\begin{aligned}
&\frac{\partial}{\partial b}\Big\{ \sum_{m=0}^{\infty} \frac{(b)_m}{(c)_m} \Big\} = \sum_{m=0}^{\infty} \frac{\partial}{\partial b}\Big\{ \frac{(b)_m}{(c)_m} \Big\} = \sum_{m=0}^{\infty} \frac{(b)_m}{(c)_m} \{\psi(b+m) - \psi(b)\} \\
&= \frac{\partial}{\partial b}\Big\{ \frac{c-1}{c-b-1} \Big\} = \frac{c-1}{(c-b-1)^2},
\end{aligned}$$

which is (34). □

Proposition 2. *We have, for $c > b > 0$,*

$$\sum_{m=1}^{\infty} \frac{(b)_m}{m(c)_m} = \psi(c) - \psi(c-b), \tag{35}$$

$$\sum_{m=1}^{\infty} \frac{(b)_m}{m(c)_m} \{\psi(c+m) - \psi(c)\} = \psi'(c) - \psi'(c-b), \tag{36}$$

and

$$\sum_{m=1}^{\infty} \frac{(b)_m}{m(c)_m} \{\psi(b+m) - \psi(b)\} = \psi'(c-b). \tag{37}$$

Proof. By (27) and (28), we have, for $0 \le x < 1$,

$$\begin{aligned} \frac{c}{hb}\Big\{F(h,b;c;x) - 1\Big\} &= \frac{c}{hb} \sum_{m=1}^{\infty} \frac{(h)_m (b)_m}{(c)_m} \frac{x^m}{m!} \\ &= \sum_{m=0}^{\infty} \frac{(1+h)_m (1+b)_m}{(1+c)_m} \frac{x^{m+1}}{(m+1)!}. \end{aligned}$$

whence by letting $x \uparrow 1$ and making use of (28),

$$\begin{aligned} \frac{c}{hb}\Big\{F(h,b;c;1) - 1\Big\} &= \frac{c}{hb}\Big\{\frac{\Gamma(c)\Gamma(c-h-b)}{\Gamma(c-h)\Gamma(c-b)} - 1\Big\} \\ &= \sum_{m=0}^{\infty} \frac{(1+h)_m (b+1)_m}{(c+1)_m} \frac{1}{(m+1)!}. \end{aligned}$$

When $h \downarrow 0$, we have, for each $m \ge 1$,

$$\frac{(1+h)_m}{(m+1)!} \downarrow \frac{1}{m+1},$$

so that

$$\begin{aligned} \lim_{h\downarrow 0} \sum_{m=0}^{\infty} \frac{(1+h)_m (b+1)_m}{(m+1)!(c+1)_m} &= \sum_{m=0}^{\infty} \frac{(b+1)_m}{(c+1)_m} \frac{1}{m+1} \\ &= \frac{c}{b} \lim_{h\downarrow 0} \frac{1}{h}\Big\{\frac{\Gamma(c)\Gamma(c-h-b)}{\Gamma(c-h)\Gamma(c-b)} - 1\Big\}. \end{aligned}$$

Next, we make use of (16), which yields the expansions

$$\frac{\Gamma(c-h)}{\Gamma(c)} = 1 - h(1+o(1))\psi(c) \quad \text{as } h \downarrow 0,$$

and

$$\frac{\Gamma(c-h-b)}{\Gamma(c-b)} = 1 - h(1+o(1))\psi(c-b) \quad \text{as } h \downarrow 0.$$

It follows readily that

$$\lim_{h\downarrow 0} \frac{1}{h}\Big\{\frac{\Gamma(c)\Gamma(c-h-b)}{\Gamma(c-h)\Gamma(c-b)} - 1\Big\} = \psi(c) - \psi(c-b).$$

By all this, we obtain

$$\sum_{m=0}^{\infty} \frac{(b)_m}{m(c)_m} = \frac{b}{c} \sum_{m=0}^{\infty} \frac{(b+1)_m}{(c+1)_m} \frac{1}{m+1} = \psi(c) - \psi(c-b),$$

which is (35). Given (35), we infer from (25) and (35) that

$$\psi'(c) - \psi'(c-b) = \frac{\partial}{\partial c}\Big\{\psi(c) - \psi(c-b)\Big\}$$
$$= \lim_{h\downarrow 0} \frac{1}{h} \sum_{m=1}^{\infty} \Big\{\frac{(b)_m}{m(c+h)_m} - \frac{(b)_m}{m(c)_m}\Big\}$$
$$= -\sum_{m=1}^{\infty} \frac{(b)_m}{m}\Big\{\lim_{h\downarrow 0}\frac{1}{h}\Big[\frac{1}{(c+h)_m} - \frac{1}{(c)_m}\Big]\Big\}$$
$$= \sum_{m=1}^{\infty} \frac{(b)_m}{m(c)_m^2}\frac{\mathrm{d}}{\mathrm{d}c}(c)_m = \sum_{m=1}^{\infty} \frac{(b)_m}{m(c)_m}\{\psi(c+m) - \psi(c)\},$$

which is (36). Likewise, we infer from (25) and (35) that

$$\psi'(c-b) = \frac{\partial}{\partial b}\Big\{\psi(c) - \psi(c-b)\Big\} = \lim_{h\downarrow 0}\frac{1}{h}\sum_{m=1}^{\infty}\Big\{\frac{(b+h)_m}{m(c)_m} - \frac{(b)_m}{m(c)_m}\Big\}$$
$$= \sum_{m=1}^{\infty}\frac{1}{m(c)_m}\Big\{\lim_{h\downarrow 0}\frac{1}{h}\Big[(b+h)_m - (b)_m\Big]\Big\} = \sum_{m=1}^{\infty}\frac{1}{m(c)_m}\frac{\mathrm{d}}{\mathrm{d}b}(b)_m$$
$$= \sum_{m=1}^{\infty}\frac{(b)_m}{m(c)_m}\{\psi(b+m) - \psi(b)\},$$

which yields (37). □

2.2. Preliminary Results and Moment Calculations

The special case where X follows a uniform distribution on $(0,1)$ will play an instrumental role in our proofs. For a general F, keeping in mind that the existence of $f(x) = \frac{\mathrm{d}}{\mathrm{d}x}F(x)$ implies that F is continuous, we set $U_1 = F(X_1), U_2 = F(X_2), \ldots$, and we observe that these random variables are independent, each with a uniform distribution on $(0,1)$. For each $n \geq 1$, we denote by

$$U_{0,n} := 0 < U_{1,n} = F(X_{1,n}) < \ldots < U_{n,n} = F(X_{n,n}) < U_{n+1,n} := 1, \tag{38}$$

the order statistics of $0, 1, U_1, \ldots, U_n$, with the convention that $U_{0,n} = F(X_{0,n}) = F(a) = 0$ and $U_{n+1,n} = F(X_{n+1,n}) = F(b) = 1$ for $n \geq 0$. We note that the inequalities in (38) hold a.s. We therefore assume that, without the loss of generality, they are fulfilled on the probability space on which $\{X_n : n \geq 1\}$ is defined. The *uniform k-spacings* are then given for $1 \leq k \leq n+1$ by

$$\Delta_{i,n}^{(k)} = U_{i+k-1,n} - U_{i-1,n} \quad \text{for} \quad i = 1, \ldots, n-k+2. \tag{39}$$

For $r \geq 0$, denote by $S_r \stackrel{d}{=} \boldsymbol{\Gamma}(r)$ a random variable following a *Gamma distribution* with mean r. Namely, $S_0 := 0$, and, for $r > 0$, S_r has density on $\mathbb{R}$, given by

$$h_r(s) := \begin{cases} \frac{s^{r-1}}{\Gamma(r)}e^{-s} & \text{for} \quad s > 0, \\ 0 & \text{for} \quad s \leq 0. \end{cases} \tag{40}$$

where $\Gamma(r) := \int_0^\infty s^{r-1}e^{-s}\mathrm{d}s$ for $r > 0$. When $r = 1$, $S_1 \stackrel{d}{=} \boldsymbol{\Gamma}(1)$ is *exponentially distributed* with a unit mean. In this special case, we use the alternative notation $S_1 \stackrel{d}{=} \mathbf{E}(1)$. In general, for $\lambda > 0$, we denote by $Z \stackrel{d}{=} \mathbf{E}(\lambda)$ an exponentially distributed r.v. Z with mean $1/\lambda$, fulfilling $\lambda Z \stackrel{d}{=} \mathbf{E}(1)$. For $p > 0$ and $q > 0$, we denote by $R_{p,q} \stackrel{d}{=} \boldsymbol{\beta}(p,q)$ a random variable following a *Beta distribution* with parameters p and q, meaning that $R_{p,q}$ has density given by

$$g_{p,q}(s) := \begin{cases} \frac{s^{p-1}(1-s)^{q-1}}{\beta(p,q)} & \text{for} \quad 0 < s < 1, \\ 0 & \text{for} \quad s \notin (0,1). \end{cases} \tag{41}$$

The functions $\beta(\cdot,\cdot)$ and $\Gamma(\cdot)$ are related by *Euler's formula*. For any $p > 0$ and $q > 0$, we have

$$\beta(p,q) := \int_0^1 u^{p-1}(1-u)^{q-1}\mathrm{d}u = \frac{\Gamma(p)\Gamma(q)}{\Gamma(p+q)}. \tag{42}$$

We extend this definition when either $p = 0$ or $q = 0$ by setting

$$R_{0,q} = 0 \stackrel{d}{=}: \boldsymbol{\beta}(0,q) \quad (q > 0) \quad \text{and} \quad R_{p,0} = 1 \stackrel{d}{=}: \boldsymbol{\beta}(p,0) \quad (p > 0). \tag{43}$$

We refer to Ch. 17, 19, and 25 in Johnson, Kotz, and Balakrishnan [18,19] for useful details concerning the Gamma, exponential, and Beta distributions. In particular, we have the following useful distributional identity (see, e.g., p.12 in David [20]). For any $0 \le j \le j + i \le n+1$,

$$U_{i+j,n} - U_{j,n} \stackrel{d}{=} \boldsymbol{\beta}(i, n-i+1). \tag{44}$$

In particular, we have the distributional identity, for any $0 \le i \le n+1$,

$$U_{i,n} \stackrel{d}{=} 1 - U_{n-i+1,n} \stackrel{d}{=} \boldsymbol{\beta}(i, n-i+1). \tag{45}$$

The following lemma plays an instrumental role in our proofs.

Lemma 1. *For $p > 0$, $q > 0$, and $r > 0$, let $S_p \stackrel{d}{=} \boldsymbol{\Gamma}(p)$, $S'_q \stackrel{d}{=} \boldsymbol{\Gamma}(q)$, and $S''_r \stackrel{d}{=} \boldsymbol{\Gamma}(r)$ be three independent*

Gamma-distributed r.v.'s. Then, the r.v.'s

$$R_{p,q} := \frac{S_p}{S_p + S'_q} \stackrel{d}{=} \boldsymbol{\beta}(p,q) \quad \textit{and} \quad T_{p,q} := S_p + S'_q \stackrel{d}{=} \boldsymbol{\Gamma}(p+q), \tag{46}$$

are independent and follow $\boldsymbol{\beta}(p,q)$ and $\boldsymbol{\Gamma}(p+q)$ distributions, respectively. Set further

$$R'_{p,q,r} := \frac{S_p + S'_q}{S_p + S'_q + S''_r} \stackrel{d}{=} \boldsymbol{\beta}(p+q, r), \tag{47}$$

$$R''_{p,q,r} := \frac{S_p + S''_r}{S_p + S'_q + S''_r} \stackrel{d}{=} \boldsymbol{\beta}(p+r, q), \tag{48}$$

and

$$T'_{p,q,r} := S_p + S'_q + S''_r \stackrel{d}{=} \boldsymbol{\Gamma}(p+q+r). \tag{49}$$

Then, the r.v. $T'_{p,q,r}$ is independent of the random pair $(R'_{p,q,r}, R''_{p,q,r})$.

Proof. Several variants of the above results have been given in the literature (see, e.g., §25.2, p. 212 in Johnson, Kotz and Balakrishnan [19]). As the proofs are simple, we give details, limiting ourselves to (46). By the change of the variables $u = s/(s+t)$ and $v = s+t \Leftrightarrow s = uv$ and $t = (1-u)v$, the joint density of $(R_{p,q}, T_{p,q})$ is given by

$$\begin{aligned} g(u,v) &= h_p(uv)h_q((1-u)v)\left|\det\begin{bmatrix} \frac{\partial s}{\partial u} & \frac{\partial s}{\partial v} \\ \frac{\partial t}{\partial u} & \frac{\partial t}{\partial v} \end{bmatrix}\right| \\ &= \left\{\frac{v^{p+q-1}e^{-v}}{\Gamma(p+q)}\right\}\left\{\frac{u^{p-1}(1-u)^{q-1}}{\beta(p,q)}\right\}\left\{\frac{\beta(p,q)}{\Gamma(p)\Gamma(q)}\right\}\frac{1}{v}\left|\det\begin{bmatrix} v & u \\ -v & 1-u \end{bmatrix}\right| \\ &= h_{p+q}(u)g_{p,q}(v), \end{aligned}$$

which is sufficient for our needs. □

In view of (38), set $Y_1 = -\log U_1, Y_2 = -\log U_2, \ldots$, and observe that $Y_1, Y_2, \ldots$ constitutes a sequence of independent $\mathbf{E}(1)$, unit mean exponential random variables. For each $n \geq 1$, the order statistics of $Y_1, \ldots, Y_n$ fulfill the relations

$$\begin{aligned} 0 < Y_{1,n} = -\log U_{n,n} < \ldots &< Y_{i,n} = -\log U_{n-i+1,n} < \ldots \\ &< Y_{n,n} = -\log U_{1,n} < \infty. \end{aligned} \tag{50}$$

Set, for convenience, $Y_{0,n} = -\log U_{n+1,n} = 0$ for $n \geq 1$. We will need the following useful fact, closely related to Lemma 1 (refer to Sukhatme [21] and Malmquist [22], and see, e.g., pp. 20–21 in David [20]):

Fact 1. *For each $n \geq 1$, the random variables*

$$\omega_{i,n} := (n-i+1)\{Y_{i,n} - Y_{i-1,n}\} \stackrel{d}{=} \mathbf{E}(1), \quad i = 1, \ldots, n, \tag{51}$$

are independent, each following an exponential $\mathbf{E}(1)$ distribution.

It will be convenient, later on, to make use of the relation following from (51),

$$Y_{i,n} = -\log U_{n-i+1,n} = \sum_{j=1}^{i} \frac{\omega_{j,n}}{n-j+1}, \quad i = 1, \ldots, n. \tag{52}$$

In Lemma 2 below, we evaluate the moments of the logarithms of Gamma-distributed random variables, which will play an instrumental role later on. As usual, we make use of the convention that $\sum_{\varnothing}(\cdot) = 0$.

Lemma 2. *Let $k \geq 1$ be an integer, and let $S_k \stackrel{d}{=} \mathbf{\Gamma}(k)$ be a Gamma-distributed random variable with mean k. Then, for each $k \geq 1$,*

$$\gamma_k := \mathbb{E}\big(-\log S_k\big) = -\psi(k) = \gamma - \sum_{j=1}^{k-1} \frac{1}{j}, \tag{53}$$

$$\begin{aligned} r_k &:= \mathbb{E}\big(-S_k \log S_k\big) = -k\psi(k) - 1 \\ &= k\gamma_k - 1 = k\gamma - k\sum_{j=1}^{k-1}\frac{1}{j} - 1, \end{aligned} \tag{54}$$

and

$$
\begin{aligned}
s_k &:= \mathbb{E}(\{-\log S_k\}^2) = \psi(k)^2 + \psi'(k) \\
&= \zeta(2) - \sum_{j=1}^{k-1} \frac{1}{j^2} + \gamma_k^2 = \sum_{j=k}^{\infty} \frac{1}{j^2} + \Big\{\gamma - \sum_{j=1}^{k-1} \frac{1}{j}\Big\}^2 \\
&= \frac{\pi^2}{6} - \sum_{j=1}^{k-1} \frac{1}{j^2} + \Big\{\gamma - \sum_{j=1}^{k-1} \frac{1}{j}\Big\}^2.
\end{aligned}
\tag{55}
$$

Proof. Recalling the definition (40) of $h_r(s)$ for $r > 0$ and the definition (53) of γ_k, we obtain that, by integrating by parts, for $k \geq 2$,

$$
\begin{aligned}
\gamma_k &= \int_0^\infty \{-\log s\} h_k(s) \mathrm{d}s = \int_0^\infty \{-\log s\} \frac{s^{k-1}}{(k-1)!} \mathrm{d}\{-e^{-s}\} \\
&= -\Big[\{-\log s\} \frac{s^{k-1}}{(k-1)!} e^{-s}\Big]_{s=0}^{s=\infty} \\
&+ \int_0^\infty \{-\log s\} \frac{s^{k-2}}{(k-2)!} \mathrm{d}\{-e^{-s}\} \\
&- \int_0^\infty \frac{s^{k-2}}{(k-1)!} e^{-s} \mathrm{d}s = \gamma_{k-1} - \frac{1}{k-1}.
\end{aligned}
\tag{56}
$$

For $k = 1$, these relations reduce to (see, e.g., Formula 4.331, p. 573, in Gradshteyn and Ryzhik [16])

$$
\gamma_1 = \int_0^\infty \{-\log s\} h_1(s) ds = \int_0^\infty \{-\log s\} e^{-s} ds = \gamma. \tag{57}
$$

Recalling the definition (18) of $\psi(m)$ for $m = 1, 2, \ldots$, and the definition (53) of γ_k, by a straightforward induction on k, we infer from the above relations that, for an arbitrary (integer) $k \geq 1$,

$$
\gamma_k = \gamma_{k-1} - \frac{1}{k-1} = \ldots = \gamma_1 - \sum_{j=1}^{k-1} \frac{1}{j} = -\psi(k), \tag{58}
$$

which is (53). Likewise, in view of (54) and (56), by integrating by parts, we see that, for $k \geq 2$,

$$
\begin{aligned}
r_k &= \int_0^\infty s\{-\log s\} h_k(s) \mathrm{d}s = \int_0^\infty \{-\log s\} \frac{s^k}{(k-1)!} \mathrm{d}\{-e^{-s}\} \\
&= -\Big[\{-\log s\} \frac{s^k}{(k-1)!} e^{-s}\Big]_{s=0}^{s=\infty} \\
&+ \int_0^\infty \{-\log s\} \frac{k s^{k-1}}{(k-1)!} \mathrm{d}\{-e^{-s}\} \\
&- \int_0^\infty \frac{s^{k-1}}{(k-1)!} e^{-s} \mathrm{d}s = k\gamma_k - 1 = k\gamma - k \sum_{j=1}^{k-1} \frac{1}{j} - 1,
\end{aligned}
$$

which is (54). In the same spirit, to establish (56), we integrate by parts to obtain the recursion formula, for $k \geq 2$,

$$
\begin{aligned}
s_k &= \int_0^\infty \{-\log s\}^2 h_k(s)\mathrm{d}s = \int_0^\infty \{-\log s\}^2 \frac{s^{k-1}}{(k-1)!}\mathrm{d}\{-e^{-s}\} \\
&= -\Big[\{-\log s\}^2 \frac{s^{k-1}}{(k-1)!} e^{-s}\Big]_{s=0}^{s=\infty} \\
&\quad + \int_0^\infty \{-\log s\}^2 \frac{s^{k-2}}{(k-2)!}\mathrm{d}\{-e^{-s}\} \\
&\quad - \frac{2}{k-1}\int_0^\infty \{-\log s\} \frac{s^{k-2}}{(k-2)!}\mathrm{d}\{-e^{-s}\} \\
&= s_{k-1} - \frac{2\gamma_{k-1}}{k-1}\,.
\end{aligned} \tag{59}
$$

By combining (58) with (60), we readily obtain that

$$
\begin{aligned}
s_k - \gamma_k^2 &= s_k - \Big\{\gamma_{k-1} - \frac{1}{k-1}\Big\}^2 \\
&= s_{k-1} - \frac{2\gamma_{k-1}}{k-1} - \Big\{\gamma_{k-1} - \frac{1}{k-1}\Big\}^2 \\
&= s_{k-1} - \gamma_{k-1}^2 - \Big\{\frac{1}{k-1}\Big\}^2 \\
&= s_{k-2} - \gamma_{k-2}^2 - \Big\{\frac{1}{k-2}\Big\}^2 - \Big\{\frac{1}{k-1}\Big\}^2 \\
&= \ldots = s_1 - \gamma_1^2 - \sum_{j=1}^{k-1}\frac{1}{j^2}.
\end{aligned} \tag{60}
$$

For $k = 1$, we combine (57) with the fact that (see, e.g., Formula 4.335, p. 574, in Gradshteyn and Ryzhik [16])

$$
s_1 - \gamma_1^2 = \int_0^\infty \{-\log s\}^2 e^{-s}\mathrm{d}s - \gamma^2 = \frac{\pi^2}{6} = \zeta(2) = \sum_{j=1}^\infty \frac{1}{j^2}. \tag{61}
$$

In view of (53), (60) and (61), the relation (56) is straightforward. □

Lemma 3. *Let $S_k \overset{d}{=} \mathbf{\Gamma}(k)$ denote a Gamma-distributed random variable with expectation k. Then, for each integer $k \geq 1$, we have*

$$
\begin{aligned}
\sigma_k^2 &:= \mathrm{Var}\big(-\log S_k\big) = s_k - \gamma_k^2 = \psi'(k) \\
&= \zeta(2) - \sum_{i=1}^{k-1}\frac{1}{i^2} = \frac{\pi^2}{6} - \sum_{i=1}^{k-1}\frac{1}{i^2} = \sum_{i=k}^{\infty}\frac{1}{i^2}.
\end{aligned} \tag{62}
$$

Proof. Even though the relation (62) is a direct consequence of (53) and (56), below, we give an alternate proof of this statement based upon Lemma 1. The corresponding arguments will be instrumental for the proof of the forthcoming Proposition 3. We may write, making use of (46) in Lemma 3, for each integer $m \geq 1$ and $\ell \geq 1$,

$$
-\log S_m = -\log\Big(\frac{S_m}{S_m + S'_\ell}\Big) + \log\big(S_m + S'_\ell\big) =: V_1 - V_2,
$$

where

$$
V_1 := -\log\Big(\frac{S_m}{S_m + S'_\ell}\Big) \overset{d}{=} -\log Z, \tag{63}
$$

with $Z \stackrel{d}{=} \beta(m,\ell)$, and

$$V_2 := -\log\left(S_m + S'_\ell\right) \stackrel{d}{=} -\log Y, \tag{64}$$

with $Y \stackrel{d}{=} \Gamma(m+\ell)$, are independent r.v.'s. Following the arguments of Lemma 1, we note that, in the above relations, $S_m \stackrel{d}{=} \Gamma(m)$ and $S'_\ell \stackrel{d}{=} \Gamma(\ell)$ are two independent Gamma-distributed random variables, with expectations equal to m and ℓ, respectively. In view of (50), by combining (44) with (45) and (46), we readily obtain that

$$\begin{aligned} V_1 &= -\log\left(\frac{S_m}{S_m + S'_\ell}\right) \\ &\stackrel{d}{=} -\log U_{m,m+\ell-1} = Y_{\ell,m+\ell-1} = \sum_{j=1}^{\ell} \frac{\omega_{j,m+\ell-1}}{m+\ell-j} \\ &\stackrel{d}{=} -\log\left(1 - U_{\ell,m+\ell-1}\right) = -\log\left(1 - \exp(-Y_{m,m+\ell-1})\right) \\ &= -\log\left(1 - \exp\left\{-\sum_{j=1}^{m} \frac{\omega_{j,m+\ell-1}}{m+\ell-j}\right\}\right). \end{aligned} \tag{65}$$

Set for convenience $\rho_p := \sigma_p^2 = \mathrm{Var}(-\log S_p)$, with $S_p \stackrel{d}{=} \Gamma(p)$ for $p \geq 1$; we infer from (63) and (64) that

$$\begin{aligned} \rho_m &= \mathrm{Var}(V_2) + \mathrm{Var}(V_1) = \rho_{m+\ell} + \mathrm{Var}(V_1) \\ &= \rho_{m+\ell} + \sum_{j=1}^{\ell} \frac{1}{(m+\ell-j)^2} = \rho_{m+\ell} + \sum_{i=m}^{m+\ell-1} \frac{1}{i^2}. \end{aligned} \tag{66}$$

By combining (57) and (61) with (62), we see that $\rho_1 = \zeta(2)$. Therefore, (62) follows readily from (66), taken with $m = 1$ and $m + \ell = k$. □

Lemma 4. *Let $Z \stackrel{d}{=} \beta(m,\ell)$, where $m \geq 1$ and $\ell \geq 1$ are integers. Then,*

$$\mathbb{E}(-\log Z) = \sum_{i=m}^{m+\ell-1} \frac{1}{i} = \psi(m+\ell) - \psi(m), \tag{67}$$

and

$$\mathrm{Var}(-\log Z) = \sum_{i=m}^{m+\ell-1} \frac{1}{i^2} = \psi'(m) - \psi'(m+\ell). \tag{68}$$

Proof. We may write, by (19) and (20),

$$\begin{aligned} \mathbb{E}(-\log Z) &= \mathbb{E}(V_1) = \mathbb{E}\left(\sum_{j=1}^{\ell} \frac{\omega_{j,m+\ell-1}}{m+\ell-j}\right) = \sum_{j=1}^{\ell} \frac{1}{m+\ell-j} \\ &= \psi(m+\ell) - \psi(m), \end{aligned}$$

and

$$\begin{aligned} \mathrm{Var}(-\log Z) &= \mathrm{Var}(V_1) = \mathrm{Var}\left(\sum_{j=1}^{\ell} \frac{\omega_{j,m+\ell-1}}{m+\ell-j}\right) = \sum_{j=1}^{\ell} \frac{1}{(m+\ell-j)^2} \\ &= \psi'(m) - \psi'(m+\ell), \end{aligned}$$

as sought. □

Lemma 5. *Let $\{\omega_m : m \geq 1\}$ denote an i.i.d. sequence of exponentially distributed $\mathbf{E}(1)$ random variables. For any $m \geq 1$, set $S_m = \omega_1 + \ldots \omega_m \stackrel{d}{=} \boldsymbol{\Gamma}(m)$ and $U^*_{m,n} := S_m / S_{n+1} \stackrel{d}{=} \boldsymbol{\beta}(m, n-m+1)$. Then, for any $1 \leq k \leq n+1$, we have*

$$\mathbb{E}\Big(\Big\{-\log S_k\Big\}\Big\{-\log S_{n+1}\Big\}\Big) = \psi(k)\psi(n+1) + \psi'(n+1), \tag{69}$$

and

$$\mathrm{Cov}\Big(\Big\{-\log S_k\Big\}, \Big\{-\log S_{n+1}\Big\}\Big) = \psi'(n+1). \tag{70}$$

Proof. We have

$$\begin{aligned} & \mathbb{E}\Big(\Big\{-\log S_k\Big\}\Big\{-\log S_{n+1}\Big\}\Big) \\ = \;& \mathbb{E}\Big(\Big\{-\log\Big(\frac{S_k}{S_{n+1}}\Big) + \Big\{-\log S_{n+1}\Big\}\Big\}\Big\{-\log S_{n+1}\Big\}\Big) \\ = \;& \mathbb{E}\Big(\Big\{\Big\{-\log U^*_{k,n}\Big\} + \Big\{-\log S_{n+1}\Big\}\Big\}\Big\{-\log S_{n+1}\Big\}\Big)\Big\}\Big). \end{aligned}$$

Since $U^*_{k,n}$ and S_{n+1} are independent, it follows that

$$\begin{aligned} & \mathbb{E}\Big(\Big\{-\log S_k\Big\}\Big\{-\log S_{n+1}\Big\}\Big) \\ = \;& \mathbb{E}\Big\{-\log U^*_{k,n}\Big\}\mathbb{E}\Big\{-\log S_{n+1}\Big\} + \mathbb{E}\Big(\Big\{-\log S_{n+1}\Big\}^2\Big). \end{aligned}$$

Making use of (67) and (57), we see that $\mathbb{E}\{-\log U^*_{k,n}\} = \psi(n+1) - \psi(k)$, $\mathbb{E}\{-\log S_k\} = -\psi(k)$, $\mathbb{E}\{-\log S_{n+1}\} = -\psi(n+1)$, and $\mathbb{E}(\{-\log S_{n+1}\}^2) = \psi(n+1)^2 + \psi'(n+1)$. By all this, we obtain

$$\begin{aligned} & \mathbb{E}\Big(\Big\{-\log S_k\Big\}\Big\{-\log S_{n+1}\Big\}\Big) \\ & = -\psi(n+1)^2 + \psi(k)\psi(n+1) + \psi(n+1)^2 + \psi'(n+1), \end{aligned}$$

which is (69). Given (69), the proof of (70) follows from the relations $\mathbb{E}\{-\log S_k\} = -\psi(k)$ and $\mathbb{E}\{-\log S_{n+1}\} = -\psi(n+1)$. We note that, when $k = n+1$, (69) yields

$$\mathbb{E}(\{-\log S_{n+1}\}^2) = \psi(n+1)^2 + \psi'(n+1),$$

which is in agreement with (56). $\square$

Proposition 3. *Let $0 \leq \ell \leq k$ be an integer, and let $S_{k-\ell} \stackrel{d}{=} \boldsymbol{\Gamma}(k-\ell)$, $S'_\ell \stackrel{d}{=} \boldsymbol{\Gamma}(\ell)$, and $S''_\ell \stackrel{d}{=} \boldsymbol{\Gamma}(\ell)$ be independent Gamma-distributed random variables. Then, we have*

$$\begin{aligned} s_{k,\ell} \;&:=\; \mathbb{E}\Big(\Big\{-\log\{S_{k-\ell} + S'_\ell\}\Big\}\Big\{-\log\{S_{k-\ell} + S''_\ell\}\Big\}\Big) \\ &=\; \psi(k)^2 - \psi'(k+\ell) - \Big\{\psi(k+\ell) - \psi(k)\Big\}^2 \\ &\quad + \sum_{m=1}^{\infty} \frac{(\ell)_m}{m(k+\ell)_m}\Big\{\psi(k+\ell+m) - \psi(k+m)\Big\}. \end{aligned} \tag{71}$$

Proof. Set for convenience $j = k - \ell$. When $\ell = 0$, we have $S'_\ell = S''_\ell = 0$, and, therefore, by (7), $s_{k,0} = \psi(k)^2\psi'(k)$, which is in agreement with (71). Likewise, when $\ell = k$, $S_{k-\ell} = 0$, and, hence, $s_{k,k} = \gamma_k^2 = \psi(k)^2$, which is also in agreement with (71). In fact, when $k = \ell$, (71) may be rewritten into

$$
\begin{aligned}
s_{k,k} &= \psi(k)^2 - \psi'(2k) - \Big\{\psi(2k) - \psi(k)\Big\}^2 \\
&\quad + \sum_{m=1}^{\infty} \frac{(k)_m}{m(2k)_m} \Big\{\psi(2k+m) - \psi(k+m)\Big\}, \\
&= \psi(k)^2 - \psi'(2k) - \Big\{\psi(2k) - \psi(k)\Big\}^2 \\
&\quad + \sum_{m=1}^{\infty} \frac{(k)_m}{m(2k)_m} \Big\{\psi(2k+m) - \psi(2k)\Big\} \\
&\quad + \Big\{\psi(2k) - \psi(k)\Big\} \sum_{m=1}^{\infty} \frac{(k)_m}{m(2k)_m} \\
&\quad - \sum_{m=1}^{\infty} \frac{(k)_m}{m(2k)_m} \Big\{\psi(k+m) - \psi(2k)\Big\} \\
&= \psi(k)^2 - \psi'(2k) - \Big\{\psi(2k) - \psi(k)\Big\}^2 \\
&\quad + \psi'(2k) - \psi'(k) + \Big\{\psi(2k) - \psi(k)\Big\}^2 + \psi'(k) = \psi(k)^2,
\end{aligned} \tag{72}
$$

where we have made use of (35), (36) and (37), taken with $b = k$ and $c = 2k$. Given that the values of $s_{k,0} = 0$ and $s_{k,k} = \psi(k)^2$ are in agreement with (71), we may limit ourselves to establish this relation when ℓ and j fulfill $1 \le \ell, j \le k$. In the remainder of our proof, we therefore assume that this condition is fulfilled.

We make use of the notation and conclusions of Lemma 1 to write that

$$
\begin{aligned}
\Sigma &:= \mathbb{E}\Big(\Big\{-\log\{S_j + S'_\ell\}\Big\}\Big\{-\log\{S_j + S''_\ell\}\Big\}\Big) \\
&= \mathbb{E}\Big(\Big\{-\log\{R'_{j,\ell,\ell} T'_{j,\ell,\ell}\}\Big\}\Big\{-\log\{R''_{j,\ell,\ell} T'_{j,\ell,\ell}\}\Big\}\Big) \\
&= \mathbb{E}\Big(\Big\{-\log T'_{j,\ell,\ell}\Big\}^2\Big) + \mathbb{E}\Big(-\log T'_{j,\ell,\ell}\Big)\Big\{\mathbb{E}\Big(-\log R'_{j,\ell,\ell}\Big) \\
&+ \mathbb{E}\Big(-\log R''_{j,\ell,\ell}\Big)\Big\} + \mathbb{E}\Big(\Big\{-\log R'_{j,\ell,\ell}\Big\}\Big\{-\log R''_{j,\ell,\ell}\Big\}\Big),
\end{aligned} \tag{73}
$$

where the random pair

$$
R'_{j,\ell,\ell} := \frac{S_j + S'_\ell}{S_j + S'_\ell + S''_\ell} \stackrel{d}{=} \beta(j+\ell, \ell), \tag{74}
$$

$$
R''_{j,\ell,\ell} := \frac{S_j + S''_\ell}{S_j + S'_\ell + S''_\ell} \stackrel{d}{=} \beta(j+\ell, \ell), \tag{75}
$$

is independent of

$$
T'_{j,\ell,\ell} := S_j + S'_\ell + S''_\ell \stackrel{d}{=} \Gamma(j+2\ell). \tag{76}
$$

Now, since $T'_{j,\ell,\ell} \stackrel{d}{=} S_{j+2\ell} \stackrel{d}{=} \Gamma(j+2\ell) \stackrel{d}{=} \Gamma(k+\ell)$, we infer from (53) and (56) that

$$
\mathbb{E}(-\log T'_{j,\ell,\ell}) = \psi(k+\ell), \tag{77}
$$

and

$$
\mathbb{E}(\{-\log T'_{j,\ell,\ell}\}^2) = \psi(k+\ell)^2 - \psi'(k+\ell). \tag{78}
$$

Next, set

$$W_1 \;:=\; -\log R'_{j,\ell,\ell} = -\log\Big(\frac{S_j + S'_\ell}{S_j + S'_\ell + S''_\ell}\Big),$$

and

$$W_2 \;:=\; -\log R''_{j,\ell,\ell} = -\log\Big(\frac{S_j + S''_\ell}{S_j + S'_\ell + S''_\ell}\Big).$$

We infer from (74) and (75), in combination with (67) and (68), taken with the formal change of (m,ℓ) into $(j+\ell,\ell)$, that

$$\begin{aligned}\mathbb{E}(W_1) = \mathbb{E}(W_2) &= \mathbb{E}(-\log R'_{j,\ell,\ell}) = \mathbb{E}(-\log R''_{j,\ell,\ell}) \\ &= \psi(j+2\ell) - \psi(j+\ell) = \psi(k+\ell) - \psi(k). \end{aligned} \tag{79}$$

By all this, we infer from (74), (77) and (78) that

$$\begin{aligned}\Sigma &= \psi(k+\ell)^2 - \psi'(k+\ell) - 2\psi(k+\ell)\{\psi(k+\ell) - \psi(k)\} \\ &\quad + \mathbb{E}(W_1 W_2) \\ &= \psi(k)^2 - \{\psi(k+\ell) - \psi(k)\}^2 - \psi'(k+\ell) + \mathbb{E}(W_1 W_2). \end{aligned} \tag{80}$$

Next, we observe that the joint distribution of (W_1, W_2) coincides with that of $(W_1^{(*)}, W_2^{(*)})$, where

$$\begin{aligned} W_1^* &= -\log\left(U_{j+\ell,j+2\ell-1}\right), \\ W_2^* &= -\log\left(1 - U_{\ell,j+2\ell-1}\right). \end{aligned}$$

We then observe that

$$U := \frac{U_{\ell,j+2\ell-1}}{U_{j+\ell,j+2\ell-1}} \overset{d}{=} U_{\ell,j+\ell-1} \overset{d}{=} \beta(\ell,j),$$

is independent of $V := U_{j+\ell,j+2\ell-1} \overset{d}{=} \beta(j+\ell,\ell)$. Given this fact, we make use of the Taylor expansion of

$$-\log(1-uv) = \sum_{m=1}^{\infty} \frac{u^m v^m}{m} \quad \text{for} \quad |uv| < 1,$$

to obtain that

$$\begin{aligned} &\mathbb{E}(W_1 W_2) = \mathbb{E}(W_1^* W_2^*) = \mathbb{E}\Big(\{-\log V\}\{-\log(1-UV)\}\Big) \\ = &\int_0^1 \Big\{ \int_0^1 \{-\log v\}\{-\log(1-uv)\} \frac{u^{\ell-1}(1-u)^{j-1}}{\beta(\ell,j)}\, du \Big\} \\ &\times \frac{v^{j+\ell-1}(1-v)^{\ell-1}}{\beta(j+\ell,\ell)}\, dv \\ = &\sum_{m=1}^{\infty} \frac{1}{m} \Big\{ \int_0^1 \frac{u^{\ell+m-1}(1-u)^{j-1}}{\beta(\ell,j)}\, du \Big\} \\ &\times \int_0^1 \{-\log v\} \Big\{ \frac{v^{j+\ell+m-1}(1-v)^{\ell-1}}{\beta(j+\ell,\ell)} \Big\} dv. \end{aligned} \tag{81}$$

Recall Euler's formula $\beta(r,s) = \Gamma(r)\Gamma(s)/\Gamma(r+s)$ and the definition of the Pochhammer symbol $(a)_m = \Gamma(a+m)/\Gamma(a)$ when $a \neq 0$ and $a \neq -m$, and, in general,

$$(a)_m = a(a+1)\ldots(a+m-1) \quad \text{for} \quad m = 1,2\ldots, \quad (a)_0 = 1.$$

Recalling that $j+\ell=k$, we infer from (81) that

$$\begin{aligned} \mathbb{E}(W_1W_2) &= \sum_{m=1}^{\infty}\frac{\beta(\ell+m,j)\beta(j+\ell+m,\ell)}{m\beta(\ell,j)\beta(j+\ell,\ell)}\Big\{\psi(k+\ell+m)-\psi(k+m)\Big\} \\ &= \sum_{m=1}^{\infty}\frac{\Gamma(\ell+m)\Gamma(k+\ell)}{m\Gamma(\ell)\Gamma(k+\ell+m)}\Big\{\psi(k+\ell+m)-\psi(k+m)\Big\} \\ &= \sum_{m=1}^{\infty}\frac{(\ell)_m}{m(k+\ell)_m}\Big\{\psi(k+\ell+m)-\psi(k+m)\Big\}, \end{aligned} \tag{82}$$

which, when combined with (80), readily yields (71). □

Let $k\geq 1$ be fixed, and assume that X is uniformly distributed on $(0,1)$. Set $T_n := T_n(k,1,1)$ to be as in (5).

Proposition 4. *Under the assumptions above, we have*

$$n^{1/2}\Big\{T_n(k)-\log k+\psi(k)\Big\}\overset{d}{\to}N\Big(0,\psi'(k)+1\Big). \tag{83}$$

Proof. Denote by $\{\omega_n : n\geq 1\}$ an i.i.d. sequence of exponentially distributed $\mathbf{E}(1)$ r.v.'s, with mean 1. For each $n\geq 0$, set

$$S_n := \sum_{i=1}^{n}\omega_i \overset{d}{=} \mathbf{\Gamma}(n),$$

and set, in view of Lemma 1, for each $1\leq i\leq k\leq n+2$,

$$\Delta_{i,n}^{(k)*} := \frac{S_{i+k-1}-S_{i-1}}{S_{n+1}} \overset{d}{=} U_{k,n} \overset{d}{=} \beta(k,n-k+1).$$

We keep in mind that $\{\Delta_{i,n}^{(k)*} : 0\leq i\leq n-k+2\} \overset{d}{=} \{\Delta_{i,n}^{(k)} : 0\leq i\leq n-k+2\}$ and that $\{\Delta_{i,n}^{(k)*} : 0\leq i\leq n-k+2\}$ is independent of $S_{n+1}\overset{d}{=}\mathbf{\Gamma}(n+1)$. Set further

$$\begin{aligned} \mathcal{T}_n^*(k) &:= \sum_{i=1}^{n-k+1}\Big\{-\log\Big(\frac{1}{k}S_{n+1}\Delta_{i,n}^{(k)*}\Big)\Big\} \\ &= \sum_{i=1}^{n-k+1}\Big\{-\log\Big(\frac{1}{k}(S_{i+k-1}-S_{i-1})\Big)\Big\} \\ &= \sum_{i=1}^{n-k+1}\Big\{-\log\Big(S_{i+k-1}-S_{i-1}\Big)+\log k\Big\}, \end{aligned} \tag{84}$$

and

$$\mathcal{T}_n^{**}(k) := (n-k)\Big\{-\log n-\Big(-\log S_{n+1}\Big)\Big\}. \tag{85}$$

Set, likewise,

$$\begin{aligned} T_n^*(k) &:= \sum_{i=1}^{n-k+1}\Big\{-\log\Big(\frac{n}{k}\Delta_{i,n}^{(k)*}\Big)\Big\} \\ &= \sum_{i=1}^{n-k+1}\Big\{-\log\Big(S_{i+k-1}-S_{i-1}\Big)+\log k-\log n-\Big(-\log S_{n+1}\Big)\Big\} \\ &= \mathcal{T}_n^*(k)+\mathcal{T}_n^{**}(k). \end{aligned} \tag{86}$$

Observe that $T_n^*(k) \stackrel{d}{=} T_n(k)$. Moreover, the r.v.'s $T_n^*(k)$ and $\mathcal{T}_n^{**}(k)$ are independent. Note further that, for each $0 \leq i \leq n-k+2$, $S_{i+k-1} - S_{i-1} \stackrel{d}{=} \boldsymbol{\Gamma}(k)$ and $S_{n+1} \stackrel{d}{=} \boldsymbol{\Gamma}(n+1)$. By (53), it follows that, for each $0 \leq i \leq n-k+2$,

$$\mathbb{E}\big(-\log\left(S_{i+k-1} - S_{i-1}\right)\big) = -\psi(k) \quad \text{and} \quad \mathbb{E}\big(-\log S_{n+1}\big) = -\psi(n+1),$$

whence

$$\mathbb{E}\Big(\mathcal{T}_n^*(k)\Big) = (n-k)\Big\{-\psi(k) + \log k\Big\}$$

and

$$\mathbb{E}\Big(\mathcal{T}_n^{**}(k)\Big) = (n-k)\Big\{-\log n + \psi(n+1)\Big\}.$$

We have, therefore,

$$\begin{aligned} \mathbb{E}\Big(T_n^*(k)\Big) &= \mathbb{E}\Big(\mathcal{T}_n^*(k)\Big) + \mathbb{E}\Big(\mathcal{T}_n^{**}(k)\Big) \\ &= (n-k)\Big\{-\psi(k) + \log k + \psi(n+1) - \log n\Big\}. \end{aligned}$$

Next, we note that the $\mathbb{R}^2$-valued r.v.'s $\{(-\log\left(S_{i+k-1} - S_{i-1}\right), S_i - S_{i-1} : i \geq 1\}$ form a stationary k-dependent sequence. Since, by (53) and (56), for all $i \geq 1$,

$$\mathrm{Var}\big(-\log\left(S_{i+k-1} - S_{i-1}\right)\big) = \psi'(k) \quad \text{and} \quad \mathrm{Var}(S_i - S_{i-1}) = 1,$$

the partial sums of this sequence are asymptotically normal in $\mathbb{R}^2$. It follows readily that, as $n \to \infty$,

$$\begin{aligned} & n^{-1/2}\Big(\mathcal{T}_n^*(k) - \mathbb{E}\Big\{\mathcal{T}_n^*(k)\Big\}, \mathcal{T}_n^{**}(k) - \mathbb{E}\Big\{\mathcal{T}_n^{**}(k)\Big\}\Big) \\ = \;& n^{-1/2}\sum_{i=1}^{n-k+1}\Big\{-\log\Big(S_{i+k-1} - S_{i-1}\Big) + \psi(k) - \log k \\ & -\log n + \psi(n+1) - \Big(-\log S_{n+1}\Big)\Big\} \\ \xrightarrow{d} \;& N\left(\begin{bmatrix} 0 \\ 0 \end{bmatrix}, \begin{bmatrix} \psi'(k) & 0 \\ 0 & 1 \end{bmatrix}\right). \end{aligned} \tag{87}$$

Here, we have made use of the fact that, as $n \to \infty$,

$$\psi(n+1) - \log n = \frac{1 + o(1)}{2n},$$

so that, in (88),

$$n^{-1/2}\psi(n+1) \to 0.$$

Likewise, making use of (70), we see that

$$\begin{aligned} \mathrm{Cov}\Big(\mathcal{T}_n^*(k), \mathcal{T}_n^{**}(k)\Big) &= \sum_{i=1}^{n-k+1}\mathrm{Cov}\Big(-\log\left(S_{i+k-1} - S_{i-1}\right), -\log S_{n+1}\Big) \\ = \;& (n-k)\mathrm{Cov}\Big(-\log S_k, -\log S_{n+1}\Big) = (n-k)\psi'(n+1) \to 1 \quad \text{as} \quad n \to \infty, \end{aligned}$$

Making use of (69), an easy argument shows that, in turn,

$$n^{-1/2}\sum_{i=1}^{n-k+1}\Big\{-\log\Big(S_{i+k-1}-S_{i-1}\Big)+\psi(k)-\log k$$
$$-\log n-\Big(-\log S_{n+1}\Big)\Big\} \quad \overset{d}{\to} \quad N\Big(0,1+\psi'(k)\Big). \tag{88}$$

In view of (87), we readily obtain (83) from this last relation. □

Remark 3. *Let $G(u) := \inf\{x : F(x) \geq u\}$ for $0 < u < 1$ denote the quantile function of X. Assume that both $F(\cdot)$ and $G(\cdot)$ are continuous. In this case, we may define the quantile density function of X by $g(u) = 1/f(G(u))$, which is continuous for $0 < u < 1$. We may then set, for $1 \leq i \leq n$,*

$$\begin{aligned} X_{i+k-1,n}-X_{i-1,n} &= G(U_{i+k-1,n})-G(U_{i-1,n}) \\ &= \frac{1+o_P(1)}{f(G(i/n))}\{U_{i+k-1,n}-U_{i-1,n}\}. \end{aligned}$$

Having proved Theorem 1 for $f(x) = 1$, the conclusion for a general f follows by routine arguments based on this observation, relating uniform spacings to general spacings. We omit the details.

Funding: This research received no external funding.

Institutional Review Board Statement: Not applicable.

Data Availability Statement: The original contributions presented in this study are included in the article. Further inquiries can be directed to the corresponding author.

Acknowledgments: I am honored to dedicate this modest contribution to the memory of Pàl Révész who has inspired my own research in probability and statistics for many decades. His celebrated book [23] was the starting point of a number of investigations related to empirical processes. His scientific influence in the field goes beyond description. I also thank the referees for their careful reading of the manuscript and insightful comments.

Conflicts of Interest: The authors declare no conflicts of interest.

References

Darling, D.A. On a class of problems related to the random division of an interval. *Ann. Math. Stat.* **1953**, *24*, 239–253. [CrossRef]

Blumenthal, S. Logarithms of sample spacings. *SIAM J. Appl. Math.* **1968**, *16*, 1184–1191. [CrossRef]

Deheuvels, P.; Derzko, G. Exact laws for products of uniform spacings. *Austrian J. Stat.* **2003**, *32*, 29–47.

Hájek, J.; Šidák, Z. *Theory of Rank Tests*; Academic Press: New York, NY, USA, 1967.

Pyke, R. Spacings. *J. R. Stat. Soc. B* **1965**, *27*, 395–436. [CrossRef]

Pyke, R. Spacings revisited. In *Proceedings of the 6th Berkeley Symposium*; University of California Press: Berkeley, CA, USA, 1972; Volume 1, pp. 417–427.

Deheuvels, P. Spacings and applications. In Proceedings of the 4th Pannonian Symposium on Mathematical Statistics, Bad Tatzmannsdorf, Austria, 4–10 September 1983; pp. 1–30.

Cressie, N. On the logarithms of high-order spacings. *Biometrika* **1976**, *63*, 343–355. [CrossRef]

Cressie, N. Power results for tests based on high-order gaps. *Biometrika* **1978**, *65*, 214–218. [CrossRef]

10. Shao, Y.; Hahn, M.G. Limit theorems for the logarithm of sample spacings. *Stat. Probab. Lett.* **1995**, *24*, 121–132. [CrossRef]

11. Deheuvels, P.; Derzko, G. Tests of fit based on products of spacings. In *Probability, Statistics and Modelling in Public Health*; Springer: Boston, MA, USA, 2005.

12. del Pino, G. On the asymptotic distribution of some goodness of fit tests based on spacings. *Bull. Inst. Math. Stat.* **1975**, *4*, 137.

13. del Pino, G. On the asymptotic distribution of k-spacings with application to goodness-of-fit tests. *Ann. Stat.* **1979**, *7*, 1058–1075. [CrossRef]

14. Czekała, F. Normalizing constants for a statistic based on logarithm of disjoint m-spacings. *Appl. Math.* **1996**, *23*, 405–416. [CrossRef]

15. Spanier, J.; Oldham, K.B. *An Atlas of Functions*; Hemisphere Publ. Co.: Washington, DC, USA, 1987.
16. Gradshteyn, I.S.; Ryzhik, I.M. *Tables of Integrals, Series and Products*; Academic Press: New York, NY, USA, 1965.
17. Abramowitz, M.; Stegun, I.A. *Handbook of Mathematical Functions*; Dover: New York, NY, USA, 1970.
18. Johnson, N.J.; Kotz, S.; Balakrishnan, N. *Continuous Univariate Distributions, Volume 1*, 2nd ed.; Wiley: New York, NY, USA, 19
19. Johnson, N.J.; Kotz, S.; Balakrishnan, N. *Continuous Univariate Distributions, Volume 2*, 2nd ed.; Wiley: New York, NY, USA, 19
20. David, H.A. *Order Statistics*, 2nd ed.; Wiley: New York, NY, USA, 1981.
21. Sukhatme, P.V. Tests of significance for samples of the χ^2 population with two degrees of freedom. *Ann. Eugen.* **1937**, *8*, 52–
    [CrossRef]
22. Malmquist, S. On a property of order statistics from a rectangular distribution. *Skand. Aktuarietidskr.* **1950**, *33*, 214–222. [CrossR
23. Csörgő, M.; Révész, P. *Strong Approximations in Probability and Statistics*; Akadémiai Kiadó, Budapest, and Academic Pre
    New York, NY, USA, 1981.

entropy

MDPI

Article

On the Convergence Rate for the Longest at Most T-Contaminated Runs of Heads

István Fazekas [1,*], Borbála Fazekas [2] and László Fórián [1]

1 Faculty of Informatics, University of Debrecen, Kassai Street 26, 4028 Debrecen, Hungary; forian.laszlo@inf.unideb.hu
2 Institute of Mathematics, University of Debrecen, Egyetem Square 1, 4032 Debrecen, Hungary; borbala.fazekas@science.unideb.hu
* Correspondence: fazekas.istvan@inf.unideb.hu

Abstract: In this paper, we study the usual coin tossing experiment. We call a run at most T-contaminated, if it contains at most T tails. We approximate the distribution of the length of the longest at most T-contaminated runs. We offer a more precise approximation than the previous one.

Keywords: coin tossing; longest head run; asymptotic distribution; rate of convergence

MSC: 60F05

1. Introduction

Consider the usual coin tossing experiment. Let p be the probability of heads and $q = 1 - p$ be the probability of tails. Here, p is a fixed number with $0 < p < 1$. We toss a coin N times independently. We write 1 for heads and 0 for tails. Therefore, we consider independent identically distributed random variables $X_1, X_2, \ldots, X_N$ with distribution $P(X_i = 1) = p$ and $P(X_i = 0) = q = 1 - p$, $i = 1, 2, \ldots, N$.

Let T be a fixed non-negative integer. We shall study the length of at most T-contaminated (in other words, at most T-interrupted) runs of heads. It means that there are at most T zeros in an m-length sequence of ones and zeros.

There are several well-known results on the length of the pure head runs. Fair coins were studied in the paper of Erdős and Rényi [1]. Almost sure limit results for the length of the longest runs containing at most T tails were obtained in [2]. Földes [3] presented asymptotic results for the distribution of the number of T-contaminated head runs, the first hitting time of a T-contaminated head run having a fixed length, and the length of the longest T-contaminated head run. Móri [4] proved an almost sure limit theorem for the longest T-contaminated head run.

Gordon, Schilling, and Waterman [5] applied extreme value theory to obtain the asymptotic behaviour of the expectation and the variance of the length of the longest T-contaminated head run. Then, accompanying distributions were obtained for the length of the longest T-contaminated head run. Ref. [6] proved results on the accuracy of the approximation to the distribution of the length of the longest head run in a Markov chain.

In this paper, we follow the lines of Arratia, Gordon, and Waterman [7], where Poisson approximation was used to find the asymptotic behaviour of the length of the longest at most T-contaminated head run. We shall use the basic results presented in [7], and give a new approximation for the distribution of the length of the longest at most T-contaminated head run. We show that for $T > 0$ the rate of the approximation in our new result is $O(1/(\log(n))^2)$, where log denotes the logarithm to base $1/p$. Here and in what follows, $f(n) = O(h(n))$ means that $f(n)/h(n)$ is bounded as $n \to \infty$. We shall see that for $T > 0$ the rate of the approximation offered by [7] is $O(\log(\log(n))/\log(n))$, so our result considerably improves the former result. In our opinion the much better rate $O(\log(n)/n)$ presented without detailed proof in [7] is just a misprint, that is true only for $T = 0$. The main result is Theorem 1. For completeness, we give a proof of the former result, see Proposition 1. In Section 4, we present some simulation results supporting our theorem.

For $T = 1$ and $T = 2$, our result is the same as our former result in [8], where a powerful lemma by Csáki, Földes and Komlós [9] was used in the proof.

2. The Approximation of Arratia, Gordon, and Waterman

Using the notation of [7], let $S_i = X_1 + \cdots + X_i$, and let $S_{n,t}$ be the largest increment in the sequence S_i in t steps; more precisely, $S_{n,t}$ is the maximal number of heads in a window of length t starting in the first n tosses. Let $R_n(T)$ be the length of the longest at most T-interrupted runs of heads starting in the first n tosses. (One can see that $R_n(T)$ is the length of the longest precisely T-interrupted runs of heads starting in the first n tosses.) Then,

$$\{R_n(T) < t\} = \{S_{n,t} < t - T\}.$$

According to Theorem 1 of [7], for the distribution of $S_{n,t}$, we have the following approximation. For positive integers n, s, and t with $s \le t$ and $s/t > p$,

$$|P(S_{n,t} < s) - e^{-EW}| \le 7tP(X_1 + \cdots + X_t = s) + P(X_1 + \cdots + X_t > s), \tag{1}$$

$$e^{-n\left(\frac{s}{t}-p\right)P(X_1+\cdots+X_t=s)} \cdot e^{-2n\left(1-\frac{s}{t}\right)P(X_1+\cdots+X_t=s)P(X_1+\cdots+X_t>s)} \le e^{-EW} \le e^{-n\left(\frac{s}{t}-p\right)P(X_1+\cdots+X_t=s)}. \tag{2}$$

In the above inequalities EW is the expectation of the random variable W defined in [7]. We shall use inequalities (1) and (2) with $s = t - T$. Using notation $\alpha = n\left(\frac{s}{t} - p\right)P(X_1 + \cdots + X_t = s)$ and $\beta = 2n\left(1 - \frac{s}{t}\right)P(X_1 + \cdots + X_t = s)P(X_1 + \cdots + X_t > s)$, the above inequality is of the form

$$e^{-\alpha}e^{-\beta} \le e^{-EW} \le e^{-\alpha}. \tag{3}$$

In this paper, the approximation of $e^{-\alpha}$ will serve as the main term.

Now, we shall analyse that approximation of $R_n(T)$ which was proposed in [7]. The centering constant in [7] is

$$c_n(T) = \log n + T\log\log n - \log(T!) + \log(q^{T+1}p^{-T}). \tag{4}$$

Let x be a fixed number so that $c_n(T) + x = t$ is an integer. We want to estimate $P(R_n(T) - c_n(T) < x) = P(S_{n,t} < t - T)$. In the following we shall use both $\exp(x)$ and e^x for the usual exponential function.

Proposition 1. *Let $[c_n(T)]$ be the integer part of $c_n(T)$ and $\{c_n(T)\} = c_n(T) - [c_n(T)]$ be its fractional part.*

If $T = 0$, then for any integer l,

$$P(R_n(T) - [c_n(0)] < l) = \exp\left(-p^{l-\{c_n(0)\}}\right)\left(1 + O\left(\frac{\log n}{n}\right)\right). \tag{5}$$

If $T > 0$, then for any integer l,

$$P(R_n(T) - [c_n(T)] < l) = \exp\left(-p^{l-\{c_n(T)\}}\right)\left(1 + \mathrm{O}\left(\frac{\log\log n}{\log n}\right)\right). \tag{6}$$

Remark 1. *In Corollary 3 of [7], the same remainder term $\mathrm{O}\left(\frac{\log n}{n}\right)$ is given for the case $T > 0$, too. However, in our opinion, it contains only a part of the remainder terms.*

Proof of Proposition 1. As our remainder term and the remainder term offered by [7] are different, we give the details of the more or less simple calculation. First, we calculate the right hand side of inequality (1) for $s = t - T$ and $t = c_n(T) + x$, where x is chosen so that t is an integer.

$$P(X_1 + \cdots + X_t = t - T) = \binom{t}{T} p^t (q/p)^T \le \kappa \frac{(\log n)^T}{(1/p)^{\log n + T\log\log n}} = \mathrm{O}\left(\frac{1}{n}\right).$$

Here and in what follows, κ is an appropriate finite positive constant. Therefore,

$$7tP(X_1 + \cdots + X_t = t - T) = \mathrm{O}\left(\frac{\log n}{n}\right).$$

For $T > 0$, we have

$$P(X_1 + \cdots + X_t > t - T) \le T\binom{t}{t - T + 1} p^{t-T+1} \le \kappa t^{T-1} p^t$$
$$\le \kappa \frac{(\log n)^{T-1}}{n(\log n)^T} = \mathrm{O}\left(\frac{1}{n\log n}\right).$$

So we obtain

$$|P(S_{n,t} < t - T) - e^{-EW}| = \mathrm{O}\left(\frac{\log n}{n}\right). \tag{7}$$

This last formula is valid for $T = 0$, too.

Now, we turn to the other parts of the approximation. First, consider $T = 0$. Then, the main term of the approximation, i.e., $e^{-\alpha}$ in Formula (3) is

$$e^{-\alpha} = e^{-n\left(\frac{t}{t} - p\right)P(X_1 + \cdots + X_t = t)} = e^{-p^{-\log(nq)+t}}.$$

We have to approximate $P(R_n(0) - [c_n(0)] < l)$, where l is an integer, $c_n(0) = \log n + \log q$, and $[.]$ denotes the integer part. So, we should apply the previous equality with $t = [c_n(0)] + l$, so we obtain

$$e^{-\alpha} = e^{-p^{l-\{c_n(0)\}}},$$

where $\{.\}$ denotes the fractional part. We see that, if $T = 0$, then $\beta = 0$, so in inequality (3), we have equality. So, for $T = 0$, this part of the approximation is precise, i.e., the main term does not contain a remainder part.

Now, we consider the approximation of the main term for $T > 0$.

$$e^{-\alpha} = e^{-n\left(\frac{t-T}{t} - p\right)P(X_1 + \cdots + X_t = t - T)} = e^{-n\left(q - \frac{T}{t}\right)\binom{t}{T} q^T p^{t-T}}.$$

Now, denote by L the base $1/p$ logarithm of the negative of the exponent, that is, $L = \log \alpha$. So,

$$L = \log n + \log(q - T/t) + \log(t(t-1)\cdots((t - T + 1)) - \log T! + T\log q + T - t.$$

We shall use $t = c_n(T) + x$. Applying Taylor's expansion of the logarithm function, $\log(x_0 + y) = \log x_0 + \frac{y}{cx_0} - \frac{y^2}{2c\tilde{x}_0^2}$, where $\tilde{x}_0$ is between x_0 and $x_0 + y$, and where $c = \ln(1/p)$, we obtain

$$L = \log n + \log q - \frac{T}{cqt} - O\left(\frac{1}{t^2}\right) + \log t^T - \frac{t^{T-1}\binom{T}{2}}{ct^T} + O\left(\frac{1}{t^2}\right) - \log T! + T\log q + T - t$$

$$= \log n + T\log t - \frac{1}{ct}\left(\frac{T}{q} + \binom{T}{2}\right) + O\left(\frac{1}{t^2}\right) - \log T! + (T+1)\log q + T - t.$$

We insert $t = c_n(T) + x = \log n + T\log\log n + E$, where E is defined by the equation at hand so it does not depend on n. Using again Taylor's expansions of the logarithm function as $\log(x_0 + y) = \log x_0 + \frac{y}{cx_0} - \frac{y^2}{2cx_0^2} + \frac{y^3}{3c\tilde{x}_0^3}$, where $\tilde{x}_0$ is between x_0 and $x_0 + y$, and for the $1/t$ function, as $\frac{1}{x_0+y} = \frac{1}{x_0} - \frac{y}{x_0^2} + \frac{y^2}{\tilde{x}_0^3}$, where $\tilde{x}_0$ is between x_0 and $x_0 + y$, we obtain

$$\begin{aligned} & L \\ = {} & \log n + T\left(\log\log n + \frac{T\log\log n + E}{c\log n} - \frac{(T\log\log n + E)^2}{2c(\log n)^2} + O\left(\frac{(\log\log n)^3}{(\log n)^3}\right)\right) \\ - {} & \frac{1}{c}\left(\frac{T}{q} + \binom{T}{2}\right)\left(\frac{1}{\log n} - \frac{T\log\log n + E}{(\log n)^2} O\left(\frac{(\log\log n)^2}{(\log n)^3}\right)\right) + \\ + {} & O\left(\frac{1}{t^2}\right) - \log T! + (T+1)\log q + T - t. \end{aligned}$$

Now, using $t = c_n(T) + x$ and inserting the value of $c_n(T)$, we obtain

$$L = -x + \frac{T^2\log\log n}{c\log n} + O\left(\frac{1}{\log n}\right),$$

which implies that

$$L = -x + O\left(\frac{\log\log n}{\log n}\right),$$

and this rate is not improvable. We remark that this relation is valid for $T = 1$, too.

Therefore, by applying the Taylor series expansion $e^y = 1 + y + e^{\tilde{y}}\frac{y^2}{2}$ twice, where $\tilde{y}$ is between 0 and y, we obtain

$$e^{-\alpha} = e^{-(1/p)^L} = e^{-p^x}\left(1 - \ln\left(\frac{1}{p}\right)\frac{T^2\log\log n}{c\log n} + O\left(\frac{1}{\log n}\right)\right) \tag{8}$$

$$= e^{-p^{l-\{c_n(T)\}}}\left(1 + O\left(\frac{\log\log n}{\log n}\right)\right), \tag{9}$$

and this rate is not improvable.

Now, we consider the $e^{-\beta}$ part. Here,

$$\beta = 2\frac{T}{t}\sum_{i=t-T+1}^{t}\binom{t}{i}p^i q^{t-i} n\binom{t}{T}p^{t-T}q^T$$

with $t = c_n(T) + x = \log n + T\log\log n + E$. The largest term in the above sum is the first one, and it is

$$\binom{t}{T-1}p^t\left(\frac{q}{p}\right)^{T-1} = O\left(\frac{1}{n\log n}\right).$$

Then,

$$\binom{t}{T}p^{t-T}q^T = O\left(\frac{1}{n}\right).$$

Using Taylor's expansion,

$$\frac{T}{t} = \mathrm{O}\Big(\frac{1}{\log n}\Big).$$

So, $\beta = \mathrm{O}(1/n(\log n)^2)$, and

$$e^{-\beta} = 1 - \mathrm{O}\Big(\frac{1}{n(\log n)^2}\Big).$$

Therefore,

$$\begin{aligned} e^{-\alpha}e^{-\beta} &= e^{-p^{l-\{c_n(T)\}}}\Big(1+\mathrm{O}\Big(\frac{\log\log n}{\log n}\Big)\Big)\Big(1-\mathrm{O}\Big(\frac{1}{n(\log n)^2}\Big)\Big) \\ &= e^{-p^{l-\{c_n(T)\}}}\Big(1+\mathrm{O}\Big(\frac{\log\log n}{\log n}\Big)\Big). \end{aligned} \tag{10}$$

□

3. A New Approximation

Theorem 1. *Let $T \geq 1$ be an integer. Let*

$$\begin{aligned} \tilde{c}_n(T) &= \log(qn) + T\log(\log(qn)) \\ &+ T^2\frac{\log(\log(qn))}{c\log(qn)} - \frac{T}{cq_0\log(qn)} - \frac{T^3}{2c}\Big(\frac{\log(\log(qn))}{\log(qn)}\Big)^2 \\ &+ T^2\frac{\log(\log(qn))}{cq_0(\log(qn))^2} + T^3\frac{\log(\log(qn))}{(c\log(qn))^2} \\ &+ \Big(T\log\Big(\frac{q}{p}\Big) - \log(T!)\Big)\Big(1+\frac{T}{c\log(qn)} - T^2\frac{\log(\log(qn))}{c(\log(qn))^2}\Big), \end{aligned} \tag{11}$$

where log *denotes the logarithm to base $1/p$, $c = \ln(1/p)$,* ln *denotes the natural logarithm to base e, and $q_0 = \frac{2q}{2+Tq-q}$. Let $[\tilde{c}_n(T)]$ denote the integer part of $\tilde{c}_n(T)$, while $\{\tilde{c}_n(T)\}$ denotes the fractional part of $\tilde{c}_n(T)$, i.e. $\{\tilde{c}_n(T)\} = \tilde{c}_n(T) - [\tilde{c}_n(T)]$.*

Then,

$$\begin{aligned} &P(R_n(T) - [\tilde{c}_n(T)] < l) \\ &= \exp\Big(-p^{(l-\{\tilde{c}_n(T)\})\left(1-\frac{T}{c\log(qn)}+T^2\frac{\log(\log(qn))}{c(\log(qn))^2}\right)}\Big)\Big(1+\mathrm{O}\Big(\frac{1}{(\log n)^2}\Big)\Big) \end{aligned} \tag{12}$$

for any integer l, where $f(n) = \mathrm{O}(h(n))$ means that $f(n)/h(n)$ is bounded as $n \to \infty$.

Proof. We use the same approach as in the previous section. First, we calculate the right hand side of inequality (1) for $s = t - T$ and $t = \tilde{c}_n(T) + x$, where x is chosen so that t is an integer. As

$$\tilde{c}_n(T) = \log(n) + T\log(\log(n)) + \mathrm{O}(1),$$

we obtain

$$P(X_1 + \cdots + X_t = t - T) = \binom{t}{T}p^t(q/p)^T \leq \kappa\frac{(\log n)^T}{(1/p)^{\log n + T\log\log n}} = \mathrm{O}\Big(\frac{1}{n}\Big).$$

Therefore,

$$7tP(X_1 + \cdots + X_t = t - T) = \mathrm{O}\Big(\frac{\log n}{n}\Big).$$

Similarly,

$$P(X_1 + \cdots + X_t > t - T) \leq \kappa t^{T-1} p^t = \mathrm{O}\left(\frac{1}{n \log n}\right).$$

So,

$$|P(S_{n,t} < t - T) - e^{-EW}| = \mathrm{O}\left(\frac{\log n}{n}\right). \tag{13}$$

Now, we turn to the approximation of the main term $e^{-\alpha}$. Denote by L again the base $1/p$ logarithm of the negative of the exponent, so

$$\begin{aligned} L &= \log \alpha \\ &= \log n + \log(q - T/t) + \log(t(t-1)\dots((t-T+1)) - \log T! + T \log q + T - t. \end{aligned}$$

We shall apply it for $t = \tilde{c}_n(T) + x$. Therefore,

$$\begin{aligned} &L \\ &= \log\left(q - \frac{T}{t}\right) + \log n + \log\left(t^T - \frac{T(T-1)}{2} t^{T-1} + \mathrm{O}(t^{T-2})\right) - t \\ &\quad + \log((q/p)^T) - \log(T!) \\ &= \log\left(q - \frac{T}{t}\right) + \log n + \log(t^T) - \frac{\frac{T(T-1)}{2} t^{T-1}}{ct^T} + \mathrm{O}\left(\frac{1}{t^2}\right) - t \\ &\quad + \log((q/p)^T) - \log(T!) \\ &= \log q - \frac{T}{cqt} + \log n + T \log t - \frac{\frac{T(T-1)}{2}}{ct} - t \\ &\quad + \log((q/p)^T) - \log(T!) + \mathrm{O}\left(\frac{1}{(\log n)^2}\right) \\ &= \log(qn) - \frac{T}{cq_0 t} + T \log t - t + \log((q/p)^T) - \log(T!) + \mathrm{O}\left(\frac{1}{(\log n)^2}\right), \end{aligned}$$

where we applied Taylor's expansion of the log function up to the second order and used the notation $q_0 = \frac{2q}{2+Tq-q}$.

Introduce notation

$$\begin{aligned} D &= -\frac{T^3}{2c}\left(\frac{\log(\log(qn))}{\log(qn)}\right)^2 + T^2 \frac{\log(\log(qn))}{cq_0(\log(qn))^2} + T^3 \frac{\log(\log(qn))}{(c\log(qn))^2} \\ &+ \left(T \log\left(\frac{q}{p}\right) - \log(T!)\right)\left(\frac{T}{c\log(qn)} - T^2 \frac{\log(\log(qn))}{c(\log(qn))^2}\right), \end{aligned} \tag{14}$$

$$B = T^2 \frac{\log(\log(qn))}{c\log(qn)} - \frac{T}{cq_0 \log(qn)} + D \tag{15}$$

and

$$A = T \log(\log(qn)) + B.$$

Then, $t = \tilde{c}_n(T) + x = \tilde{c}_n(T) + l - \{\tilde{c}_n(T)\}$, where l is an integer, so

$$t = T \log\left(\frac{q}{p}\right) - \log(T!) + \log(qn) + A + l - \{\tilde{c}_n(T)\}.$$

Inserting this value of t into the term $-t$ of L, we obtain

$$L = -\frac{T}{cq_0 t} + T \log t - A - l + \{\tilde{c}_n(T)\} + \mathrm{O}\left(\frac{1}{(\log n)^2}\right).$$

Then, use Taylor's expansion for the function $1/t$ to obtain

$$\begin{aligned} L &= -\frac{T}{cq_0\log(qn)} + T^2\frac{\log(\log(qn))}{cq_0(\log(qn))^2} \\ &+ T\log\big(\log(qn) + T\log(\log(qn)) + B + \log((q/p)^T) - \log(T!) + l - \{\tilde{c}_n(T)\}\big) \\ &- A - l + \{\tilde{c}_n(T)\} + O\Big(\frac{1}{(\log n)^2}\Big). \end{aligned}$$

Now, by Taylor's expansion for the $\log(x)$ function, we obtain

$$\begin{aligned} L = &- \frac{T}{cq_0\log(qn)} + T^2\frac{\log(\log(qn))}{cq_0(\log(qn))^2} + T\log(\log(qn)) \\ &+ \frac{T(T\log(\log(qn)) + B + \log((q/p)^T) - \log(T!) + l - \{\tilde{c}_n(T)\})}{c\log(qn)} \\ &- \frac{1}{2}\frac{T\big(T\log(\log(qn)) + B + \log((q/p)^T) - \log(T!) + l - \{\tilde{c}_n(T)\}\big)^2}{c(\log(qn))^2} \\ &- A - l + \{\tilde{c}_n(T)\} + O\Big(\frac{1}{(\log n)^2}\Big). \end{aligned}$$

Now, we can omit B from the quadratic term. Then, we apply $A = T\log(\log(qn)) + B$, so we obtain

$$\begin{aligned} L = &- \frac{T}{cq_0\log(qn)} + \frac{T^2\log(\log(qn))}{cq_0(\log(qn))^2} + \frac{T^2\log(\log(qn))}{c\log(qn)} \\ &+ \frac{T(\log((q/p)^T) - \log(T!))}{c\log(qn)} + \frac{T^3\log(\log(qn))}{(c\log(qn))^2} - \frac{T^2}{q_0(c\log(qn))^2} + \frac{TD}{c\log(qn)} \\ &+ \frac{T(l - \{\tilde{c}_n(T)\})\})}{c\log(qn)} - \frac{1}{2}\frac{T^3(\log(\log(qn)))^2}{c(\log(qn))^2} \\ &- \frac{1}{2}\frac{T\big(\log((q/p)^T) - \log(T!) + l - \{\tilde{c}_n(T)\}\big)^2}{c(\log(qn))^2} \\ &- \frac{2T}{2}\frac{T\log(\log(qn))(\log((q/p)^T) - \log(T!) + l - \{\tilde{c}_n(T)\})}{c(\log(qn))^2} \\ &- B - l + \{\tilde{c}_n(T)\} + O\Big(\frac{1}{(\log n)^2}\Big) \\ = &\ (l - \{\tilde{c}_n(T)\})\Big(\frac{T}{c\log(qn)} - \frac{T^2\log(\log(qn))}{c(\log(qn))^2} - 1\Big) + O\Big(\frac{1}{(\log n)^2}\Big). \end{aligned}$$

So,

$$e^{-\alpha} = e^{-p^{(l-\{\tilde{c}_n(T)\})\left(1-\frac{T}{c\log(qn)}+\frac{T^2\log(\log(qn))}{c(\log(qn))^2}\right)+O\left(\frac{1}{(\log n)^2}\right)}}.$$

Using Taylor's expansion again,

$$e^{-\alpha} = e^{-p^{(l-\{\tilde{c}_n(T)\})\left(1-\frac{T}{c\log(qn)}+\frac{T^2\log(\log(qn))}{c(\log(qn))^2}\right)}}\Big(1 + O\Big(\frac{1}{(\log n)^2}\Big)\Big).$$

Now, turn to the $e^{-\beta}$ part, where

$$\beta = 2\frac{T}{t}\sum_{i=t-T+1}^{t}\binom{t}{i}p^i q^{t-i} n\binom{t}{T}p^{t-T}q^T$$

and $t = \tilde{c}_n(T) + x$. Simple calculations shows that $\beta \le \kappa(1/n(\log n)^2)$, and so

$$e^{-\beta} = 1 + \mathrm{O}\left(\frac{1}{n(\log n)^2}\right).$$

Therefore,

$$e^{-\alpha}e^{-\beta} = e^{-p^{(l-\{\hat{c}_n(T)\})\left(1-\frac{T}{c\log(qn)}+\frac{T^2\log(\log(qn))}{c(\log(qn))^2}\right)}}\left(1+\mathrm{O}\left(\frac{1}{(\log n)^2}\right)\right).$$

□

4. Simulation Results

We performed several computer simulation studies for certain fixed values of p and T. Here, we present the results of three simulations. The length of each simulated sequence was $N = 10^6$, and $s = 2000$ was the number of repetitions of the N-length sequences in each case. In each case, the number of contaminations was $T = 3$.

Figures 1–3 present the results of the simulations. The left hand side of each figure shows the empirical distribution function of the longest at most T-contaminated run and its approximation suggested by our Theorem 1. The asterisk (i.e., $*$) denotes the result of the simulation, i.e., the empirical distribution of the longest at most T-contaminated run, and the circle ($\circ$) denotes the approximation offered by Theorem 1. The right hand side of each figure shows the approximation by the former result. The asterisk denotes the result of the simulation again, and the circle ($\circ$) denotes the approximation offered by Proposition 1. The simulation results support that our new theorem offers a better approximation than the previous one.

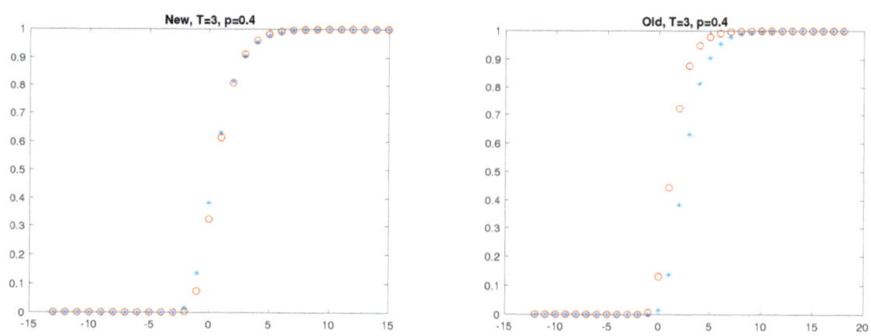

(**a**) New theorem (**b**) Previous result

Figure 1. Longest at most $T = 3$ contaminated run when $p = 0.4$.

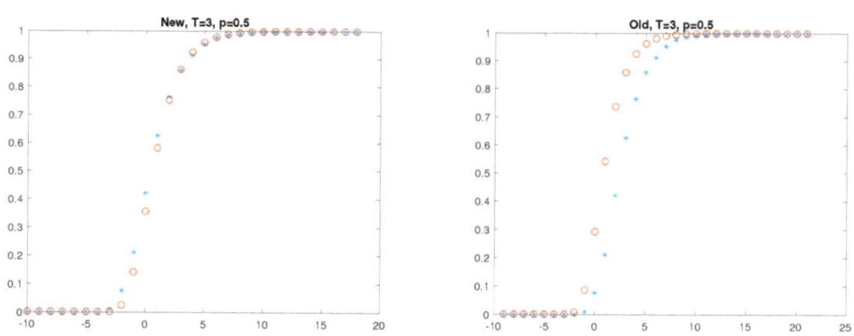

(**a**) New theorem (**b**) Previous result

Figure 2. Longest at most $T = 3$ contaminated run when $p = 0.5$.

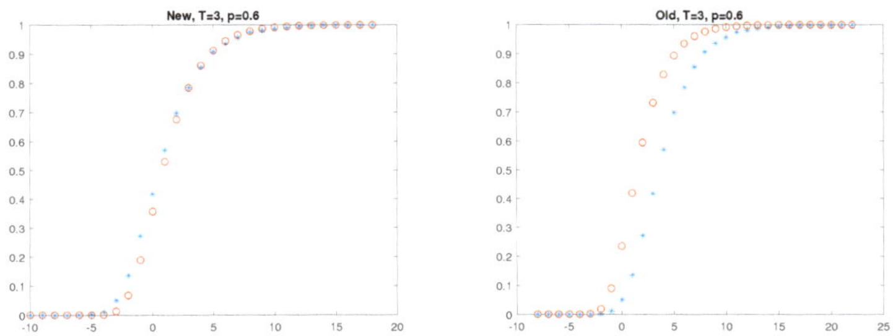

(a) New theorem (b) Previous result

Figure 3. Longest at most $T = 3$ contaminated run when $p = 0.6$.

5. Discussion

We were able to obtain a practically applicable approximation for the distribution of the longest at most T-contaminated head-run. We presented both detailed mathematical proof and simulation evidence.

Author Contributions: Conceptualization, I.F.; methodology, I.F.; software, L.F.; validation, B.F.; formal analysis, I.F., B.F. and L.F.; investigation, I.F., B.F. and L.F.; writing—original draft preparation, I.F., B.F. and L.F.; writing—review and editing, I.F.; visualization, L.F.; supervision, I.F. All authors have read and agreed to the published version of the manuscript.

Funding: This research received no external funding.

Institutional Review Board Statement: Not applicable.

Data Availability Statement: The original contributions presented in this study are included in the article. Further inquiries can be directed to the corresponding author.

Conflicts of Interest: The authors declare no conflicts of interest.

References

Erdős, P.; Rényi, A. On a new law of large numbers. *J. Analyse Math.* **1970**, *23*, 103–111. [CrossRef]
Erdős, P.; Révész, P. On the length of the longest head-run. In *Topics in Information Theory (Second Colloq., Keszthely, 1975)*; Colloq. Math. Soc. János Bolyai; North-Holland: Amsterdam, The Netherlands, 1977; Volume 16, pp. 219–228.
Földes, A. The limit distribution of the length of the longest head-run. *Period. Math. Hungar.* **1979**, *10*, 301–310. [CrossRef]
Móri, T.F. The a.s. limit distribution of the longest head run. *Canad. J. Math.* **1993**, *45*, 1245–1262. [CrossRef]
Gordon, L.; Schilling, M.F.; Waterman, M.S. An extreme value theory for long head runs. *Probab. Theory Relat. Fields* **1986**, *72*, 279–287. [CrossRef]
Novak, S.Y. On the length of the longest head run. *Statist. Probab. Lett.* **2017**, *130*, 111–114. [CrossRef]
Arratia, R.; Gordon, L.; Waterman, M.S. The Erdős-Rényi Law in Distribution, for Coin Tossing and Sequence Matching. *Ann. Statist.* **2008**, *18*, 539–570. [CrossRef]
Fazekas, I.; Fazekas, B.; Ochieng Suja, M. Convergence rate for the longest T-contaminated runs of heads. *Statist. Probab. Lett.* **2024**, *208*, 110059. [CrossRef]
Csáki, E.; Földes, A.; Komlós, J. Limit theorems for Erdős-Rényi type problems. *Studia Sci. Math. Hungar.* **1987**, *22*, 321–332.

entropy

MDPI

Article

Self-Normalized Moderate Deviations for Degenerate *U*-Statistic

Lin Ge [1], Hailin Sang [2,*] and Qi-Man Shao [3]

1 Division of Arts and Sciences, Mississippi State University at Meridian, Meridian, MS 39307, USA; lge@meridian.msstate.edu
2 Department of Mathematics, University of Mississippi, University, MS 38677, USA
3 Department of Statistics and Data Science, Shenzhen International Center for Mathematics, Southern University of Science and Technology, Shenzhen 518055, China; shaoqm@sustech.edu.cn
* Correspondence: sang@olemiss.edu

Abstract: In this paper, we study self-normalized moderate deviations for degenerate U-statistics of order 2. Let $\{X_i, i \geq 1\}$ be i.i.d. random variables and consider symmetric and degenerate kernel functions in the form $h(x,y) = \sum_{l=1}^{\infty} \lambda_l g_l(x) g_l(y)$, where $\lambda_l > 0$, $Eg_l(X_1) = 0$, and $g_l(X_1)$ is in the domain of attraction of a normal law for all $l \geq 1$. Under the condition $\sum_{l=1}^{\infty} \lambda_l < \infty$ and some truncated conditions for $\{g_l(X_1) : l \geq 1\}$, we show that $\log P\left(\frac{\sum_{1\leq i\neq j\leq n} h(X_i,X_j)}{\max_{1\leq l<\infty} \lambda_l V_{n,l}^2} \geq x_n^2\right) \sim -\frac{x_n^2}{2}$ for $x_n \to \infty$ and $x_n = o(\sqrt{n})$, where $V_{n,l}^2 = \sum_{i=1}^{n} g_l^2(X_i)$. As application, a law of the iterated logarithm is also obtained.

Keywords: moderate deviation; degenerate U-statistics; law of the iterated logarithm; self-normalization

MSC: 60F15; 60F10; 62E20

1. Introduction and Main Results

The recent three decades have witnessed significant developments on self-normalized limit theory, especially on large deviations, Cramér-type moderate deviations, and the law of the iterated logarithm. Compared with the classical limit theorems, these self-normalized limit theorems usually require much less moment assumptions.

Let $X, X_1, X_2, \ldots$ be independent identically distributed (i.i.d.) random variables. Set

$$S_n = \sum_{i=1}^{n} X_i \text{ and } V_n^2 = \sum_{i=1}^{n} X_i^2.$$

Griffin and Kuelbs [1] obtained a law of the iterated logarithm (LIL) for the self-normalized sum of i.i.d. random variables with distributions in the domain of attraction of a normal or stable law. They proved that

1. If $EX = 0$ and X is in the domain of attraction of a normal law, then

$$\limsup_{n\to\infty} \frac{S_n}{V_n(2\log\log n)^{1/2}} = 1 \ a.s. \quad (1)$$

2. If X is symmetric and is in the domain of attraction of a stable law, then there exists a positive constant C such that

$$\limsup_{n\to\infty} \frac{S_n}{V_n(2\log\log n)^{1/2}} = C \ \ a.s. \tag{2}$$

Shao [2] obtained the following self-normalized moderate deviations and specified the constant C in (2). Let $\{x_n, n \geq 1\}$ be a sequence of positive numbers such that $x_n \to \infty$ and $x_n = o(\sqrt{n})$ as $n \to \infty$.

1. If $EX = 0$ and X is in the domain of attraction of a normal law, then

$$\lim_{n\to\infty} x_n^{-2} \log P\left(\frac{S_n}{V_n} \geq x_n\right) = -\frac{1}{2}. \tag{3}$$

2. If X is in the domain of attraction of a stable law such that $EX = 0$ with index $1 < \alpha < 2$, or X_1 is symmetric with index $\alpha = 1$, then

$$\lim_{n\to\infty} x_n^{-2} \log P\left(\frac{S_n}{V_n} \geq x_n\right) = -\beta(\alpha, c_1, c_2),$$

where $\beta(\alpha, c_1, c_2)$ is a constant depending on the tail distribution; see [2] for an explicit definition.

Shao [3] refined (3) and obtained the following Cramér-type moderate deviation theorem under a finite third moment: if $EX = 0$ and $E|X|^3 < \infty$, then

$$\frac{P(S_n/V_n \geq x_n)}{P(Z \geq x_n)} \to 1 \tag{4}$$

for any $x_n \in [0, o(n^{1/6}))$, where Z is the standard normal random variable.

Jing, Shao and Wang [4] further extended (4) to general independent random variables under a Lindeberg-type condition, while Shao and Zhou [5] established the result for self-normalized non-linear statistics, which include U-statistics as a special case.

The U-statistics were introduced by Halmos [6] and Hoeffding [7]. The LIL for nondegenerate U-statistics was obtained by Serfling [8]. The LIL for degenerate U-statistics was studied by Dehling, Denker and Philipp ([9,10]), Dehling [11], Arcones and Giné [12], Teicher [13], Giné and Zhang [14], and others. Giné, Kwapień, Latała and Zinn [15] provided necessary and sufficient conditions for the LIL of degenerate U-statistics of order 2, which was extended to any order by Adamczak and Latała [16].

The main purpose of this paper is to study the self-normalized moderate deviations and the LIL for degenerate U-statistics of order 2. Let

$$U_n = \frac{1}{n(n-1)} \sum_{1\leq i\neq j\leq n} h(X_i, X_j),$$

where

$$h(x,y) = \sum_{l=1}^{\infty} \lambda_l g_l(x) g_l(y). \tag{5}$$

A motivation example for the LIL is the one with the kernel $h(x,y) = xy$. Obviously, $V_n^2/(2V_n^2 \log\log n) \to 0$. Then, via (1) and (2), we have

1. If $EX = 0$ and X is in the domain of attraction of a normal law, then

$$\limsup_{n\to\infty} \frac{1}{2V_n^2 \log\log n}\left|\sum_{1\le i\ne j\le n} X_i X_j\right|$$
$$= \limsup_{n\to\infty}\left[\frac{S_n}{V_n(2\log\log n)^{1/2}}\right]^2 = 1 \ \ a.s. \tag{6}$$

2. If X is symmetric and is in the domain of attraction of a stable law, then there exists a positive constant C such that

$$\limsup_{n\to\infty} \frac{1}{2V_n^2 \log\log n}\left|\sum_{1\le i\ne j\le n} X_i X_j\right|$$
$$= \limsup_{n\to\infty}\left[\frac{S_n}{V_n(2\log\log n)^{1/2}}\right]^2 = C^2 \ \ a.s.$$

For the general degenerate kernel h defined in (5), we have

$$\begin{aligned} n(n-1)U_n &= \sum_{l=1}^{\infty}\lambda_l \sum_{1\le i\ne j\le n} g_l(X_i)g_l(X_j) \\ &= \sum_{l=1}^{\infty}\lambda_l\Big(\Big(\sum_{i=1}^{n} g_l(X_i)\Big)^2 - \sum_{i=1}^{n} g_l^2(X_i)\Big). \end{aligned}$$

Suppose that $g_l(X)$ is in the domain of attraction of a normal law for every $l \ge 1$. Then, $L_l(x) := Eg_l^2(X_1)I(|g_l(X_1)| \le x)$ is a slowly varying function for all $l \ge 1$ as $x \to \infty$. Let $\{x_n, n \ge 1\}$ be a sequence of positive numbers such that $x_n \to \infty$ and $x_n = o(\sqrt{n})$ as $n \to \infty$. For each $l \ge 1$, set

$$\begin{aligned} b_l &= \inf\Big\{x \ge 1 : L_l(x) > 0\Big\}, \\ z_{n,l} &= \inf\Big\{s : s \ge b_l + 1, \frac{L_l(s)}{s^2} \le \frac{x_n^2}{n}\Big\}. \end{aligned} \tag{7}$$

Write

$$W_n = \frac{n(n-1)U_n}{\max_{1\le l<\infty}\lambda_l \sum_{i=1}^{n} g_l^2(X_i)}.$$

We have the following self-normalized moderate deviation:

Theorem 1. *Let $Eg_l(X) = 0$ and $\lambda_l \ge 0$ for every $l \ge 1$.*

$$\sup_{x\in R}\frac{\sum_{l=m+1}^{\infty}\lambda_l g_l^2(x)}{\sum_{1\le l<\infty}\lambda_l g_l^2(x)} \to 0 \ \ as \ \ m \to \infty \tag{8}$$

and

$$\lim_{n\to\infty}\frac{Eg_l(X)I(|g_l(X)| \le z_{n,l})g_k(X)I(|g_k(X)| \le z_{n,k})}{\sqrt{L_l(z_{n,l})L_k(z_{n,k})}} \to 0 \tag{9}$$

for any $l \ne k$. Then, for $x_n \to \infty$ and $x_n = o(\sqrt{n})$,

$$\lim_{n\to\infty} x_n^{-2}\log P\Big(W_n \ge x_n^2\Big) = -\frac{1}{2}.$$

As an application, we have the following self-normalized LIL:

Theorem 2. *Under the assumptions in Theorem 1, and instead of* (8), *we assume that for each* $l \in [1, \infty)$, *there is a constant* $c_l > 0$ *such that*

$$\sup_{x \in R} \frac{\lambda_l g_l^2(x)}{\sum_{l=1}^{\infty} \lambda_l g_l^2(x)} \le c_l \text{ and } \sum_{l=1}^{\infty} c_l < \infty. \tag{10}$$

Then,

$$\limsup_{n \to \infty} \frac{W_n}{\log \log n} = 2 \ a.s. \tag{11}$$

Remark 1. *We use an example to show that (9) cannot be removed. Let* $g_1(x) = x$, $g_2(x) = x^3$ *and* $\lambda_1 = \lambda_2 = 1$, $\lambda_l = 0$ *for* $l \ge 3$. *Let X be a Rademacher random variable. Then,* $n(n-1)U_n = \sum_{1 \le i \ne j \le n} (X_i X_j + X_i^3 X_j^3) = 2 \sum_{1 \le i \ne j \le n} X_i X_j$ *and* $W_n = 2 \sum_{1 \le i \ne j \le n} X_i X_j / \sum_{i=1}^n X_i^2$. *By (6),* $\limsup_{n \to \infty} W_n / \log \log n = 4$ *a.s. which contradicts (11).*

2. Proofs

In the proofs of theorems, we will use the following properties for the slowly varying functions g_l (e.g., Bingham et al. [17]). As $x \to \infty$,

$$P(|g_l(X)| \ge x) = o(L_l(x)/x^2), \tag{12}$$

$$E|g_l(X)| I(|g_l(X)| \ge x) = o(L_l(x)/x), \tag{13}$$

$$E|g_l(X)|^p I(|g_l(X)| \le x) = o(x^{p-2} L_l(x)), \quad p > 2. \tag{14}$$

Since $L_l(s)/s^2 \to 0$ as $s \to \infty$ and $L_l(x)$ is right continuous, in (7), $z_{n,l} \to \infty$ and for all sufficiently large n values, we have

$$n L_l(z_{n,l}) = x_n^2 z_{n,l}^2. \tag{15}$$

2.1. The Upper Bound of Theorem 1

For each $l \ge 1$ and $i \ge 1$, denote the truncated function

$$\bar{g}_l(X_i) = g_l(X_i) I(|g_l(X_i)| \le z_{n,l}).$$

Since $E g_l(X_i) = 0$, we have

$$E\bar{g}_l(X_i) = o(L_l(z_{n,l})/z_{n,l}) = o(x_n \sqrt{L_l(z_{n,l})}/\sqrt{n}) \tag{16}$$

by (13) and (15). For each $l \ge 1$, write

$$Y_{n,l} = \sum_{i=1}^n g_l(X_i), \ \bar{Y}_{n,l} = \sum_{i=1}^n \bar{g}_l(X_i) \text{ and } V_{n,l}^2 = \sum_{i=1}^n g_l^2(X_i).$$

By Condition (8), for each $0 < \varepsilon < 1$, there exists $1 \le m < \infty$ such that

$$m \max_{1 \le l < \infty} \lambda_l V_{n,l}^2 \ge \sum_{l=1}^m \lambda_l V_{n,l}^2 \ge (1-\varepsilon) \sum_{l=1}^{\infty} \lambda_l V_{n,l}^2. \tag{17}$$

Hence, for $x_n \to \infty$,

$$P\Big(W_n \geq (1+\varepsilon)x_n^2\Big) \leq P\Big(\frac{\sum_{l=1}^{\infty}\lambda_l Y_{n,l}^2}{\max_{1\leq l<\infty}\lambda_l V_{n,l}^2} \geq x_n^2\Big). \tag{18}$$

Observe that for any random variables $\{U_l\}_{l=1}^{\infty}$ and $\{Z_l\}_{l=1}^{\infty}$ and any constants $x > 0$ and $0 < a < 1/3$, we have the following via the Cauchy inequality:

$$\begin{aligned}
& P\Big(\sum_l (U_l + Z_l)^2 \geq x\Big) \\
\leq\ & P\Big(\sum_l U_l^2 \geq (1-a)^2 x\Big) + P\Big(\sum_l Z_l^2 \geq a^2 x\Big) \\
\leq\ & P\Big(\sum_l U_l^2 \geq (1-2a) x\Big) + P\Big(\sum_l Z_l^2 \geq a^2 x\Big).
\end{aligned} \tag{19}$$

For any $0 < \varepsilon < 1/3$, by (18) and (19), we have

$$\begin{aligned}
& P\Big(W_n \geq (1+\varepsilon)x_n^2\Big) \\
\leq\ & P\Big(\frac{\sum_{l=1}^{\infty}\lambda_l(\sum_{i=1}^{n} g_l(X_i) I(|g_l(X_i)| > z_{n,l}))^2}{\max_{1\leq l<\infty}\lambda_l V_{n,l}^2} \geq \varepsilon^2 x_n^2\Big) \\
& + P\Big(\frac{\sum_{l=1}^{\infty}\lambda_l \bar{Y}_{n,l}^2}{\max_{1\leq l<\infty}\lambda_l V_{n,l}^2} \geq (1-2\varepsilon)x_n^2\Big).
\end{aligned} \tag{20}$$

For any integer $m \geq 1$ and any constant $C_1 > 0$ with $C_1\varepsilon < 1$, we have

$$\begin{aligned}
& P\Big(\frac{\sum_{l=1}^{\infty}\lambda_l \bar{Y}_{n,l}^2}{\max_{1\leq l<\infty}\lambda_l V_{n,l}^2} \geq (1-2\varepsilon)x_n^2\Big) \\
\leq\ & P\Big(\max_{1\leq l<\infty}\lambda_l V_{n,l}^2 \leq \frac{n}{\varepsilon}\sum_{l=m+1}^{\infty}\lambda_l L_l(z_{n,l})\Big) \\
& + P\Big(\max_{1\leq l<\infty}\lambda_l V_{n,l}^2 \leq (1-\varepsilon)n \max_{1\leq l\leq m}\lambda_l L_l(z_{n,l})\Big) \\
& + P\Big(\frac{\sum_{l=m+1}^{\infty}\lambda_l \bar{Y}_{n,l}^2}{(n/\varepsilon)\sum_{l=m+1}^{\infty}\lambda_l L_l(z_{n,l})} \geq C_1\varepsilon(1-2\varepsilon)x_n^2\Big) \\
& + P\Big(\frac{\sum_{l=1}^{m}\lambda_l \bar{Y}_{n,l}^2}{(1-\varepsilon)n \max_{1\leq l\leq m}\lambda_l L_l(z_{n,l})} \geq (1-C_1\varepsilon)(1-2\varepsilon)x_n^2\Big).
\end{aligned} \tag{21}$$

Applying (21) to (20), we have

$$
\begin{aligned}
& P\Big(W_n \geq (1+\varepsilon)x_n^2\Big) \\
\leq\ & P\Big(\max_{1\leq l<\infty} \lambda_l V_{n,l}^2 \leq \frac{n}{\varepsilon}\sum_{l=m+1}^{\infty} \lambda_l L_l(z_{n,l})\Big) \\
& +P\Big(\max_{1\leq l<\infty} \lambda_l V_{n,l}^2 \leq (1-\varepsilon)n \max_{1\leq l\leq m} \lambda_l L_l(z_{n,l})\Big) \\
& +P\Big(\frac{\sum_{l=1}^{\infty}\lambda_l(\sum_{i=1}^{n} g_l(X_i)I(|g_l(X_i)|>z_{n,l}))^2}{\max_{1\leq l<\infty}\lambda_l V_{n,l}^2} \geq \varepsilon^2 x_n^2\Big) \\
& +P\Big(\frac{\sum_{l=m+1}^{\infty}\lambda_l \bar{Y}_{n,l}^2}{n\sum_{l=m+1}^{\infty}\lambda_l L_l(z_{n,l})} \geq C_1(1-2\varepsilon)x_n^2\Big) \\
& +P\Big(\frac{\sum_{l=1}^{m}\lambda_l \bar{Y}_{n,l}^2}{n\max_{1\leq l\leq m}\lambda_l L_l(z_{n,l})} \geq (1-C_1\varepsilon)(1-2\varepsilon)^2 x_n^2\Big) \\
:=\ & I_{1,1}+I_{1,2}+I_2+I_3+I_4.
\end{aligned} \tag{22}
$$

2.2. Estimation of $I_{1,1}$ and $I_{1,2}$

Proposition 1. *For $m \geq 1$ that is sufficiently large,*

$$
I_{1,1} = P\Big(\max_{1\leq l<\infty} \lambda_l V_{n,l}^2 \leq \frac{n}{\varepsilon}\sum_{l=m+1}^{\infty} \lambda_l L_l(z_{n,l})\Big) \leq \exp(-2x_n^2) \tag{23}
$$

and for any constants $\delta > 0$ and $0 < \eta < 1$,

$$
P\Big(2m \max_{1\leq l<\infty} \lambda_l V_{n,l}^2 \leq (1-\eta)n \sum_{1\leq l<\infty} \lambda_l L_l(z_{n,l})\Big) \leq \exp(-2x_n^2), \tag{24}
$$

$$
\begin{aligned}
& P\Big(\max_{1\leq l<\infty} \lambda_l \sum_{i=1}^{n} g_l^2(X_i)I(|g_l(X_i)| \leq \delta z_{n,l}) \leq (1-\eta)n \max_{1\leq l<\infty} \lambda_l L_l(z_{n,l})\Big) \\
\leq\ & \exp(-2x_n^2).
\end{aligned} \tag{25}
$$

In particular,

$$
I_{1,2} \leq P\Big(\max_{1\leq l<\infty} \lambda_l V_{n,l}^2 \leq (1-\varepsilon)n \max_{1\leq l<\infty} \lambda_l L_l(z_{n,l})\Big) \leq \exp(-2x_n^2).
$$

Proof. We shall apply the following exponential inequality (see, e.g., Theorem 2.19 of de la Peña, Lai and Shao [18]). If $Y_1, \ldots, Y_n$ are independent random variables with $Y_i \geq 0$, $\mu_n = \sum_{i=1}^{n} EY_i$ and $B_n^2 = \sum_{i=1}^{n} EY_i^2 < \infty$, then for $0 < x < \mu_n$,

$$
P\Big(\sum_{i=1}^{n} Y_i \leq x\Big) \leq \exp\Big(-\frac{(\mu_n - x)^2}{2B_n^2}\Big).
$$

By (8), $\sum_{l=m+1}^{\infty} \lambda_l V_{n,l}^2 / \sum_{l=1}^{\infty} \lambda_l V_{n,l}^2 \to 0$ as $m \to \infty$. Then, by (17),

$$
\frac{\sum_{l=m+1}^{\infty} \lambda_l V_{n,l}^2}{\max_{1\leq l<\infty} \lambda_l V_{n,l}^2} \to 0 \quad as \quad m \to \infty. \tag{26}
$$

Hence,

$$\varepsilon \max_{1\le l<\infty} \lambda_l V_{n,l}^2 \ge 2 \sum_{l=m+1}^{\infty} \lambda_l V_{n,l}^2 \ge 2 \sum_{l=m+1}^{\infty} \lambda_l \sum_{i=1}^{n} \bar{g}_l^2(X_i).$$

Then,

$$\begin{aligned} I_{1,1} &\le P\left(\sum_{l=m+1}^{\infty} \lambda_l \sum_{i=1}^{n} \bar{g}_l^2(X_i) \le \frac{n}{2} \sum_{l=m+1}^{\infty} \lambda_l L_l(z_{n,l}) \right) \\ &\le \exp\left(-\frac{(n\sum_{l=m+1}^{\infty} \lambda_l L_l(z_{n,l})/2)^2}{2nE(\sum_{l=m+1}^{\infty} \lambda_l \bar{g}_l^2(X_1))^2} \right). \end{aligned} \tag{27}$$

By Minkowski's integral inequality, (14) and (15),

$$\begin{aligned} E\left(\sum_{l=m+1}^{\infty} \lambda_l \bar{g}_l^2(X_1) \right)^2 &\le \left\{ \sum_{l=m+1}^{\infty} \lambda_l (E\bar{g}_l^4(X_1))^{1/2} \right\}^2 \\ &= o\left(\frac{\sqrt{n}}{x_n} \sum_{l=m+1}^{\infty} \lambda_l L_l(z_{n,l}) \right)^2. \end{aligned} \tag{28}$$

Therefore, (23) follows from (27) and (28). To show (24), notice that by (17),

$$m \max_{1\le l<\infty} \lambda_l V_{n,l}^2 \ge (1-\eta) \sum_{l=1}^{\infty} \lambda_l V_{n,l}^2 \ge (1-\eta) \sum_{l=1}^{\infty} \lambda_l \sum_{i=1}^{n} \bar{g}_l^2(X_i).$$

Then,

$$\begin{aligned} & P\left(2m \max_{1\le l<\infty} \lambda_l V_{n,l}^2 \le (1-\eta)n \sum_{1\le l<\infty} \lambda_l L_l(z_{n,l}) \right) \\ \le\ & P\left(\sum_{l=1}^{\infty} \lambda_l \sum_{i=1}^{n} \bar{g}_l^2(X_i) \le \frac{n}{2} \sum_{l=1}^{\infty} \lambda_l L_l(z_{n,l}) \right) \\ \le\ & \exp\left(-\frac{((\frac{n}{2}\sum_{l=1}^{\infty} \lambda_l L_l(z_{n,l}))^2}{2nE(\sum_{l=1}^{\infty} \lambda_l \bar{g}_l^2(X_1))^2} \right). \end{aligned}$$

Similar to the proof of $I_{1,1}$ as in (27) and (28), we have (24).

To show (25), let

$$l_n = \min\left\{ l : \lambda_l L_l(z_{n,l}) = \max_{1\le l<\infty} \lambda_l L_l(z_{n,l}) \right\}.$$

Then,

$$\begin{aligned} & P\left(\max_{1\le l<\infty} \lambda_l \sum_{i=1}^{n} g_l^2(X_i) I(|g_l(X_i)| \le \delta z_{n,l}) \le (1-\eta)n \max_{1\le l<\infty} \lambda_l L_l(z_{n,l}) \right) \\ \le\ & P\left(\sum_{i=1}^{n} \lambda_{l_n} g_{l_n}^2(X_i) I(|g_{l_n}(X_i)| \le \delta z_{n,l_n}) \le (1-\eta) n\lambda_{l_n} L_{l_n}(z_{n,l_n}) \right) \\ \le\ & \exp\left(-\frac{(1-(1-\eta))^2 (n\lambda_{l_n} L_{l_n}(z_{n,l_n}))^2}{2n\lambda_{l_n}^2 E g_{l_n}^4(X_1) I(|g_{l_n}(X_1)| \le \delta z_{n,l_n})} \right) \\ =\ & \exp\left(-\frac{\eta^2 (n\lambda_{l_n} L_{l_n}(z_{n,l_n}))^2}{2n\lambda_{l_n}^2 o(nL_{l_n}^2(\delta z_{n,l_n})/x_n^2)} \right). \end{aligned}$$

Since $L_l(\delta z_{n,l})/L_l(z_{n,l}) \to 1$, (25) follows. □

2.3. Estimation of I_2

Proposition 2.

$$I_2 = P\left(\frac{\sum_{l=1}^{\infty} \lambda_l \{\sum_{i=1}^{n} g_l(X_i) I(|g_l(X_i)| > z_{n,l})\}^2}{\max_{1\le l<\infty} \lambda_l V_{n,l}^2} \ge \varepsilon^2 x_n^2\right) \le \exp(-2x_n^2).$$

Proof. Via the Cauchy–Schwarz inequality,

$$\begin{aligned} & \frac{\sum_{l=1}^{\infty} \lambda_l \{\sum_{i=1}^{n} |g_l(X_i)| I(|g_l(X_i)| > z_{n,l})\}^2}{\max_{1\le l<\infty} \lambda_l V_{n,l}^2} \\ \le & \frac{\sum_{l=1}^{\infty} \lambda_l \sum_{i=1}^{n} g_l^2(X_i) \sum_{i=1}^{n} I(|g_l(X_i)| > z_{n,l})}{\max_{1\le l<\infty} \lambda_l V_{n,l}^2}. \end{aligned}$$

By (17), the sum of the diagonal terms is as follows:

$$\frac{\sum_{l=1}^{\infty} \lambda_l \sum_{i=1}^{n} g_l^2(X_i) I(|g_l(X_i)| > z_{n,l})}{\max_{1\le l<\infty} \lambda_l V_{n,l}^2} \le \frac{\varepsilon^2 x_n^2}{2}.$$

$$\begin{aligned} I_2 \le & P\left(\frac{\sum_{1\le i\ne j\le n} \sum_{l=1}^{\infty} \lambda_l g_l^2(X_i) I(|g_l(X_j)| > z_{n,l})}{\max_{1\le l<\infty} \lambda_l \sum_{i=1}^{n} g_l^2(X_i)} \ge \frac{\varepsilon^2 x_n^2}{2}\right) \\ \le & P\left(\frac{\sum_{1\le i<j\le n} \sum_{l=1}^{\infty} \lambda_l g_l^2(X_i) I(|g_l(X_j)| > z_{n,l})}{\max_{1\le l<\infty} \lambda_l \sum_{i=1}^{n} g_l^2(X_i)} \ge \frac{\varepsilon^2 x_n^2}{4}\right) \\ + & P\left(\frac{\sum_{1\le j<i\le n} \sum_{l=1}^{\infty} \lambda_l g_l^2(X_i) I(|g_l(X_j)| > z_{n,l})}{\max_{1\le l<\infty} \lambda_l \sum_{i=1}^{n} g_l^2(X_i)} \ge \frac{\varepsilon^2 x_n^2}{4}\right) \\ \le & P\left(\sum_{2\le j\le n} \frac{\sum_{1\le i<j} \sum_{l=1}^{\infty} \lambda_l g_l^2(X_i) I(|g_l(X_j)| > z_{n,l})}{\max_{1\le l<\infty} \lambda_l \sum_{1\le i<j} g_l^2(X_i)} \ge \frac{\varepsilon^2 x_n^2}{4}\right) \\ + & P\left(\sum_{1\le j<n} \frac{\sum_{j<i\le n} \sum_{l=1}^{\infty} \lambda_l g_l^2(X_i) I(|g_l(X_j)| > z_{n,l})}{\max_{1\le l<\infty} \lambda_l \sum_{j<i\le n} g_l^2(X_i)} \ge \frac{\varepsilon^2 x_n^2}{4}\right) \\ = & I_{2,1} + I_{2,2}. \end{aligned} \tag{29}$$

Let

$$\phi_j = \frac{\sum_{1\le i<j} \sum_{l=1}^{\infty} \lambda_l g_l^2(X_i) I(|g_l(X_j)| > z_{n,l})}{\max_{1\le l<\infty} \lambda_l \sum_{1\le i<j} g_l^2(X_i)}.$$

Then, for any constant $t > 0$,

$$I_{2,1} \le E e^{t \sum_{j=2}^{n} \phi_j} e^{-t\varepsilon^2 x_n^2/4}. \tag{30}$$

Let E_j be the expectation of X_j for $2 \le j \le n$. Then,

$$E e^{t \sum_{j=2}^{n} \phi_j} = E(e^{t \sum_{j=2}^{n-1} \phi_j} E_n e^{t\phi_n}). \tag{31}$$

Since $|e^s - 1| \le e^{0 \vee s}|s|$ for any $s \in R$ and $0 \le \phi_n \le m$ for some sufficiently large m value, then

$$\begin{aligned}\left|E_n e^{t\phi_n} - 1\right| &\le e^{mt} t E_n \phi_n \\ &= \frac{e^{mt} t \sum_{1\le i<n} \sum_{l=1}^{\infty} \lambda_l g_l^2(X_i) P(|g_l(X_n)| > z_{n,l})}{\max_{1\le l<\infty} \lambda_l \sum_{1\le i<n} g_l^2(X_i)}.\end{aligned}$$

By (12) and (15), we have $P(|g_l(X_n)| > z_{n,l}) = o(x_n^2/n)$. Then, together with (17),

$$E_n e^{t\phi_n} = 1 + o(x_n^2/n) = e^{o(x_n^2/n)}. \tag{32}$$

Applying (32) to (31), we have

$$Ee^{t\sum_{j=2}^{n}\phi_j} = e^{o(x_n^2/n)} Ee^{t\sum_{j=2}^{n-1}\phi_j}.$$

Similarly,

$$\begin{aligned}Ee^{t\sum_{j=2}^{n-1}\phi_j} &= E(e^{t\sum_{j=2}^{n-2}\phi_j} E_{n-1} e^{t\phi_{n-1}}) \\ &= e^{o(x_n^2/n)} Ee^{t\sum_{j=2}^{n-2}\phi_j}.\end{aligned}$$

Continue this process from X_n to X_1. We conclude that

$$Ee^{t\sum_{j=2}^{n}\phi_j} = e^{n\times o(x_n^2/n)} = e^{o(x_n^2)}. \tag{33}$$

Applying (33) to (30) and letting $t = 16/\varepsilon^2$, we have

$$I_{2,1} \le \exp(-3x_n^2). \tag{34}$$

By the same argument,

$$I_{2,2} \le \exp(-3x_n^2). \tag{35}$$

Combining (29), (34) and (35), we obtain the proposition. □

2.4. Estimation of I_3

Let $Y_1, \ldots, Y_n$ be an independent copy of $X_1, \ldots, X_n$. We will use the following lemma which is a Bernstein-type exponential inequality for degenerate U-statistics.

Lemma 1 ((3.5) of Giné, Latała and Zinn [19]). *For bounded degenerate kernel $h_{i,j}(X_i, Y_j)$, let*

$$A = \max_{i,j} \left\|h_{i,j}(X_i, Y_j)\right\|_\infty, \quad C^2 = \sum_{i,j} Eh_{i,j}^2(X_i, Y_j),$$

$$B^2 = \max_{i,j}\left\{\left\|\sum_i Eh_{i,j}^2(X_i, y)\right\|_\infty, \left\|\sum_j Eh_{i,j}^2(x, Y_j)\right\|_\infty\right\}.$$

Then, there is a universal constant K such that

$$Pr\left\{\left|\sum_{i,j} h_{i,j}(X_i, Y_j)\right| > x\right\} \le K\exp\left\{-\frac{1}{K}\min\left[\frac{x}{C}, \left(\frac{x}{B}\right)^{2/3}, \left(\frac{x}{A}\right)^{1/2}\right]\right\}.$$

Recall (16). Hence, by (19) and the definition of I_3 in (22),

$$I_3 \le P\left(\frac{\sum_{l=m+1}^{\infty}\lambda_l(\bar{Y}_{n,l}-E\bar{Y}_{n,l})^2}{\sum_{l=m+1}^{\infty}\lambda_l L_l(z_{n,l})} \ge C_1 n(1-2\varepsilon)^2 x_n^2\right). \tag{36}$$

Let

$$h_m(X_i,Y_j) = \sum_{l=m+1}^{\infty}\lambda_l(\bar{g}_l(X_i)-E\bar{g}_l(X_i))(\bar{g}_l(Y_j)-E\bar{g}_l(Y_j)). \tag{37}$$

In addition to the estimate of I_3, we include (40) in the following proposition which will be used in the proof of Theorem 2, where

$$\begin{aligned} & h_{(\beta)}(X_i,Y_j) \\ = & \sum_{l=1}^{\infty}\lambda_l\{(g_l(X_i)I(|g_l(X_i)|\le\beta z_{n,l}) - Eg_l(X_i)I(|g_l(X_i)|\le\beta z_{n,l})\} \\ & \times\{(g_l(Y_j)I(|g_l(Y_j)|\le\beta z_{n,l}) - Eg_l(Y_j))I(|g_l(Y_j)|\le\beta z_{n,l})\}. \end{aligned} \tag{38}$$

Proposition 3. *For a sufficiently large constant $C_2 > 0$,*

$$P\left(\frac{\sum_{1\le i,j\le n} h_m(X_i,Y_j)}{n\sum_{l=m+1}^{\infty}\lambda_l L_l(z_{n,l})} \ge C_2 x_n^2\right) \le \exp(-3x_n^2), \tag{39}$$

Then, by (36) and the decoupling inequalities of de la Peña and Montgomery-Smith [20], for a sufficiently large $C_1 > 0$,

$$I_3 \le P\left(\frac{\sum_{1\le i,j\le n} h_m(X_i,X_j)}{n\sum_{l=m+1}^{\infty}\lambda_l L_l(z_{n,l})} \ge C_1(1-2\varepsilon)^2 x_n^2\right) \le \exp(-2x_n^2).$$

Suppose that $\lambda_l > 0$ for all $1 \le l < \infty$ and $d > 0$ is a constant. For constants $0 < \alpha, \beta \le 1$ that are sufficiently small,

$$P\left(\frac{\sum_{1\le i,j\le[\alpha n]} h_{(\beta)}(X_i,Y_j)}{n\sum_{l=1}^{\infty}\lambda_l L_l(z_{n,l})} \ge d x_n^2\right) \le \exp(-2x_n^2). \tag{40}$$

Proof. We will prove (39) and (40) simultaneously. By (15) and (37),

$$A_n \;:=\; \|h_m(X_i,Y_j)\|_\infty \le 4\sum_{l=m+1}^{\infty}\lambda_l z_{n,l}^2 = 4\sum_{l=m+1}^{\infty}\lambda_l\frac{nL_l(z_{n,l})}{x_n^2}. \tag{41}$$

By (15) and (38),

$$A_{n,(\beta)} := \left\|h_{(\beta)}(X_i,Y_j)\right\|_\infty \le 4\sum_{l=1}^{\infty}\lambda_l\beta^2 z_{n,l}^2 = \frac{4\beta^2 n\sum_{l=1}^{\infty}\lambda_l L_l(z_{n,l})}{x_n^2}. \tag{42}$$

Let

$$B_n^2 := \max\left\{\Big\|\sum_{1\le i\le n} Eh_m^2(X_i,y)\Big\|_\infty, \Big\|\sum_{1\le j\le n} Eh_m^2(x,Y_j)\Big\|_\infty\right\}.$$

Since $|\bar{g}_l(Y_j)| \leq z_{n,l}$, then by Cauchy–Schwarz inequality, (15) and (37),

$$\begin{aligned}
&\Big\| \sum_{1\leq i\leq n} Eh_m^2(X_i, y)\Big\|_\infty \leq nE\Big(2\sum_{l=m+1}^{\infty} \lambda_l |\bar{g}_l(X_1) - E\bar{g}_l(X_1)| z_{n,l}\Big)^2 \\
\leq\ & 4nE\sum_{l=m+1}^{\infty} \lambda_l \big(\bar{g}_l(X_1) - E\bar{g}_l(X_1)\big)^2 \sum_{l=m+1}^{\infty} \lambda_l z_{n,l}^2 \\
\leq\ & 4n\sum_{l=m+1}^{\infty} \lambda_l L_l(z_{n,l}) \sum_{l=m+1}^{\infty} \lambda_l \frac{nL_l(z_{n,l})}{x_n^2}.
\end{aligned}$$

The same result can be obtained for $\| \sum_{1\leq j\leq n} Eh_m^2(x, Y_j)\|_\infty$. Therefore,

$$B_n^2 \leq \frac{4n^2(\sum_{l=m+1}^{\infty} \lambda_l L_l(z_{n,l}))^2}{x_n^2}. \tag{43}$$

Similarly,

$$\begin{aligned}
B_{n,\alpha,(\beta)}^2 &:= \max\Big\{\Big\| \sum_{1\leq i\leq [\alpha n]} Eh_{(\beta)}^2(X_i, y)\Big\|_\infty, \Big\| \sum_{1\leq j\leq [\alpha n]} Eh_{(\beta)}^2(x, Y_j)\Big\|_\infty\Big\} \\
&\leq 4\alpha n\sum_{l=1}^{\infty} \lambda_l L_l(\beta z_{n,l}) \sum_{l=1}^{\infty} \lambda_l \beta^2 \frac{nL_l(z_{n,l})}{x_n^2}.
\end{aligned}$$

Since $0 < \beta \leq 1$, then $L_l(\beta z_{n,l})/L_l(z_{n,l}) \leq 1$. Hence,

$$B_{n,\alpha,(\beta)}^2 \leq \frac{4\alpha\beta^2 n^2(\sum_{l=1}^{\infty} \lambda_l L_l(z_{n,l}))^2}{x_n^2}.$$

By (37) and the Cauchy–Schwarz inequality,

$$\begin{aligned}
C_n^2 &:= \sum_{1\leq i,j\leq n} Eh_m^2(X_i, Y_j) \\
&\leq \sum_{1\leq i,j\leq n}\sum_{l=m+1}^{\infty} \lambda_l E\big(\bar{g}_l(X_i) - E\bar{g}_l(X_i)\big)^2 \sum_{l=m+1}^{\infty} \lambda_l E\big(\bar{g}_l(Y_j) - E\bar{g}_l(Y_j)\big)^2 \\
&\leq n^2\Big(\sum_{l=m+1}^{\infty} \lambda_l L_l(z_{n,l})\Big)^2.
\end{aligned} \tag{44}$$

Similarly,

$$\begin{aligned}
C_{n,\alpha,(\beta)}^2 &:= \sum_{1\leq i\neq j\leq [\alpha n]} Eh_{(\beta)}^2(X_i, Y_j) \\
&\leq \alpha^2 n^2\Big(\sum_{l=1}^{\infty} \lambda_l L_l(\beta z_{n,l})\Big)^2 \\
&\leq \alpha^2 n^2\Big(\sum_{l=1}^{\infty} \lambda_l L_l(z_{n,l})\Big)^2.
\end{aligned} \tag{45}$$

Now let

$$x = C_2 n x_n^2 \sum_{l=m+1}^{\infty} \lambda_l L_l(z_{n,l}). \tag{46}$$

By (41) and (46),

$$\left(\frac{x}{A_n}\right)^{1/2} \geq \left(\frac{C_2 n x_n^2 \sum_{l=m+1}^{\infty} \lambda_l L_l(z_{n,l})}{4n \sum_{l=m+1}^{\infty} \lambda_l L_l(z_{n,l})/x_n^2}\right)^{1/2} = (C_2/4)^{1/2} x_n^2.$$

By (43) and (46),

$$\left(\frac{x}{B_n}\right)^{2/3} \geq \left(\frac{C_2 n x_n^2 \sum_{l=m+1}^{\infty} \lambda_l L_l(z_{n,l})}{2n \sum_{l=m+1}^{\infty} \lambda_l L_l(z_{n,l})/x_n}\right)^{2/3} = (C_2/2)^{2/3} x_n^2.$$

By (44) and (46),

$$\frac{x}{C_n} \geq \frac{C_2 n x_n^2 \sum_{l=m+1}^{\infty} \lambda_l L_l(z_{n,l})}{n \sum_{l=m+1}^{\infty} \lambda_l L_l(z_{n,l})} = C_2 x_n^2.$$

Then, (39) follows from Lemma 1 for a sufficiently large C_2 value. Similarly, let

$$x_d = d n x_n^2 \sum_{l=1}^{\infty} \lambda_l L_l(z_{n,l}). \tag{47}$$

By (42) and (47),

$$\left(\frac{x_d}{A_{n,(\beta)}}\right)^{1/2} \geq \left(\frac{d n x_n^2 \sum_{l=1}^{\infty} \lambda_l L_l(z_{n,l})}{4\beta^2 n \sum_{l=1}^{\infty} \lambda_l L_l(z_{n,l})/x_n^2}\right)^{1/2} = \frac{\sqrt{d}}{2\beta} x_n^2.$$

By (44) and (47),

$$\left(\frac{x_d}{B_{n,\alpha,(\beta)}}\right)^{2/3} \geq \left(\frac{d n x_n^2 \sum_{l=1}^{\infty} \lambda_l L_l(z_{n,l})}{2\sqrt{\alpha}\beta n \sum_{l=1}^{\infty} \lambda_l L_l(z_{n,l})/x_n}\right)^{2/3} = \left(\frac{d}{2\sqrt{\alpha}\beta}\right)^{2/3} x_n^2.$$

By (45) and (47),

$$\frac{x_d}{C_{n,\alpha,(\beta)}} \geq \frac{d n x_n^2 \sum_{l=1}^{\infty} \lambda_l L_l(z_{n,l})}{\alpha n \sum_{l=1}^{\infty} \lambda_l L_l(z_{n,l})} = \frac{d}{\alpha} x_n^2.$$

Therefore, (40) follows from Lemma 1 for α and β values that are sufficiently small. □

2.5. Estimation of I_4

Lemma 2 below follows Corollary 1(b) of Einmahl [21] and Lemma 4.2 of Lin and Liu [22]. However, we add the condition $\sum_{i=1}^{k_n} E\|\xi_{n,i}\|^2 \leq b_n^2$, and our result is in a form of an exponential inequality for independent random vectors. We use the same positive constants c_{17}, c_{20} and c_{22} (depending only on the vector dimension d) in Einmahl [21].

Lemma 2. *Let $\xi_{n,1}, \ldots, \xi_{n,k_n}$ be independent random vectors with a mean of zero and values in $\mathbb{R}^d$ such that $\|\xi_{n,i}\| \leq A_n$ and $\sum_{i=1}^{k_n} E\|\xi_{n,i}\|^2 \leq b_n^2$, where $\|\cdot\|$ denotes the Euclidean norm. Let $S_n = \sum_{i=1}^{k_n} \xi_{n,i}$. Suppose that*

$$Cov(S_n) = B_n I_d \tag{48}$$

where $B_n > 0$, I_d *is a* $d \times d$ *identity matrix, and* α_n *is a positive sequence such that* $\alpha_n B_n^{1/2} \to \infty$ *and*

$$\alpha_n \sum_{i=1}^{k_n} E\Big\{ \|\xi_{n,i}\|^3 \exp(\alpha_n \|\xi_{n,i}\|) \Big\} \leq B_n. \tag{49}$$

Let

$$\beta_n = B_n^{-3/2} \sum_{i=1}^{k_n} E\Big\{ \|\xi_{n,i}\|^3 \exp(\alpha_n \|\xi_{n,i}\|) \Big\}. \tag{50}$$

Then, for any $0 < \gamma < 1$, *there exists* n_γ *such that for all* $n \geq n_\gamma$,

$$\begin{aligned} P(\|S_n\| \geq x) \quad \leq \quad & \exp\Big\{ c_{20}\beta_n \Big(c_{17}^3 \alpha_n^3 B_n^{3/2} + 1 \Big) \Big\} \\ & \times \Big\{ \exp\Big(-\frac{(1-\gamma)^6 x^2}{2B_n} \Big) + \exp\Big(-\frac{\gamma^3 (1-\gamma)^3 x^2}{2c_{22} B_n \beta_n^2 \log(1/\beta_n)} \Big) \Big\} \\ & + 2d \exp\left(-\frac{(1-\gamma)^2 c_{17}^2 \alpha_n^2 B_n^2}{2(d^2 b_n^2 + d c_{17} A_n \alpha_n B_n)} \right) \end{aligned}$$

uniformly for $x \in [e_n B_n^{1/2}, c_{17}\alpha_n B_n]$, *where* $\{e_n\}_{n \geq 1}$ *can be any sequence with* $e_n \to \infty$ *and* $e_n \leq c_{17}\alpha_n B_n^{1/2}$.

Proof. Let $\eta_{n,i}$, $1 \leq i \leq k_n$, be independent $N(0, \sigma^2 Cov(\xi_{n,i}))$ random vectors, which are independent of the $\xi_{n,i}$s, where

$$\sigma^2 = c_{22}\beta_n^2 \log(1/\beta_n). \tag{51}$$

By (49) and (50), we have $\beta_n \leq \alpha_n^{-1} B_n^{-1/2} \to 0$ as $n \to \infty$. Hence, $\sigma \to 0$ as $n \to \infty$. Let $p_n(y)$ be the probability density of $B_n^{-1/2} \sum_{i=1}^{k_n} (\xi_{n,i} + \eta_{n,i})$ and $\phi_{(1+\sigma^2)I_d}$ be the density of $N(0, (1+\sigma^2)I_d)$. By Corollary 1(b) in Einmahl [21] (together with the Remark on page 32), for $\|y\| \leq c_{17}\alpha_n B_n^{1/2}$,

$$p_n(y) = \phi_{(1+\sigma^2)I_d}(y) \exp(T_n(y)) \quad \text{with} \quad |T_n(y)| \leq c_{20}\beta_n (\|y\|^3 + 1). \tag{52}$$

For any $0 < \gamma < 1$ and $x \in [e_n B_n^{1/2}, c_{17}\alpha_n B_n]$,

$$\begin{aligned}
& P(\|S_n\| \geq x) \\
\leq\ & P\Big(\Big\|S_n + \sum_{i=1}^{k_n} \eta_{n,i}\Big\| \geq (1-\gamma)x\Big) + P\Big(\Big\|\sum_{i=1}^{k_n} \eta_{n,i}\Big\| \geq \gamma x\Big) \\
=\ & P\Big((1-\gamma)x \leq \Big\|S_n + \sum_{i=1}^{k_n} \eta_{n,i}\Big\| < c_{17}\alpha_n B_n\Big) \\
& + P\Big(\Big\|S_n + \sum_{i=1}^{k_n} \eta_{n,i}\Big\| \geq c_{17}\alpha_n B_n\Big) + P\Big(\Big\|\sum_{i=1}^{k_n} \eta_{n,i}\Big\| \geq \gamma x\Big) \\
\leq\ & P\Big((1-\gamma)x \leq \Big\|S_n + \sum_{i=1}^{k_n} \eta_{n,i}\Big\| < c_{17}\alpha_n B_n\Big) \\
& + P(\|S_n\| \geq (1-\gamma)c_{17}\alpha_n B_n) \\
& + P\Big(\Big\|\sum_{i=1}^{k_n} \eta_{n,i}\Big\| \geq \gamma c_{17}\alpha_n B_n\Big) + P\Big(\Big\|\sum_{i=1}^{k_n} \eta_{n,i}\Big\| \geq \gamma x\Big) \\
\leq\ & P\Big((1-\gamma)x \leq \Big\|S_n + \sum_{i=1}^{k_n} \eta_{n,i}\Big\| < c_{17}\alpha_n B_n\Big) + 2P\Big(\Big\|\sum_{i=1}^{k_n} \eta_{n,i}\Big\| \geq \gamma x\Big) \\
& + P(\|S_n\| \geq (1-\gamma)c_{17}\alpha_n B_n) \\
:=\ & J_1 + J_2 + J_3.
\end{aligned} \tag{53}$$

Let N denote a centered normal random vector with covariance matrix I_d. Then, by (52),

$$\begin{aligned}
& J_1 = \int_{(1-\gamma)x/B_n^{1/2} < \|y\| \leq c_{17}\alpha_n B_n^{1/2}} \phi_{(1+\sigma^2)I_d}(y) \exp(T_n(y))dy \\
& \leq \exp\Big\{c_{20}\beta_n\Big(c_{17}^3\alpha_n^3 B_n^{3/2} + 1\Big)\Big\} \int_{\|y\| \geq (1-\gamma)x/B_n^{1/2}} \phi_{(1+\sigma^2)I_d}(y)dy \\
& \leq \exp\Big\{c_{20}\beta_n\Big(c_{17}^3\alpha_n^3 B_n^{3/2} + 1\Big)\Big\} \times \\
& \Big\{P\Big(\|N\| \geq (1-\gamma)^2 x/B_n^{1/2}\Big) + P\Big(\sigma\|N\| \geq \gamma(1-\gamma)x/B_n^{1/2}\Big)\Big\}.
\end{aligned} \tag{54}$$

Observe that $\|N\|^2$ has a χ_d^2 distribution. It is well known that for a χ_d^2 random variable Y, $P(Y > y) \leq (ye^{1-y/d}/d)^{d/2}$ for $y > d$. Hence,

$$\begin{aligned}
& P\Big(\|N\| \geq (1-\gamma)^2 x/B_n^{1/2}\Big) \\
& \leq \left(\frac{(1-\gamma)^4 x^2}{dB_n} \exp\left(1 - \frac{(1-\gamma)^4 x^2}{dB_n}\right)\right)^{d/2} \\
& = \frac{(1-\gamma)^{2d} x^d}{d^{d/2} B_n^{d/2}} \exp\left(d/2 - \frac{(1-\gamma)^4 x^2}{2B_n}\right) \\
& \leq \exp\left(-\frac{(1-\gamma)^6 x^2}{2B_n}\right)
\end{aligned} \tag{55}$$

by $x^2/B_n \to \infty$. Similarly,

$$\begin{aligned}
& P\Big(\sigma\|N\| \geq \gamma(1-\gamma)x/B_n^{1/2}\Big) \leq \exp\left(-\frac{\gamma^3(1-\gamma)^3 x^2}{2B_n\sigma^2}\right) \\
=\ & \exp\left(-\frac{\gamma^3(1-\gamma)^3 x^2}{2c_{22}B_n\beta_n^2 \log(1/\beta_n)}\right)
\end{aligned} \tag{56}$$

by (51). Then, by (54)–(56), we have

$$J_1 \le \exp\Big\{c_{20}\beta_n\Big(c_{17}^3\alpha_n^3 B_n^{3/2}+1\Big)\Big\} \times\Big\{\exp\Big(-\frac{(1-\gamma)^6x^2}{2B_n}\Big)+\exp\Big(-\frac{\gamma^3(1-\gamma)^3x^2}{2c_{22}B_n\beta_n^2\log(1/\beta_n)}\Big)\Big\}. \tag{57}$$

Since the distribution of $\eta_{n,i}$ is $N(0,\sigma^2 Cov(\xi_{n,i}))$, the distribution of $\sum_{i=1}^{k_n}\eta_{n,i}$ is $N(0,\sigma^2\sum_{i=1}^{k_n}Cov(\xi_{n,i}))$. Since the $\xi_{n,i}$s are independent, $\sum_{i=1}^{k_n}Cov(\xi_{n,i}) = Cov(\sum_{i=1}^{k_n}\xi_{n,i}) = B_n I_d$ by (48). Hence, the distribution of $\sum_{i=1}^{k_n}\eta_{n,i}$ is $N(0,\sigma^2 B_n I_d)$. Then, similar to (56),

$$\begin{aligned} J_2 &= 2P\Big(\Big\|\sum_{i=1}^{k_n}\eta_{n,i}\Big\|\ge\gamma x\Big) = 2P\Big(\sigma\|N\|\ge\gamma x/B_n^{1/2}\Big) \\ &\le 2\exp\Big(-\frac{\gamma^3x^2}{2B_nc_{22}\beta_n^2\log(1/\beta_n)}\Big). \end{aligned} \tag{58}$$

By (57) and (58), we have

$$J_1+J_2 \le \exp\Big\{c_{20}\beta_n\Big(c_{17}^3\alpha_n^3 B_n^{3/2}+1\Big)\Big\} \times\Big\{\exp\Big(-\frac{(1-\gamma)^6x^2}{2B_n}\Big)+3\exp\Big(-\frac{\gamma^3(1-\gamma)^3x^2}{2c_{22}B_n\beta_n^2\log(1/\beta_n)}\Big)\Big\}. \tag{59}$$

Next, we estimate J_3. For each $1\le i\le n$, let $\xi_{n,i}=(\xi_{n,i}^{(1)},\ldots,\xi_{n,i}^{(d)})^T$, where $\boldsymbol{a}^T$ denote the transpose of a vector $\boldsymbol{a}$. Then

$$\|S_n\| = \Big\|\sum_{i=1}^{k_n}\xi_{n,i}\Big\| = \Big(\sum_{l=1}^{d}\Big(\sum_{i=1}^{k_n}\xi_{n,i}^{(l)}\Big)^2\Big)^{1/2} \le \sum_{l=1}^{d}\Big|\sum_{i=1}^{k_n}\xi_{n,i}^{(l)}\Big|.$$

Hence,

$$\begin{aligned} J_3 &= P(\|S_n\|\ge(1-\gamma)c_{17}\alpha_nB_n) \\ &\le P\Big(\sum_{l=1}^{d}\Big|\sum_{i=1}^{k_n}\xi_{n,i}^{(l)}\Big|\ge(1-\gamma)c_{17}\alpha_nB_n\Big) \\ &\le \sum_{l=1}^{d}P\Big(\Big|\sum_{i=1}^{k_n}\xi_{n,i}^{(l)}\Big|\ge\frac{(1-\gamma)c_{17}\alpha_nB_n}{d}\Big). \end{aligned}$$

Since $\|\xi_{n,i}\|\le A_n$ and $\sum_{i=1}^{k_n}E\|\xi_{n,i}\|^2\le b_n^2$, then $|\xi_{n,i}^{(l)}|\le\|\xi_{n,i}\|\le A_n$ and $\sum_{i=1}^{k_n}E(\xi_{n,i}^{(l)})^2\le\sum_{i=1}^{k_n}E\|\xi_{n,i}\|^2\le b_n^2$ for each $1\le l\le d$. By Bernstein's inequality (e.g., (2.17) of de la Peña, Lai and Shao [18]),

$$J_3 \le 2d\exp\Big(-\frac{(1-\gamma)^2c_{17}^2\alpha_n^2B_n^2}{2d^2(b_n^2+c_{17}A_n\alpha_nB_n/d)}\Big). \tag{60}$$

Then, the lemma follows by applying (59) and (60) to (53). □

Now, we estimate I_4 in the following proposition, which uses some ideas in Liu and Shao [23]:

Proposition 4.

$$
\begin{aligned}
I_4 &\leq P\Big(\sum_{l=1}^{m}\lambda_l(\bar{Y}_{n,l}-E\bar{Y}_{n,l})^2 \geq (1-C_1\varepsilon)(1-2\varepsilon)^3 n x_n^2 \max_{1\leq l\leq m}\lambda_l L_l(z_{n,l})\Big)\\
&\leq \exp\Big(-\frac{(1-C_1\varepsilon)(1-2\varepsilon)^4 x_n^2}{2(1+\varepsilon)}\Big).
\end{aligned}
$$

Proof. For each $1 \leq i \leq n$, let

$$
\boldsymbol{G}_{n,i} = \Big(\sqrt{\lambda_1}(\bar{g}_1(X_i) - E\bar{g}_1(X_i)), \ldots, \sqrt{\lambda_m}(\bar{g}_m(X_i) - E\bar{g}_m(X_i))\Big)^T.
$$

Let $B_n = n$ and Σ be the covariance matrix of $\boldsymbol{G}_{n,1}$. For $1 \leq i \leq n$, let

$$
\xi_{n,i} = \Sigma^{-1/2}\boldsymbol{G}_{n,i}. \tag{61}
$$

Then,

$$
\begin{aligned}
&Cov(\xi_{n,1} + \cdots + \xi_{n,n})\\
&= E\Big\{\Big(\Sigma^{-1/2}(\boldsymbol{G}_{n,1} + \cdots + \boldsymbol{G}_{n,n})\Big)\Big(\Sigma^{-1/2}(\boldsymbol{G}_{n,1} + \cdots + \boldsymbol{G}_{n,n})\Big)^T\Big\}\\
&= \Sigma^{-1/2}E\Big\{(\boldsymbol{G}_{n,1} + \cdots + \boldsymbol{G}_{n,n})(\boldsymbol{G}_{n,1} + \cdots + \boldsymbol{G}_{n,n})^T\Big\}\Sigma^{-1/2}\\
&= \Sigma^{-1/2}\sum_{1\leq i,j\leq n} E\Big\{\boldsymbol{G}_{n,i}\boldsymbol{G}_{n,j}^T\Big\}\Sigma^{-1/2}.
\end{aligned}
$$

Since the X_is are independent, then

$$
\begin{aligned}
Cov(\xi_{n,1} + \cdots + \xi_{n,n}) &= \Sigma^{-1/2}\sum_{i=1}^{n} E\Big\{\boldsymbol{G}_{n,i}\boldsymbol{G}_{n,i}^T\Big\}\Sigma^{-1/2}\\
&= nI_m = B_n I_m.
\end{aligned}
$$

Hence, Condition (48) in Lemma 2 is satisfied. Let

$$
\alpha_n = \frac{C_m x_n}{n^{1/2}}
$$

where $C_m > 0$ is a finite constant depending only on m. We shall verify Condition (49). By (61),

$$
\|\xi_{n,i}\|^2 = \Big(\Sigma^{-1/2}\boldsymbol{G}_{n,i}\Big)^T\Big(\Sigma^{-1/2}\boldsymbol{G}_{n,i}\Big) = \boldsymbol{G}_{n,i}^T\Sigma^{-1}\boldsymbol{G}_{n,i}. \tag{62}
$$

Observe that Σ is positive definite by Assumption (9). Then, by the identity

$$
\boldsymbol{x}^T\boldsymbol{A}^{-1}\boldsymbol{x} = \max_{\|\vartheta\|=1}\frac{(\boldsymbol{x}^T\vartheta)^2}{\vartheta^T\boldsymbol{A}\vartheta} \tag{63}
$$

for any $m \times m$ positive definite matrix $\boldsymbol{A}$, we have

$$
\|\xi_{n,i}\|^2 = \boldsymbol{G}_{n,i}^T\Sigma^{-1}\boldsymbol{G}_{n,i} = \max_{\|\vartheta\|=1}\frac{(\boldsymbol{G}_{n,i}^T\vartheta)^2}{\vartheta^T\Sigma\vartheta}. \tag{64}
$$

Let $\vartheta^* = (\vartheta_1^*, \ldots, \vartheta_m^*)$ such that $\|\vartheta^*\| = 1$ and $(G_{n,i}^T\vartheta^*)^2 = \max_{\|\vartheta\|=1}(G_{n,i}^T\vartheta)^2$. Then, for any $\vartheta = (\vartheta_1, \ldots, \vartheta_m) \in l^2$, by the Cauchy–Schwarz inequality,

$$\begin{aligned}
(G_{n,i}^T\vartheta)^2 &= \left(\sum_{l=1}^m \sqrt{\lambda_l}(\bar{g}_l(X_i) - E\bar{g}_l(X_i))\vartheta_l\right)^2 \\
&= \left(\sum_{l=1}^m \frac{\bar{g}_l(X_i) - E\bar{g}_l(X_i)}{\sqrt{L_l(z_{n,l})}}\vartheta_l\sqrt{\lambda_l L_l(z_{n,l})}\right)^2 \\
&\leq \sum_{l=1}^m \frac{(\bar{g}_l(X_i) - E\bar{g}_l(X_i))^2}{L_l(z_{n,l})} \sum_{l=1}^m \vartheta_l^2\lambda_l L_l(z_{n,l}).
\end{aligned} \tag{65}$$

Since $Eg_l(X_1) = 0$ for all $l \geq 1$, then $E\bar{g}_l(X_1) = o(x_n\sqrt{L_l(z_{n,l})}/\sqrt{n})$ by (13) and (15). By Assumption (9),

$$\begin{aligned}
\vartheta^T\Sigma\vartheta &= \sum_{1\leq l,l'\leq m} \vartheta_l\vartheta_{l'}\sqrt{\lambda_l\lambda_{l'}}E(\bar{g}_l(X_1) - E\bar{g}_l(X_1))(\bar{g}_{l'}(X_1) - E\bar{g}_{l'}(X_1)) \\
&= \sum_{l=1}^m \vartheta_l^2\lambda_l E\bar{g}_l^2(X_1) - \sum_{l=1}^m \vartheta_l^2\lambda_l(E\bar{g}_l(X_1))^2 \\
&\quad + \sum_{1\leq l\neq l'\leq m} \vartheta_l\vartheta_{l'}\sqrt{\lambda_l\lambda_{l'}}E\bar{g}_l(X_1)\bar{g}_{l'}(X_1) \\
&\quad - \sum_{1\leq l\neq l'\leq m} \vartheta_l\vartheta_{l'}\sqrt{\lambda_l\lambda_{l'}}E\bar{g}_l(X_1)E\bar{g}_{l'}(X_1) \\
&= \sum_{l=1}^m \vartheta_l^2\lambda_l L_l(z_{n,l}) - \sum_{l=1}^m \vartheta_l^2\lambda_l \times o\left(\frac{x_n^2 L_l(z_{n,l})}{n}\right) \\
&\quad + o(1)\sum_{1\leq l\neq l'\leq m} \vartheta_l\vartheta_{l'}\sqrt{\lambda_l\lambda_{l'}L_l(z_{n,l})L_{l'}(z_{n,l'})} \\
&\quad - \sum_{1\leq l\neq l'\leq m} \vartheta_l\vartheta_{l'}\sqrt{\lambda_l\lambda_{l'}} \times o\left(\frac{x_n\sqrt{L_l(z_{n,l})}}{\sqrt{n}}\right)o\left(\frac{x_n\sqrt{L_{l'}(z_{n,l'})}}{\sqrt{n}}\right).
\end{aligned}$$

By the Cauchy–Schwarz inequality,

$$\sum_{1\leq l\neq l'\leq m} \vartheta_l\vartheta_{l'}\sqrt{\lambda_l\lambda_{l'}L_l(z_{n,l})L_{l'}(z_{n,l'})} \leq m\sum_{l=1}^m \vartheta_l^2\lambda_l L_l(z_{n,l}).$$

Hence,

$$\vartheta^T\Sigma\vartheta = (1 + o(1))\sum_{l=1}^m \vartheta_l^2\lambda_l L_l(z_{n,l}). \tag{66}$$

Applying (65) and (66) to (64), we have

$$\|\xi_{n,i}\|^2 \leq 2\sum_{l=1}^m \frac{(\bar{g}_l(X_i) - E\bar{g}_l(X_i))^2}{L_l(z_{n,l})}. \tag{67}$$

Since $|\bar{g}_l(X_i)| \leq z_{n,l} = \sqrt{nL_l(z_{n,l})}/x_n$ by (15), and (16), we have

$$\|\xi_{n,i}\|^2 \leq \frac{4mn}{x_n^2}. \tag{68}$$

By (67),

$$E\|\xi_{n,i}\|^2 \le 2\sum_{l=1}^{m} \frac{E(\bar{g}_l(X_i) - E\bar{g}_l(X_i))^2}{L_l(z_{n,l})} \le 2m \tag{69}$$

and

$$E\|\xi_{n,i}\|^3 \le 2^{3/2}E\left(\sum_{l=1}^{m} \frac{(\bar{g}_l(X_i) - E\bar{g}_l(X_i))^2}{L_l(z_{n,l})}\right)^{3/2}. \tag{70}$$

By Hölder's inequality,

$$\left(\sum_{l=1}^{m} \frac{(\bar{g}_l(X_i) - E\bar{g}_l(X_i))^2}{L_l(z_{n,l})}\right)^{3/2} \le m^{1/2}\sum_{l=1}^{m} \frac{|\bar{g}_l(X_i) - E\bar{g}_l(X_i)|^3}{L_l^{3/2}(z_{n,l})}. \tag{71}$$

Combining (70) and (71), we have

$$\begin{aligned} E\|\xi_{n,i}\|^3 &\le 2^{3/2}m^{1/2}\sum_{l=1}^{m} \frac{8E|\bar{g}_l(X_i)|^3}{L_l^{3/2}(z_{n,l})} \\ &= \sum_{l=1}^{m} \frac{o(z_{n,l}L_l(z_{n,l}))}{L_l^{3/2}(z_{n,l})} = o\left(\frac{n^{1/2}}{x_n}\right) \end{aligned} \tag{72}$$

by (14) and (15). Since $B_n = n$ and $\alpha_n = C_m x_n / n^{1/2}$, then by (68) and (72), we have

$$\begin{aligned} &\alpha_n \sum_{i=1}^{n} E\left\{\|\xi_{n,i}\|^3 \exp(\alpha_n\|\xi_{n,i}\|)\right\} \\ \le\ & \frac{C_m x_n}{n^{1/2}} n \times o\left(\frac{n^{1/2}}{x_n}\right) \exp\left(\frac{C_m x_n}{n^{1/2}}\left(\frac{4mn}{x_n^2}\right)^{1/2}\right) = o(n) = o(B_n). \end{aligned}$$

Hence, Condition (49) in Lemma 2 is satisfied. Similarly,

$$\begin{aligned} \beta_n &:= B_n^{-3/2}\sum_{i=1}^{n} E\left\{\|\xi_{n,i}\|^3 \exp(\alpha_n\|\xi_{n,i}\|)\right\} \\ &= n^{-3/2} n \times o\left(\frac{n^{1/2}}{x_n}\right) \exp\left(\frac{C_m x_n}{n^{1/2}}\left(\frac{4mn}{x_n^2}\right)^{1/2}\right) \\ &= o(1/x_n). \end{aligned} \tag{73}$$

Then, $\beta_n^2 \log(1/\beta_n) = o(1/x_n)$. By (68), we have $\|\xi_{n,i}\| \le (4mn/x_n^2)^{1/2} := A_n$. By (69), we have $\sum_{i=1}^{n} E\|\xi_{n,i}\|^2 \le 2mn := b_n^2$. Then, by Lemma 2 and (73) with $B_n = n$ and $\alpha_n = C_m x_n / n^{1/2}$ for a sufficiently large C_m value, we have

$$\begin{aligned} &P\left(\|S_n\| \ge n^{1/2}x_n\right) \\ \le\ & \exp\left\{o(x_n^2)\right\}\left\{\exp\left(-\frac{(1-\gamma)^6 n x_n^2}{2n}\right) + \exp\left(-\frac{\gamma^3(1-\gamma)^3 n x_n^2}{n \times o(1/x_n)}\right)\right\} \\ & +2m\exp\left(-\frac{(1-\gamma)^2 c_{17}^2 C_m^2 x_n^2 n}{2(2m^3 n + m(4mn/x_n^2)^{1/2} c_{17} C_m x_n n^{1/2})}\right) \\ \le\ & \exp\left\{o(x_n^2)\right\}\left\{\exp\left(-\frac{(1-\gamma)^6 x_n^2}{2}\right) + \exp\left(-4x_n^2\right)\right\} + \exp\left(-4x_n^2\right) \\ \le\ & \exp\left(-\frac{(1-\gamma)^7 x_n^2}{2}\right). \end{aligned}$$

Letting $\gamma = 1 - (1-\varepsilon)^{1/7}$, we have

$$P\Big(\|S_n\| \geq n^{1/2}x_n\Big) \leq \exp\Big(-\frac{(1-\varepsilon)x_n^2}{2}\Big). \tag{74}$$

Similar to (62),

$$\begin{aligned} \|S_n\|^2 = \Big\|\sum_{i=1}^n \xi_{n,i}\Big\|^2 &= \Big(\Sigma^{-1/2}\sum_{i=1}^n \boldsymbol{G}_{n,i}\Big)^T\Big(\Sigma^{-1/2}\sum_{i=1}^n \boldsymbol{G}_{n,i}\Big) \\ &= \Big(\sum_{i=1}^n \boldsymbol{G}_{n,i}\Big)^T\Sigma^{-1}\Big(\sum_{i=1}^n \boldsymbol{G}_{n,i}\Big). \end{aligned} \tag{75}$$

We will use Identity (63) to estimate (75). Let $\vartheta^* = (\vartheta_1^*, \ldots, \vartheta_m^*)$ be such that $\|\vartheta^*\| = 1$ and

$$\Big(\sum_{i=1}^n \boldsymbol{G}_{n,i}\Big)^T\vartheta^* = \max_{\|\vartheta\|=1}\Big(\sum_{i=1}^n \boldsymbol{G}_{n,i}\Big)^T\vartheta. \tag{76}$$

Observe that

$$\max_{\|\vartheta\|=1}\Big(\sum_{i=1}^n \boldsymbol{G}_{n,i}\Big)^T\vartheta = \Big(\sum_{l=1}^m\Big(\sum_{i=1}^n \sqrt{\lambda_l}(\bar{g}_l(X_i) - E\bar{g}_l(X_i))\Big)^2\Big)^{1/2}. \tag{77}$$

By (66),

$$\begin{aligned} (\vartheta^*)^T\Sigma\vartheta^* &= (1+o(1))\sum_{l=1}^m(\vartheta_l^*)^2\lambda_l L_l(z_{n,l}) \\ &\leq (1+o(1))\max_{1\leq l\leq m}\lambda_l L_l(z_{n,l}) \end{aligned} \tag{78}$$

because $\|\vartheta^*\| = 1$. By Identity (63) and by (76)–(78),

$$\Big(\sum_{i=1}^n \boldsymbol{G}_{n,i}\Big)^T\Sigma^{-1}\Big(\sum_{i=1}^n \boldsymbol{G}_{n,i}\Big) \geq \frac{\sum_{l=1}^m(\sum_{i=1}^n \sqrt{\lambda_l}(\bar{g}_l(X_i) - E\bar{g}_l(X_i)))^2}{(1+\varepsilon)\max_{1\leq l\leq m}\lambda_l L_l(z_{n,l})}. \tag{79}$$

By (74), (75) and (79), with the application of (16) and (19),

$$\begin{aligned} I_4 &\leq P\Big(\frac{\sum_{l=1}^m\lambda_l(\sum_{i=1}^n(\bar{g}_l(X_i) - E\bar{g}_l(X_i)))^2}{\max_{1\leq l\leq m}\lambda_l L_l(z_{n,l})} \geq (1-C_1\varepsilon)(1-2\varepsilon)^3 n x_n^2\Big) \\ &\leq P\Big(\Big(\sum_{i=1}^n \boldsymbol{G}_{n,i}\Big)^T\Sigma^{-1}\Big(\sum_{i=1}^n \boldsymbol{G}_{n,i}\Big) \geq \frac{(1-C_1\varepsilon)(1-2\varepsilon)^3 n x_n^2}{1+\varepsilon}\Big) \\ &= P\Big(\|S_n\|^2 \geq \frac{(1-C_1\varepsilon)(1-2\varepsilon)^3 n x_n^2}{1+\varepsilon}\Big) \\ &\leq \exp\Big(-\frac{(1-C_1\varepsilon)(1-2\varepsilon)^4 x_n^2}{2(1+\varepsilon)}\Big). \end{aligned}$$

□

Since ε is arbitrary, then the upper bound of Theorem 1 follows from (22) and the estimates of I_1, I_2, I_3 and I_4.

3. The Lower Bound of Theorem 1

Let $0 < \varepsilon < 1$ be sufficiently small. For $1 \le m < \infty$ that is sufficiently large, by (26), $\max_{1\le l<\infty} \lambda_l V_{n,l}^2 = \max_{1\le l\le m} \lambda_l V_{n,l}^2$. Together with (17), we have

$$
\begin{aligned}
& P(W_n \ge (1-\varepsilon)x_n^2) \\
= \; & P\left(\frac{\sum_{l=1}^{\infty} \lambda_l \Big(\{\sum_{i=1}^n g_l(X_i)\}^2 - \sum_{i=1}^n g_l^2(X_i)\Big)}{\max_{1\le l<\infty} \lambda_l V_{n,l}^2} \ge (1-\varepsilon)x_n^2\right) \\
\ge \; & P\left(\frac{\sum_{l=1}^{m} \lambda_l \{\sum_{i=1}^n g_l(X_i)\}^2}{\max_{1\le l\le m} \lambda_l V_{n,l}^2} \ge x_n^2\right).
\end{aligned} \tag{80}
$$

Let $\tilde{g}_l(X_i)$ be the random variable with distribution which is of the distribution of $g_l(X_i)$ conditioned on $|g_l(X_i)| \le z_{n,l}$. Define $\tilde{Y}_{n,l} = \sum_{i=1}^n \tilde{g}_l(X_i)$ and $\tilde{V}_{n,l}^2 = \sum_{i=1}^n \tilde{g}_l^2(X_i)$. By the definition of $L_l(x)$ and (12),

$$
\begin{aligned}
& E\tilde{g}_l^2(X_i) = E\tilde{g}_l^2(X_i)/P(|g_l(X_i)| \le z_{n,l}) \\
& = L_l(z_{n,l})/P(|g_l(X_i)| \le z_{n,l}) = L_l(z_{n,l})(1+o(1)).
\end{aligned}
$$

Notice that (13) implies $E\tilde{g}_l(X_1) = o(L_l(z_{n,l})/z_{n,l})$. Then, we have

$$
\begin{aligned}
& \sigma_l^2 := E(\tilde{Y}_{n,l} - E\tilde{Y}_{n,l})^2 = nE(\tilde{g}_l(X_1) - E\tilde{g}_l(X_1))^2 \\
& = nE\tilde{g}_l^2(X_1)(1+o(1)) = nL_l(z_{n,l})(1+o(1))
\end{aligned} \tag{81}
$$

and

$$
E\tilde{V}_{n,l}^2 = nL_l(z_{n,l})(1+o(1)).
$$

Then, for $0 < \delta < 1$,

$$
\begin{aligned}
& P\left(\frac{\sum_{l=1}^{m} \lambda_l \{\sum_{i=1}^n g_l(X_i)\}^2}{\max_{1\le l\le m} \lambda_l V_{n,l}^2} \ge x_n^2\right) \\
\ge \; & P\left(\frac{\sum_{l=1}^{m} \lambda_l \{\sum_{i=1}^n g_l(X_i)\}^2}{\max_{1\le l\le m} \lambda_l V_{n,l}^2} \ge x_n^2, \max_{1\le i\le n} |g_l(X_i)| \le z_{n,l}, , 1 \le l \le m\right) \\
= \; & P\left(\frac{\sum_{l=1}^{m} \lambda_l \{\sum_{i=1}^n \tilde{g}_l(X_i)\}^2}{\max_{1\le l\le m} \lambda_l \tilde{V}_{n,l}^2} \ge x_n^2\right) P\left(\max_{1\le i\le n} |g_l(X_i)| \le z_{n,l}, , 1 \le l \le m\right) \\
\ge \; & P\left(\frac{\sum_{l=1}^{m} \lambda_l \{\sum_{i=1}^n \tilde{g}_l(X_i)\}^2}{\max_{1\le l\le m} \lambda_l \tilde{V}_{n,l}^2} \ge x_n^2, \tilde{V}_{n,l}^2 \le (1+2\delta)\sigma_l^2, 1 \le l \le m\right) \\
& \times P\left(\max_{1\le i\le n} |g_l(X_i)| \le z_{n,l}, , 1 \le l \le m\right) \\
\ge \; & P\left(\frac{\sum_{l=1}^{m} \lambda_l \{\sum_{i=1}^n \tilde{g}_l(X_i)\}^2}{\max_{1\le l\le m} \lambda_l \sigma_l^2} \ge (1+2\delta)x_n^2\right) \\
& \times P\left(\max_{1\le i\le n} |g_l(X_i)| \le z_{n,l}, , 1 \le l \le m\right) - \sum_{l=1}^{m} P(\tilde{V}_{n,l}^2 \ge (1+2\delta)\sigma_l^2).
\end{aligned} \tag{82}
$$

Without the loss of generality, assume that $\max_{1\le l\le m}\lambda_l\sigma_l^2=\lambda_1\sigma_1^2$. Then,

$$P\left(\frac{\sum_{l=1}^m \lambda_l\{\sum_{i=1}^n \tilde{g}_l(X_i)\}^2}{\max_{1\le l\le m}\lambda_l\sigma_l^2}\ge(1+2\delta)x_n^2\right)$$
$$\ge P\left(\frac{\lambda_1\{\sum_{i=1}^n \tilde{g}_1(X_i)\}^2}{\lambda_1\sigma_1^2}\ge(1+2\delta)x_n^2\right)$$
$$\ge P\left(\sum_{i=1}^n \tilde{g}_1(X_i)\ge(1+2\delta)^{1/2}\sigma_1 x_n\right).$$

Recall (15) and (81). Take $c=1/x_n$; thus, we have $|\tilde{g}_1(X_1)|\le z_{n,l}=c\sigma_l$. Therefore, by Theorem 5.2.2 in Stout [24], for any $\gamma>0$, we have

$$P\left(\sum_{i=1}^n \tilde{g}_1(X_i)\ge(1+2\delta)^{1/2}\sigma_1 x_n\right)\ge\exp(-(x_n^2/2)(1+2\delta)(1+\gamma)). \tag{83}$$

On the other hand,

$$P\left(\max_{1\le i\le n}|g_l(X_i)|\le z_{n,l},1\le l\le m\right)=[P(|g_l(X_1)|\le z_{n,l},1\le l\le m)]^n$$
$$=[1-P(|g_l(X_1)|\ge z_{n,l},\exists 1\le l\le m)]^n\ge[1-\sum_{l=1}^m P(|g_l(X_1)|\ge z_{n,l})]^n$$
$$\ge\exp(-2n\sum_{l=1}^m P(|g_l(X_1)|\ge z_{n,l}))=\exp(-o(x_n^2)). \tag{84}$$

We apply the following exponential inequality (see Lemma 2.1, Csörgő, Lin and Shao [25]; see also Pruitt [26] and Griffin and Kuelbs [1]) for the rest of the proof.

Lemma 3. *Let $\xi,\xi_1,\cdots,\xi_n$ be i.i.d. random variables. Then, for any $b,v,s>0$,*

$$P\left(\left|\sum_{i=1}^n(\xi_i I(|\xi_i|\le b)-E\xi_i I(|\xi_i|\le b))\right|\ge\frac{ve^v nE\xi_i^2 I(|\xi_i|\le b)}{2b}+\frac{sb}{v}\right)\le 2e^{-s}.$$

By (14),

$$E\tilde{g}_1^4(X_i)=o(z_{n,1}^2L_1(z_{n,1})). \tag{85}$$

In Lemma 3, we take $\xi_i=\tilde{g}_1^2(X_i),s=x_n^2,b=z_{n,1}^2$ and $v=1/\delta$. Notice that $sb/v=\delta\sigma_1^2$ and $\frac{ve^v nE\xi_i^2 I(|\xi_i|\le b)}{2b}=o(\sigma_1^2)$ by (81) and (85). Then,

$$P(\tilde{V}_{n,1}^2\ge(1+2\delta)\sigma_1^2)=P(\tilde{V}_{n,1}^2-E\tilde{V}_{n,1}^2\ge(1+2\delta)\sigma_1^2-E\tilde{V}_{n,1}^2)$$
$$\le P\left(\sum_{i=1}^n(\tilde{g}_1^2(X_i)-E\tilde{g}_1^2(X_i))\ge\delta(1+\delta)\sigma_1^2\right)$$
$$\le 2\exp(-x_n^2). \tag{86}$$

Combining (80), (82), (83), (84) and (86) and letting $\lambda,\delta\to 0$, we have

$$P(W_n\ge(1-\varepsilon)x_n^2)\ge\exp(-x_n^2/2).$$

4. The Upper Bound of Theorem 2

Lemma 4 (Lemma 2.3 of Giné, Kwapień, Latała, and Zinn [15]). *There exists a universal constant $C_3 < \infty$ such that for any kernel h and any two sequences of i.i.d. random variables, we have*

$$P\left(\max_{k\leq m,l\leq n}\left|\sum_{i\leq k,j\leq l} h(X_i,Y_j)\right|\geq t\right)\leq C_3 P\left(\left|\sum_{i\leq m,j\leq n} h(X_i,Y_j)\right|\geq t/C_3\right)$$

for all $m,n\in\mathbb{N}$ and all $t>0$.

Proposition 5. *Under the assumptions of Theorem 1,*

$$\limsup_{n\to\infty}\frac{\sum_{l=1}^{\infty}\lambda_l(\sum_{i=1}^{n}g_l(X_i))^2}{\max_{1\leq l<\infty}\lambda_l V_{n,l}^2\log\log n}\leq 2\ a.s.$$

Consequently,

$$\limsup_{n\to\infty}\frac{W_n}{\log\log n}\leq 2\ a.s.$$

Proof. Let $x_n\to\infty$ as $n\to\infty$. Let $\theta>1$ with $\theta-1$ be sufficiently small. For any positive integer $k\in(n,\theta n]$, via a similar idea as in (19) with $0<\eta<1$,

$$\begin{aligned}
&P\left(\max_{n<k\leq\theta n}\frac{\sum_{l=1}^{\infty}\lambda_l\left(\sum_{i=1}^{k}g_l(X_i)\right)^2}{\max_{1\leq l<\infty}\lambda_l V_{k,l}^2}\geq 2(1+\eta)^3x_n^2\right)\\
\leq\ & P\left(\frac{\sum_{l=1}^{\infty}\lambda_l\left(\sum_{i=1}^{n}g_l(X_i)\right)^2}{\max_{1\leq l<\infty}\lambda_l V_{n,l}^2}\geq 2(1-\eta)(1+\eta)^3x_n^2\right)\\
&+P\left(\max_{n<k\leq\theta n}\frac{\sum_{l=1}^{\infty}\lambda_l\left(\sum_{i=n+1}^{k}g_l(X_i)\right)^2}{\max_{1\leq l<\infty}\lambda_l V_{k,l}^2}\geq\frac{\eta^2(1+\eta)^3x_n^2}{2}\right)\\
:=\ & H_1+H_2.
\end{aligned}\tag{87}$$

Notice that (10) implies (8). By (17) and the upper bound of Theorem 1,

$$H_1\leq\exp\left(-(1-\eta)^{3/2}(1+\eta)^3x_n^2\right).\tag{88}$$

Let $0<\delta<1$ be a sufficiently small constant. By (19),

$$\begin{aligned}
H_2\leq\ & P\left(2m\max_{1\leq l<\infty}\lambda_l V_{n,l}^2\leq(1-\eta)n\sum_{1\leq l<\infty}\lambda_l L_l(z_{n,l})\right)\\
&+P\left(\max_{n<k\leq\theta n}\frac{\sum_{l=1}^{\infty}\lambda_l\left(\sum_{i=n+1}^{k}g_l(X_i)I(|g_l(X_i)|>\delta\eta z_{n,l})\right)^2}{\max_{1\leq l<\infty}\lambda_l V_{k,l}^2}\geq\frac{\eta^4(1+\eta)^3x_n^2}{2}\right)\\
&+P\left(\frac{\max_{n<k\leq\theta n}\sum_{l=1}^{\infty}\lambda_l\left(\sum_{i=n+1}^{k}g_l(X_i)I(|g_l(X_i)|\leq\delta\eta z_{n,l})\right)^2}{n\sum_{1\leq l<\infty}\lambda_l L_l(z_{n,l})}\right.\\
&\left.\geq\frac{(1-\eta)(1-2\eta)\eta^2(1+\eta)^3x_n^2}{4m}\right)\\
:=\ & H_{2,1}+H_{2,2}+H_{2,3}.
\end{aligned}\tag{89}$$

By (24) in Proposition 1,

$$H_{2,1} \leq \exp\big(-2x_n^2\big). \qquad (90)$$

By the Cauchy–Schwarz inequality, for each k,

$$\begin{aligned} & \frac{\sum_{l=1}^{\infty} \lambda_l \big\{\sum_{i=n+1}^{k} |g_l(X_i)| I(|g_l(X_i)| > \delta\eta z_{n,l})\big\}^2}{\max_{1\leq l<\infty} \lambda_l V_{k,l}^2} \\ \leq \; & \frac{\sum_{l=1}^{\infty} \lambda_l \sum_{i=n+1}^{k} g_l^2(X_i) \sum_{i=n+1}^{k} I(|g_l(X_i)| > \delta\eta z_{n,l})}{\max_{1\leq l<\infty} \lambda_l V_{k,l}^2}. \end{aligned} \qquad (91)$$

By (17), for some m value that is sufficiently large, the sum of the diagonal terms is as follows:

$$\frac{\sum_{l=1}^{\infty} \lambda_l \sum_{i=n+1}^{k} g_l^2(X_i) I(|g_l(X_i)| > \delta\eta z_{n,l})}{\max_{1\leq l<\infty} \lambda_l V_{k,l}^2} \leq m. \qquad (92)$$

By (91) and (92),

$$\begin{aligned} H_{2,2} \leq P\Bigg(& \max_{n<k\leq\theta n} \frac{\sum_{n+1\leq i\neq j\leq k} \sum_{l=1}^{\infty} \lambda_l g_l^2(X_i) I(|g_l(X_j)| > \delta\eta z_{n,l})}{\max_{1\leq l<\infty} \lambda_l \sum_{i=n+1}^{k} g_l^2(X_i)} \geq \frac{\eta^5(1+\eta)^3 x_n^2}{2}\Bigg) \\ \leq \; & P\Bigg(\max_{n<k\leq\theta n} \frac{\sum_{n+1\leq i<j\leq k} \sum_{l=1}^{\infty} \lambda_l g_l^2(X_i) I(|g_l(X_j)| > \delta\eta z_{n,l})}{\max_{1\leq l<\infty} \lambda_l \sum_{i=n+1}^{k} g_l^2(X_i)} \geq \frac{\eta^5(1+\eta)^3 x_n^2}{4}\Bigg) \\ + \; & P\Bigg(\max_{n<k\leq\theta n} \frac{\sum_{n+1\leq j<i\leq k} \sum_{l=1}^{\infty} \lambda_l g_l^2(X_i) I(|g_l(X_j)| > \delta\eta z_{n,l})}{\max_{1\leq l<\infty} \lambda_l \sum_{i=n+1}^{k} g_l^2(X_i)} \geq \frac{\eta^5(1+\eta)^3 x_n^2}{4}\Bigg) \\ \leq \; & P\Bigg(\max_{n<k\leq\theta n} \sum_{n+2\leq j\leq k} \frac{\sum_{n+1\leq i<j} \sum_{l=1}^{\infty} \lambda_l g_l^2(X_i) I(|g_l(X_j)| > \delta\eta z_{n,l})}{\max_{1\leq l<\infty} \lambda_l \sum_{n+1\leq i<j} g_l^2(X_i)} \geq \frac{\eta^5(1+\eta)^3 x_n^2}{4}\Bigg) \\ + \; & P\Bigg(\max_{n<k\leq\theta n} \sum_{n+1\leq j<k} \frac{\sum_{j<i\leq k} \sum_{l=1}^{\infty} \lambda_l g_l^2(X_i) I(|g_l(X_j)| > \delta\eta z_{n,l})}{\max_{1\leq l<\infty} \lambda_l \sum_{j<i\leq k} g_l^2(X_i)} \geq \frac{\eta^5(1+\eta)^3 x_n^2}{4}\Bigg) \\ = \; & H_{2,2,1} + H_{2,2,2}. \end{aligned} \qquad (9$$

Let

$$\phi_j = \frac{\sum_{n+1\leq i<j} \sum_{l=1}^{\infty} \lambda_l g_l^2(X_i) I(|g_l(X_j)| > \delta\eta z_{n,l})}{\max_{1\leq l<\infty} \lambda_l \sum_{n+1\leq i<j} g_l^2(X_i)}.$$

Then, for any constant $t > 0$,

$$\begin{aligned} H_{2,2,1} \leq \; & \Bigg(\sum_{n+2\leq j\leq[\theta n]} \frac{\sum_{n+1\leq i<j} \sum_{l=1}^{\infty} \lambda_l g_l^2(X_i) I(|g_l(X_j)| > \delta\eta z_{n,l})}{\max_{1\leq l<\infty} \lambda_l \sum_{n+1\leq i<j} g_l^2(X_i)} \geq \frac{\eta^5(1+\eta)^3 x_n^2}{4}\Bigg) \\ \leq \; & Ee^{t\sum_{j=n+2}^{[\theta n]} \phi_j} e^{-t\eta^5(1+\eta)^3 x_n^2/4}. \end{aligned} \qquad (9$$

Let E_j be the expectation of X_j for $n+2 \leq j \leq [\theta n]$. Then,

$$Ee^{t\sum_{j=n+2}^{[\theta n]} \phi_j} = E\big(e^{t\sum_{j=n+2}^{[\theta n]-1} \phi_j} E_{[\theta n]} e^{t\phi_{[\theta n]}}\big). \qquad (95)$$

Since $|e^s - 1| \leq e^{0\vee s}|s|$ for any $s \in R$ and $0 \leq \phi_{[\theta n]} \leq m$ for some m value that is sufficiently large, then

$$\begin{aligned}\left|E_{[\theta n]}e^{t\phi_{[\theta n]}} - 1\right| &\leq e^{mt}tE_{[\theta n]}\phi_{[\theta n]} \\ &= \frac{e^{mt}t\sum_{n+1\leq i<[\theta n]}\sum_{l=1}^{\infty}\lambda_l g_l^2(X_i)P(|g_l(X_{[\theta n]})| > \delta\eta z_{n,l})}{\max_{1\leq l<\infty}\lambda_l\sum_{n+1\leq i<[\theta n]}g_l^2(X_i)}.\end{aligned}$$

By (12) and (15), we have $P(|g_l(X_{[\theta n]})| > \delta\eta z_{n,l}) = o(x_n^2/n)$. Then, together with (17),

$$E_{[\theta n]}e^{t\phi_{[\theta n]}} = 1 + o(x_n^2/n) = e^{o(x_n^2/n)}. \tag{96}$$

Applying (96) to (95), we have

$$Ee^{t\sum_{j=2}^{[\theta n]}\phi_j} = e^{o(x_n^2/n)}Ee^{t\sum_{j=n+2}^{[\theta n]-1}\phi_j}.$$

Similarly,

$$\begin{aligned}Ee^{t\sum_{j=n+2}^{[\theta n]-1}\phi_j} &= E(e^{t\sum_{j=n+2}^{[\theta n]-2}\phi_j}E_{n-1}e^{t\phi_{[\theta n]-1}}) \\ &= e^{o(x_n^2/n)}Ee^{t\sum_{j=n+2}^{[\theta n]-2}\phi_j}.\end{aligned}$$

Continue this process from $X_{[\theta n]}$ to X_{n+1}. Thus, we conclude that

$$Ee^{t\sum_{j=n+2}^{[\theta n]}\phi_j} = e^{[(\theta-1)n]\times o(x_n^2/n)} = e^{o(x_n^2)}. \tag{97}$$

Applying (97) to (94) and letting $t = 8/(\eta^5(1+\eta)^3)$, we have

$$H_{2,2,1} \leq \exp(-2x_n^2). \tag{98}$$

To estimate $H_{2,2,2}$, let

$$\psi_{j,k} = \frac{\sum_{j<i\leq k}\sum_{l=1}^{\infty}\lambda_l g_l^2(X_i)I(|g_l(X_j)| > \delta\eta z_{n,l})}{\max_{1\leq l<\infty}\lambda_l\sum_{j<i\leq k}g_l^2(X_i)}.$$

Then, for any constant $t > 0$,

$$\begin{aligned}H_{2,2,2} &\leq P\left(\sum_{n+1\leq j<[\theta n]}\max_{j<k\leq\theta n}\psi_{j,k} \geq \frac{\eta^5(1+\eta)^3x_n^2}{4}\right) \\ &\leq Ee^{t\sum_{j=n+1}^{[\theta n]-1}\max_{j<k\leq\theta n}\psi_{j,k}}e^{-t\eta^5(1+\eta)^3x_n^2/4}.\end{aligned} \tag{99}$$

Let E_j be the expectation of X_j for $n+1 \leq j \leq [\theta n]$. Note $k > j$. Then,

$$\begin{aligned}&Ee^{t\sum_{j=n+1}^{[\theta n]-1}\max_{j<k\leq\theta n}\psi_{j,k}} \\ &= E(e^{t\sum_{j=n+2}^{[\theta n]-1}\max_{j<k\leq\theta n}\psi_{j,k}}E_{n+1}e^{t\max_{n+1<k\leq\theta n}\psi_{n+1,k}}).\end{aligned} \tag{100}$$

Observe that

$$\psi_{j,k} = \frac{\sum_{l=1}^{\infty}\lambda_l\left(\sum_{j<i\leq k}g_l^2(X_i)\right)I(|g_l(X_j)| > \delta\eta z_{n,l})}{\max_{1\leq l<\infty}\lambda_l\sum_{j<i\leq k}g_l^2(X_i)}. \tag{101}$$

Then, by (17), $0 \le \psi_{n+1,k} \le m$ for some m value that is sufficiently large. Since $|e^s - 1| \le e^{0 \vee s}|s|$ for any $s \in R$,

$$\left|E_{n+1}e^{t\max_{n+1<k\le\theta n}\psi_{n+1,k}} - 1\right| \le e^{mt}tE_{n+1}\max_{n+1<k\le\theta n}\psi_{n+1,k}. \tag{102}$$

Under Assumption (10), for each $l \in [1,\infty)$,

$$\lambda_l V_{n,l}^2 = \sum_{i=1}^{n}\lambda_l g_l^2(X_i) \le c_l \sum_{v=1}^{\infty}\sum_{i=1}^{n}\lambda_v g_v^2(X_i) = c_l \sum_{v=1}^{\infty}\lambda_v V_{n,v}^2.$$

Recall that (17); then, for each $l \in [1,\infty)$,

$$\frac{\lambda_l V_{n,l}^2}{\max_{1\le l<\infty}\lambda_l V_{n,l}^2} \le \frac{mc_l}{1-\varepsilon}.$$

Hence, by (101),

$$\psi_{j,k} \le \frac{m}{1-\varepsilon}\sum_{l=1}^{\infty} c_l I(|g_l(X_j)| > \delta\eta z_{n,l}).$$

Then,

$$E_{n+1}\max_{n+1<k\le\theta n}\psi_{n+1,k} \le \frac{m}{1-\varepsilon}\sum_{l=1}^{\infty} c_l P(|g_l(X_{n+1})| > \delta\eta z_{n,l}).$$

By (12) and (15), we have $P(|g_l(X_{n+1})| > \delta\eta z_{n,l}) = o(x_n^2/n)$. Then, together with (10),

$$E_{n+1}\max_{n+1<k\le\theta n}\psi_{n+1,k} = o(x_n^2/n). \tag{103}$$

Then, by (102) and (103),

$$E_{n+1}e^{t\max_{n+1<k\le\theta n}\psi_{n+1,k}} = 1 + o(x_n^2/n) = e^{o(x_n^2/n)}.$$

Continue this process from $j = n+2$ to $j = [\theta n] - 1$ and by (100),

$$Ee^{t\sum_{j=n+1}^{[\theta n]-1}\max_{j<k\le\theta n}\psi_{j,k}} = e^{o(x_n^2)}. \tag{104}$$

Applying (104) to (99) and letting $t = 8/(\eta^5(1+\eta)^3)$, we have

$$H_{2,2,2} \le \exp(-2x_n^2). \tag{105}$$

By (93), (98) and (105),

$$H_{2,2} \le 2\exp(-2x_n^2). \tag{106}$$

By the definition of $H_{2,3}$ in (89), and by Lemma 4, there is a constant $0 < C' < \infty$ such that

$$H_{2,3} \le C'P\left(\frac{\sum_{l=1}^{\infty}\lambda_l\left(\sum_{i=n+1}^{[\theta n]} g_l(X_i)I(|g_l(X_i)| \le \delta\eta z_{n,l})\right)^2}{n\sum_{l=1}^{\infty}\lambda_l L_l(z_{n,l})} \ge \frac{(1-3\eta)\eta^2 x_n^2}{4mC'}\right).$$

Similar to (36),

$$H_{2,3} \leq C'P\left(\frac{\sum_{l=1}^{\infty}\lambda_l\left(\sum_{i=n+1}^{[\theta n]}\{g_l(X_i)I(|g_l(X_i)|\leq\delta\eta z_{n,l})-Eg_l(X_i)I(|g_l(X_i)|\leq\delta\eta z_{n,l})\}\right)^2}{n\sum_{l=1}^{\infty}\lambda_l L_l(z_{n,l})} \geq \frac{(1-3\eta)^2\eta^2x_n^2}{4mC'}\right).$$

By the decoupling version of (40) in Proposition 3,

$$H_{2,3} \leq C'\exp\left(-2x_n^2\right). \tag{107}$$

Combining (89), (90), (106) and (107), we have

$$H_2 \leq (3+C')\exp\left(-2x_n^2\right). \tag{108}$$

By (87), (88) and (108),

$$P\left(\max_{n<k\leq\theta n}\frac{\sum_{l=1}^{\infty}\lambda_l\left(\sum_{i=1}^{k}g_l(X_i)\right)^2}{\max_{1\leq l<\infty}\lambda_l V_{k,l}^2} \geq 2(1+\eta)^3x_n^2\right) \leq \exp\left(-(1-\eta)^{7/4}(1+\eta)^3x_n^2\right).$$

Let $n=[\theta^j]$ for some $j\in\mathbb{N}$. We have

$$P\left(\max_{\theta^j<k\leq\theta^{j+1}}\frac{\sum_{l=1}^{\infty}\lambda_l\left(\sum_{i=1}^{k}g_l(X_i)\right)^2}{\max_{1\leq l<\infty}\lambda_l V_{k,l}^2} \geq 2(1+\eta)^3x_{[\theta^j]}^2\right) \leq \exp\left(-(1-\eta)^{7/4}(1+\eta)^3x_{[\theta^j]}^2\right).$$

Let $x_n^2=\log\log n$. Then,

$$\begin{aligned}
&\sum_{j=1}^{\infty}P\left(\max_{\theta^j<k\leq\theta^{j+1}}\frac{\sum_{l=1}^{\infty}\lambda_l\left(\sum_{i=1}^{k}g_l(X_i)\right)^2}{\max_{1\leq l<\infty}\lambda_l V_{k,l}^2\log\log k} \geq 2(1+\eta)^3\right)\\
\leq\ &\sum_{j=1}^{\infty}P\left(\max_{\theta^j<k\leq\theta^{j+1}}\frac{\sum_{l=1}^{\infty}\lambda_l\left(\sum_{i=1}^{k}g_l(X_i)\right)^2}{\max_{1\leq l<\infty}\lambda_l V_{k,l}^2} \geq 2(1+\eta)^3x_{[\theta^j]}^2\right)\\
\leq\ &\sum_{j=1}^{\infty}\exp\left(-(1-\eta)^{7/4}(1+\eta)^3\log\log[\theta^j]\right)\\
\leq\ &K\sum_{j=1}^{\infty}\exp\left(-(1-\eta)^2(1+\eta)^3\log j\right)<\infty.
\end{aligned}$$

By the Borel–Cantelli lemma,

$$\limsup_{n\to\infty}\frac{\sum_{l=1}^{\infty}\lambda_l\left(\sum_{i=1}^{n}g_l(X_i)\right)^2}{\max_{1\leq l<\infty}\lambda_l V_{n,l}^2\log\log n} \leq 2 \ \ a.s.$$

□

5. The Lower Bound of Theorem 2

Proof. By the definition of W_n,

$$\frac{W_n}{\log\log n} = \frac{\sum_{l=1}^{\infty}\lambda_l\Big(\big(\sum_{i=1}^{n} g_l(X_i)\big)^2 - \sum_{i=1}^{n} g_l^2(X_i)\Big)}{\max_{1\le l<\infty}\lambda_l V_{n,l}^2 \log\log n}$$
$$= \frac{\sum_{l=1}^{\infty}\lambda_l\big(\sum_{i=1}^{n} g_l(X_i)\big)^2}{\max_{1\le l<\infty}\lambda_l V_{n,l}^2 \log\log n} - \frac{\sum_{l=1}^{\infty}\lambda_l V_{n,l}^2}{\max_{1\le l<\infty}\lambda_l V_{n,l}^2 \log\log n}.$$

By (17), $\sum_{l=1}^{\infty}\lambda_l V_{n,l}^2/(\max_{1\le l<\infty}\lambda_l V_{n,l}^2 \log\log n) \le m/((1-\varepsilon)\log\log n) \to 0$ as $n\to\infty$, we have

$$\frac{W_n}{\log\log n} \ge \frac{\sum_{l=1}^{\infty}\lambda_l\big(\sum_{i=1}^{n} g_l(X_i)\big)^2}{\max_{1\le l<\infty}\lambda_l V_{n,l}^2 \log\log n}.$$

Then,

$$\frac{W_n}{\log\log n} \ge \sum_{k=1}^{\infty}\frac{\big(\sum_{i=1}^{n} g_k(X_i)\big)^2}{V_{n,k}^2\log\log n} I_{k=min\{j:\max_{1\le l<\infty}\lambda_l V_{n,l}^2=\lambda_j V_{n,j}^2\}}.$$

Hence, by (6),

$$\limsup_{n\to\infty}\frac{W_n}{\log\log n} \ge 2 \ a.s.$$

□

Author Contributions: Conceptualization, Q.-M.S.; methodology, L.G., H.S. and Q.-M.S.; formal analysis, L.G., H.S. and Q.-M.S.; investigation, L.G., H.S. and Q.-M.S.; writing—original draft preparation, L.G. and H.S.; writing—review and editing, Q.-M.S. All authors have read and agreed to the published version of the manuscript.

Funding: This research was partially supported by the Simons Foundation Grant 586789, USA, as well as by the National Nature Science Foundation of China NSFC 12031005 and Shenzhen Outstanding Talents Training Fund, China.

Institutional Review Board Statement: Not applicable.

Data Availability Statement: Data sharing is not applicable (only appropriate if no new data is generated or the article describes entirely theoretical research).

Conflicts of Interest: The authors declare no conflicts of interest. The funders had no role in the design of the study; in the collection, analyses, or interpretation of data; in the writing of the manuscript; or in the decision to publish the results.

References

1. Griffin, P.; Kuelbs, J. Self-normalized laws of the iterated logarithm. *Ann. Probab.* **1989**, *17*, 1571–1601. [CrossRef]
2. Shao, Q.M. Self-normalized large deviations. *Ann. Probab.* **1997**, *25*, 285–328. [CrossRef]
3. Shao, Q.M. A Cramér type large deviation result for Student's t-statistic. *J. Theoret. Probab.* **1999**, *12*, 385–398. [CrossRef]
4. Jing, B.Y.; Shao, Q.M.; Wang, Q. Self-normalized Cramér type large deviations for independent random variables. *Ann. Prob* **2003**, *31*, 2167–2215. [CrossRef]
5. Shao, Q.M.; Zhou, W.X. Cramér type moderate deviation theorems for self-normalized processes. *Bernoulli* **2016**, *22*, 2029–20 [CrossRef]
6. Halmos, P.R. The theory of unbiased estimation. *Ann. Math. Statst.* **1946**, *17*, 34–43. [CrossRef]

Hoeffding, W. A class of statistics with asymptotically normal distribution. *Ann. Math. Statst.* **1948**, *19*, 293–325. [CrossRef]

Serfling, R.J. The law of the iterated logarithm for *U*-statistics and related von Mises statistics. *Ann. Math. Statist.* **1971**, *42*, 1794.

Dehling, H.; Denker, M.; Philipp, W. Invariance principles for von Mises and *U*-statistics. *Z. Wahrscheinlichkeitstheorie Verwandte Geb.* **1984**, *67*, 139–167. [CrossRef]

0. Dehling, H.; Denker, M.; Philipp, W. A bounded law of the iterated logarithm for Hilbert space valued martingales and its application to *U*-statistics. *Probab. Theory Relat. Fields* **1986**, *72*, 111–131. [CrossRef]

1. Dehling, H. Complete convergence of triangular arrays and the law of the iterated logarithm for degenerate *U*-statistics. *Statist. Probab. Lett.* **1989**, *7*, 319–321. [CrossRef]

2. Arcones, M.; Giné, E. On the law of the iterated logarithm for canonical *U*-statistics and processes. *Stoch. Process. Appl.* **1995**, *58*, 217–245. [CrossRef]

3. Teicher, H. Moments of randomly stopped sums revisited. *J. Theoret. Probab.* **1995**, *8*, 779–794. [CrossRef]

4. Giné, E.; Zhang, C.-H. On Integrability in the LIL for Degenerate *U*-statistics. *J. Theoret. Probab.* **1996**, *9*, 385–412. [CrossRef]

5. Giné, E.; Kwapień, S.; Latała, R.; Zinn, J. The LIL for canonical *U*-statistics of order 2. *Ann. Probab.* **2001**, *29*, 520–557. [CrossRef]

6. Adamczak, R.; Latała, R. The LIL for canonical *U*-statistics. *Ann. Probab.* **2008**, *36*, 1023–1068. [CrossRef]

7. Bingham, N.H.; Goldie, C.M.; Teugels, J.L. *Regular Variation*; Cambridge University Press: Cambridge, UK, 1987.

8. de la Peña, V.H.; Lai, T.L.; Shao, Q.M. *Self-Normalized Processes: Limit Theory and Statistical Applications. Probability and Its Applications (New York)*; Springer: Berlin, Germany, 2009.

9. Giné, E.; Latała, R.; Zinn, J. Exponential and moment inequalities for *U*-statistics. In *High Dimensional Probability II*; Birkhäuser: Boston, MA, USA, 2000; pp. 13–38.

0. de la Peña, V.H.; Montgomery-Smith, S.J. Decoupling inequalities for the tail probabilities of multivariate *U*-statistics. *Ann. Probab.* **1995**, *23*, 806–816. [CrossRef]

1. Einmahl, U. Extensions of results of Komlós, Major, and Tusnády to the multivariate case. *J. Mult. Anal.* **1989**, *28*, 20–68. [CrossRef]

2. Lin, Z.; Liu, W. On maxima of periodograms of stationary processes. *Ann. Statist.* **2009**, *37*, 2676–2695. [CrossRef]

3. Liu, W.; Shao, Q.M. A Cramér moderate deviation theorem for Hotelling's T^2-statistic with applications to global tests. *Ann. Statist.* **2013**, *41*, 296–322. [CrossRef]

4. Stout, W.F. *Almost Sure Convergence*; Academic Press: New York, NY, USA, 1974.

5. Csőrgxox, M.; Lin, Z.Y.; Shao, Q.M. Studentized increments of partial sums. *Sci. China Ser. A* **1994**, *37*, 265–276.

6. Pruitt, W.E. General one-sided laws of the iterated logarithm. *Ann. Probab.* **1981**, *9*, 1–48. [CrossRef]

entropy

MDPI

Article

An Erdős-Révész Type Law for the Length of the Longest Match of Two Coin-Tossing Sequences

Karl Grill

Institute of Statistics and Mathematical Methods in Economy, TU Wien, Wiedner Hauptstraße 8-10, 1040 Vienna, Austria; karl.grill@tuwien.ac.at

Abstract: Consider a coin-tossing sequence, i.e., a sequence of independent variables, taking values 0 and 1 with probability 1/2. The famous Erdős-Rényi law of large numbers implies that the longest run of ones in the first n observations has a length R_n that behaves like $\log(n)$, as n tends to infinity (throughout this article, log denotes logarithm with base 2). Erdős and Révész refined this result by providing a description of the Lévy upper and lower classes of the process R_n. In another direction, Arratia and Waterman extended the Erdős-Rényi result to the longest matching subsequence (with shifts) of two coin-tossing sequences, finding that it behaves asymptotically like $2\log(n)$. The present paper provides some Erdős-Révész type results in this situation, obtaining a complete description of the upper classes and a partial result on the lower ones.

Keywords: coin tossing; runs; matching subsequences; strong asymptotics

1. Introduction

Consider a coin-tossing sequence (X_n), i.e., a sequence of independent random variables satisfying $\mathbb{P}(X_n = 0) = \mathbb{P}(X_n = 1) = 1/2$. Let R_n be the length of the longest head-run, i.e., the largest integer r for which there is an i, $0 \le i \le n - r$, for which $X_{i+j} = 1$ for $j = 1, \dots r$. A result of Erdős and Rényi [1] implies that

$$\lim_{n\to\infty} \frac{R_n}{\log(n)} = 1 \tag{1}$$

(throughout this paper, log will denote base 2 logarithms. The notation $\log_k$ will be used for its iterates: $\log_2(x) = \log(\log(x))$, $\log_{k+1}(x) = \log(\log_k(x))$. Also, C and c, with or without an index, are used to denote generic constants that may have different values at each occurrence). The simple result (1) has seen a number of improvements. Erdős and Révész [2] provided a detailed description of the asymptotic behavior of R_n. In order to formulate their result, let us recall

Definition 1 (Lévy classes). *Let (Y_n) be a sequence of random variables. We say that a sequence (a_n) of real numbers belongs to*

- *The upper-upper class of (Y_n) ($UUC(Y_n)$), if, with probability 1 as $n \to \infty$, $Y_n \le a_n$ eventually.*
- *The upper-lower class of (Y_n) ($ULC(Y_n)$), if, with probability 1 as $n \to \infty$, $Y_n > a_n$ for infinitely many n.*
- *The lower-upper class of (Y_n) ($LUC(Y_n)$), if, with probability 1 as $n \to \infty$, $Y_n < a_n$ for infinitely many n.*
- *The lower-lower class of (Y_n) ($LLC(Y_n)$), if, with probability 1 as $n \to \infty$, $Y_n \ge a_n$ eventually.*

Of course, these definitions work best if the sequence (Y_n) obeys some zero-one law.

Their result is as follows:

Let (a_n) be a nondecreasing integer sequence. Then

- $(a_n) \in UUC(R_n)$ if $\sum_n 2^{-a_n} < \infty$,
- $(a_n) \in ULC(R_n)$ if $\sum_n 2^{-a_n} = \infty$,
- for any $\epsilon > 0$, $a_n = \lfloor \log(n) - \log_3(n) + \log_2(e) - 1 + \epsilon \rfloor \in LUC(R_n)$,
- for any $\epsilon > 0$, $a_n = \lfloor \log(n) - \log_3(n) + \log_2(e) - 2 - \epsilon \rfloor \in LLC(R_n)$.

Arratia and Waterman [3] extend Erdős and Rényi's result in another direction: they consider two independent coin-tossing sequences, (X_n) and (Y_n), and look for the longest matching subsequences when shifting is allowed. Formally, let M_n be the the largest integer m for which there are i, j with $0 \leq i, j \leq n - m$ and $X_{i+k} = Y_{j+k}$ for all $k = 1, \ldots, m$. They prove that, with probability 1

$$\lim_{n\to\infty} \frac{M_n}{\log(n)} = 2. \tag{2}$$

In the present paper, we will make this more precise by providing a description for the upper classes of (M_n) and also some results on its lower classes:

Theorem 1. *Let (a_n) be a nondecreasing integer sequence. We have*

- $(a_n) \in UUC(M_n)$ *if* $\sum_n n2^{-a_n} < \infty$.
- $(a_n) \in ULC(M_n)$ *if* $\sum_n n2^{-a_n} = \infty$.
- *for some c,* $a_n = \lfloor 2\log(n) - \log_3(n) + c \rfloor \in LUC(M_n)$.
- *for some c,* $a_n = \lfloor 2\log(n) - 2\log_2(n) - \log_3(n) + c \rfloor \in LLC(M_n)$.

2. Discussion

We leave the proof of Theorem 1 for later and rather discuss some of the concepts that are connected to this problem. One of them is the so-called independence principle: in many, although not all, situations, one may pretend that the waiting times until a given pattern of length l is observed have an exponential distribution with parameter 2^{-l}, and that the waiting times for different patterns are independent. Móri [4] and Móri and Székely [5] provide an account of this principle and its limitations. In our case, all results but the lower-lower class one are more or less in tune with this principle.

Another question that is closely related is that of the number $N(n, l)$ of different length l subsequences of $(X_1, \ldots, X_n)$. This question does not seem to have been considered by literature very much; there is one remarkable result by Móri [6]: in the remark following the statement of Theorem 3 in that paper, he mentions that with probability one for large n, the largest l for which all 2^l possible patterns occur as subsequences of $(X_1, \ldots, X_n)$ is either $\lfloor \log(n) - \log_2(n) - \epsilon \rfloor$ or $\lfloor \log(n) - \log_2(n) + \epsilon \rfloor$ for any $\epsilon > 0$. The independence principle would suggest that $N(n, \log(n))/n$ is bounded away from 0 with probability one, and this or even the less stringent $N(n, \log(n)) \geq n(\log_2(n))^{-c}$ for large n would be an important step towards removing the double log term from the LLC result, as we conjecture that, for some $c > 0$, $\log(n) - c\log_3(n) \in LLC(M_n)$. Unfortunately, we are only able to obtain $N(n, \log(n)) \geq cn/\log(n)$, which is also implied by Móri's result.

3. Proofs

Proof of the upper-upper class result. Both upper class statements are fairly easy to prove. First, observe that under our assumptions, the convergence of

$$\sum_{n=1}^{\infty} n2^{-a_n} \tag{3}$$

is equivalent to that of

$$\sum_{k=1}^{\infty} n_k^2 2^{-a_{n_k}} \tag{4}$$

with $n_k = 2^k$.

Now, define events

$$A_k = [M_{n_k} \geq a_{n_{k-1}}]. \tag{5}$$

A_k occurs if in one of the $(n_k + 1 - a_{n_{k-1}})^2$ pairs of sequences

$$((X_{i+1}, \ldots, X_{i+a_{k-1}}), ((Y_{j+1}, \ldots, Y_{j+a_{k-1}})) \tag{6}$$

both sequences agree. That provides the trivial upper bound

$$\mathbb{P}(A_k) \leq n_k^2 2^{-a_{n_{k-1}}}, \tag{7}$$

so, by our assumptions, $\sum_n \mathbb{P}(A_k) < \infty$, and the Borel-Cantelli Lemma implies that, with probability 1, only finitely many events A_k occur. Thus, for sufficiently large k, $M_{n_k} \leq a_{n_{k-1}}$, and for $n_{k-1} \leq n \leq n_k$, we have

$$M_n \leq M_{n_k} \leq a_{n_{k-1}} \leq a_n. \tag{8}$$

This shows that $(a_n) \in UUC(M_n)$, as claimed. □

Proof of the upper-lower class result. We may assume without loss of generality that $n^2 2^{-a_n} \leq 1/4$.

Again, let $n_k = 2^k$. We want to use the second Borel-Cantelli Lemma, so we are defining independent events

$$A_k = [\exists i, j : n_{k-1} < i, j \leq n_k : X_{i+s} = Y_{j+s}, s = 0, \ldots, a_{n_k} - 1] \tag{9}$$

This is the union of the events

$$B_{ij} = [X_{i+s} = Y_{j+s}, s = 0, \ldots, a_{n_k} - 1] \tag{10}$$

with $n_{k-1} < i, j \leq n_k$. We endow the set of pairs (i, j) with the lexicographic order. For a subset I of the integers, Bonferroni's inequality provides

$$\mathbb{P}\Big(\bigcup_{(i,j) \in I \times I} B_{ij}\Big) \geq \sum_{(i,j) \in I \times I} \mathbb{P}(B_{ij}) - \sum_{(i,j),(i',j') \in I \times I, (i,j) < (i',j')} \mathbb{P}(B_{ij} \cap B_{i'j'}). \tag{11}$$

Let $d((i, j), (i', j')) = \max(|i - i'|, |j - j'|)$. If $d((i, j), (i', j')) \geq a_{n_k}$, then $\mathbb{P}(B_{ij} \cap B_{i'j'}) = 2^{-2a_{n_k}}$, otherwise $\mathbb{P}(B_{ij} \cap B_{i'j'}) = 2^{-(a_{n_k} + d((i,j),(i',j'))}$.

Let $I = \{i : n_{k-1} < i \leq n_k : 4|i\}$. Using this in (11) yields the value $|I|^2 2^{-a_{n_k}}$ for the first sum. In the second sum, for given (i, j) and $d < a_{n_k}/4$, there are no more than $2(2d + 1)$ pairs (i', j') with $d((i, j), (i', j')) = 4d$. The number of pairs of pairs $((i, j), (i', j')$ with $d((i, j), (i', j')) \geq a_{n_k}$ is trivially bounded by $|I|^4/2$. Putting these together, we arrive at the upper estimate

$$|I|^2 2^{-a_{n_k}} \Big(\sum_{d=1}^{\infty} (2d + 1) 2^{1-4d} + |I|^2 2^{-1-a_{n_k}}\Big) < \frac{1}{2} |I|^2 2^{-a_{n_k}}. \tag{12}$$

In total,

$$\mathbb{P}(A_k) \geq \frac{1}{2} |I|^2 e^{-a_{n_k}} = \frac{1}{128} n_k^2 2^{-a_{n_k}}, \tag{13}$$

keeping in mind that $|I| = n_k/8$.

and $\sum_k \mathbb{P}(A_k) = \infty$. Borel-Cantelli implies that, with probability 1, infinitely many events A_k occur. Thus, for infinitely many k, $M_{n_k} \geq a_{n_k}$, so $(a_n) \in ULC(M_n)$. □

For the lower class results, we first prove some lemmas:

Lemma 1. *With probability 1 for n sufficiently large*

$$\frac{n}{4\log(n)} \leq N(n, \lfloor \log(n) \rfloor) \leq n \tag{14}$$

Proof of Lemma 1. The lower part is a direct consequence of Móri's result: as for sufficiently large n $N(n, \lfloor \log(n) - \log_2(n) - 1 \rfloor) = 2^{\lfloor \log(n) - \log_2(n) - 1 \rfloor} \geq \frac{n}{4\log(n)}$ and, obviously $N(n, \lfloor \log(n) \rfloor) \geq N(n, \lfloor \log(n) - \log_2(n) - 1 \rfloor) - \log_2(n) - 2$, as extending two different sequences from length $\lfloor \log(n) - \log_2(n) \rfloor$ to $\lfloor \log(n) \rfloor$ keeps them different; it can only happen that some of them are extended beyond index n, but this can affect at most $\log_2(n) + 2$ of them. □

Lemma 2. *Let S be a set of $m < 2^l$ sequences of length $l < n$, and let A be the event that none of the sequences in S occurs as a subsequence of $(X_1, \ldots, X_n)$. For $l \leq n' < n$, let B be the event that some sequence from S is a subsequence of $X_1, \ldots, X_{n'}$. Then*

$$((1 - \mathbb{P}(B))^2 - \lfloor n/n' \rfloor m 2^{-l})(1 - \mathbb{P}(B))^{\lfloor n/n' \rfloor} \leq \mathbb{P}(A) \leq (1 - \mathbb{P}(B))^{\lfloor n/n' \rfloor}. \tag{15}$$

Proof of Lemma 2, upper part. Consider the $\lfloor n/n' \rfloor$ sequences $X_{kn'+1}, \ldots, X_{(k+1)n'}$ for $k = 0, \ldots \lfloor n/n' \rfloor - 1$. Each of these has probability $1 - \mathbb{P}(B)$ that it does not contain a subsequence that lies in S, and by independence

$$\mathbb{P}(A) \leq (1 - \mathbb{P}(B))^{\lfloor n/n' \rfloor}. \tag{16}$$

□

Proof of Lemma 2, lower part. Assume for simplicity that n is a multiple of n', say $n = Nn'$. Again, we split $(X_1, \ldots, X_n)$ into N blocks of length n', and the probability that none of those contains a sequence from S is

$$(1 - \mathbb{P}(B))^N. \tag{17}$$

It can still happen that there is a sequence from S that crosses one of the boundaries between the blocks. There are $N - 1$ boundaries, and for each of those, there are $l - 1$ possible subsequences of length l crossing it. The probability that this one is from S but none of the N blocks contains one can be estimated above by the probability that it is from S and none of the $N - 2$ blocks not adjacent to it contains one from S. This provides the upper bound

$$(N-1)(l-1)m2^{-l}(1 - \mathbb{P}(B))^{N-2} \tag{18}$$

for the probability that there is a subsequence from S in $(X_1, \ldots, X_n)$ but none in any of the N blocks. Subtracting this from (17), we obtain the lower bound

$$((1 - \mathbb{P}(B))^2 - (N-1)(l-1)m2^{-l})(1 - \mathbb{P}(B))^{N-2}, \tag{19}$$

and the general case is obtained by observing that the probability $\mathbb{P}(A)$ for a given n is bounded below by the one that we get for $n'\lceil n/n' \rceil$. □

In this lemma, the lower and upper bounds are rather close. Its applicability, however, depends on the availability of good estimates for the probability $\mathbb{P}(B)$. There is the trivial upper bound $n'm2^{-l}$ and an almost as simple lower bound const.$n'ml^{-1}2^{-l}$ (given $n'ml^{-1}2^{-l} < 1$). Bridging the gap between these requires deeper insight into the structure of S.

Proof of the lower-lower class result. In both the lower-lower and lower-upper parts, we consider the asymptotics of the longest match found between $(X_1, \dots, X_n)$ and $(Y_1, \dots, Y_n)$ under the condition that the sequence $(Y_n, n \in \mathbb{N})$ is given. Doing so, we may assume that $\mathbf{Y} = (Y_n, n \in \mathbb{N})$ is a "typical" coin-tossing sequence, in the sense that it possesses some property that holds with probability 1. In the sequel, all probabilities are understood as conditional with respect to such a typical sequence $\mathbf{Y}$. For the lower-lower class result, we let $n = n_l = \lceil C2^{l/2}l\sqrt{\log(l)}\rceil$, $n' = n'_l = l$, and $m = m_l = \lceil \frac{n}{4\log(n)} \rceil$ in Lemma 2. Clearly, as $(X_1, \dots, X_l)$ only has one length l subsequence, $\mathbb{P}(B)$ equals $\tilde{m}2^{-l}$, where $\tilde{m}$ is the number of different sequences of length l in $Y_1, \dots, Y_{n_l}$. For sufficiently large l, $\tilde{m} \geq m_l$ by Lemma 1, and we obtain an upper estimate

$$p_l = \exp(-m\lfloor n/l \rfloor 2^{-l}) = \exp\left(-\frac{1}{2}C^2\log(l)(1+o(1))\right) \tag{20}$$

for the probability (conditional on $\mathbf{Y}$) that there is no match of length l between $(Y_1, \dots, Y_{n_l})$ and $(X_1, \dots, X_{n_l})$. For $C > \sqrt{2/\log(e)}$, the series $\sum_l p_l$ converges, so with probability 1, we have $M(n_l) \geq l$ for all but finitely many l. Thus, for $n_{l-1} \leq n < n_l$, $M_n \geq M_{n_{l-1}} \geq l - 1$. Inverting the relationship between n_l and l yields $l = 2\log(n_l) - 2\log_2(n_l) - \log_3(n_l) + O(1)$, so, for some constant c and l large enough, we obtain $M_n \geq l - 1 \geq 2\log(n) - 2\log_2(n) - \log_3(n) - c$, which proves the lower-lower class result. □

Proof of the lower-upper class result. This time, we need to make our choice of the parameters in Lemma 2 with a little more sophistication. We start with $l = l_k = k^2$ for $k \in \mathbb{N}$. Then, $n = n_k = \lfloor C2^{l_k/2}\sqrt{\log(l_k)} \rfloor'$. As the set S, we choose the set $S_k$of all sequences of length l_k contained in $(Y_1, \dots, Y_{n_k})$. $n' = n'_k$ is chosen in such a way that $m_k n'_k 2^{-l_k} \to 0$ and $m_k n_k l_k 2^{-l_k}/n'_k \to 0$, $n'_k = \lfloor 2^{l_k/4} \rfloor$ is a possible choice.

We define the events

$$A_k = \{\text{There is no sequence from } S_k \text{ in } (X_1, \dots X_{n_k})\}, \tag{21}$$

$$\tilde{A}_k = \{\text{There is no sequence from } S_k \text{ in } (X_{n_{k-1}+1}, \dots X_{n_k})\} \tag{22}$$

$$B_k = \{\text{There is a sequence from } S_k \text{ in } (X_1, \dots X_{n'_k})\} \tag{23}$$

(this last is just the event B from Lemma 2).

Lemma 2 gives us

$$\mathbb{P}(A_k) = (1 - \mathbb{P}(B_k))^{\lfloor n_k/n'_k \rfloor}(1 + o(1)) \tag{24}$$

and

$$\mathbb{P}(\tilde{A}_k) = (1 - \mathbb{P}(B_k))^{\lfloor (n_k - n_{k-1})/n'_k \rfloor}(1 + o(1)). \tag{25}$$

The trivial estimate $\mathbb{P}(B_k) \leq m_k n'_k 2^{-l_k} \leq n_k^2 2^{-l_k}$ yields

$$\mathbb{P}(A_k) \geq e^{-2C^2\log(k)(1+o(1))}, \tag{26}$$

which diverges if we choose $C < 1/\sqrt{2\log(e)}$.

We are going to use the Borel-Cantelli Lemma in the usual form for dependent events:

Lemma 3 (Borel-Cantelli II). *If the sequence (A_n) satisfies*

$$\sum_{n \in \mathbb{N}} \mathbb{P}(A_n) = \infty \tag{27}$$

and

$$\lim_{n \to \infty} \frac{\sum_{i=1}^{n} \sum_{j=1}^{n} \mathbb{P}(A_i \cap A_j)}{(\sum_{i=1}^{n} \mathbb{P}(A_i))^2} = 1, \tag{28}$$

then

$$\mathbb{P}(\limsup_n A_n) = 1, \tag{29}$$

To this end, we need an upper bound for $\mathbb{P}(A_i \cap A_j)$ for $i < j$. We have

$$\mathbb{P}(A_i \cap A_j) \leq \mathbb{P}(A_i \cap \tilde{A}_j) = \mathbb{P}(A_i)\mathbb{P}(\tilde{A}_j). \tag{30}$$

By our Equations (24) and (25) from above

$$\mathbb{P}(\tilde{A}_j) = \mathbb{P}(A_j)(1 - \mathbb{P}(B_j))^{-n_{j-1}/n'_j}(1 + o(1)) = \mathbb{P}(A_j)e^{m_j n_{j-1} 2^{-l_j}(1+o(1))} =$$

$$\mathbb{P}(A_j)(1 + o(1)), \tag{31}$$

as $n_{j-1} \leq n_j e^{1-2j}$ and $m_j n_j 2^{-l_j} \leq n_j^2 2^{-l_j} = O(\log j)$.

This means that for any $\epsilon > 0$, there is a number j_0 such that, for $j > j_0$ and $i < j$, the inequality

$$\mathbb{P}(A_i \cap A_j) \leq (1 + \epsilon)\mathbb{P}(A_i)\mathbb{P}(A_j) \tag{32}$$

holds. Plugging this into

$$\sum_{j=1}^{n} \sum_{i=1}^{n} \mathbb{P}(A_i \cap A_j) = \sum_{i=1}^{n} \mathbb{P}(A_i) + 2 \sum_{j=2}^{n} \sum_{i=1}^{j-1} \mathbb{P}(A_i \cap A_j) \tag{33}$$

yields the estimate

$$\sum_{j=1}^{n} \sum_{i=1}^{n} \mathbb{P}(A_i \cap A_j) \leq \sum_{i=1}^{n} \mathbb{P}(A_i) + j_0^2 + (1 + \epsilon)(\sum_{i=1}^{n} \mathbb{P}(A_i))^2. \tag{34}$$

As $\sum_{i=1}^{\infty} \mathbb{P}(A_i) = \infty$, we get

$$\limsup_{n \to \infty} \frac{\sum_{i=1}^{n} \sum_{j=1}^{n} \mathbb{P}(A_i \cap A_j)}{(\sum_{i=1}^{n} \mathbb{P}(A_i))^2} \leq 1 + \epsilon. \tag{35}$$

As $\epsilon > 0$ is arbitrary, the sequence (A_k) satisfies the assumptions of Lemma 3, so, with probability 1, infinitely many of the events (A_k) occur. Thus, with probability 1 for infinitely many k, $M_{n_k} < l_k$. Observing that $l_k = 2\log(n_k) - \log_3(n_k) + O(1)$, we obtain our lower-upper class result. □

Funding: This research was funded by TU Wien Bibliothek for financial support through its Open Access Funding Programme.

Institutional Review Board Statement: Not applicable.

Data Availability Statement: No new data were created or analyzed in this study. Data sharing is not applicable.

Acknowledgments: The author acknowledges TU Wien Bibliothek for financial support through its Open Access Funding Programme.

Conflicts of Interest: The author declares no conflicts of interest.

References

1. Erdős, P.; Rényi, A. On a new law of large numbers. *J. Anal. Math.* **1970**, *23*, 103–111. [CrossRef]
2. Erdős, P.; Révész, P. On the length of the longest head-run. In *Topics in Information Theory*; Colloquia Mathematica Societatis Jar Bolyai Volume 16; Ciszár, I., Elias, P., Eds.; North-Holland: Amsterdam, The Netherlands, 1977; pp. 219–228.
3. Arratia, R.; Waterman, S. An Erdős-Rényi law with shifts. *Adv. Math.* **1985**, *55*, 13–23. [CrossRef]
4. Móri, T. Large deviation results for waiting times in repeated experiments. *Acta Math. Hung.* **1985**, *45*, 213–221. [CrossRef]
5. Móri, T.; Székely, G. Asymptotic independence of pure head stopping times. *Stat. Probab. Lett.* **1984**, *2*, 5–8. [CrossRef]
6. Móri, T. On the waiting time till each of some given patterns occurs as a run. *Probab. Theory Relat. Fields* **1991**, *87*, 313–3 [CrossRef]

entropy

MDPI

rticle

wo Monotonicity Results for Beta Distribution Functions

urt Hornik

Institute for Statistics and Mathematics, WU Wirtschaftsuniversität Wien, Welthandelsplatz 1, A-1020 Wien, Austria; kurt.hornik@wu.ac.at

Abstract: Write $\text{pbeta}(\cdot, \alpha, \beta)$ for the distribution function of the Beta distribution with parameters α and β. We show that $\alpha \mapsto \text{pbeta}(\alpha/(\alpha+\beta), \alpha, \beta)$ is decreasing and $\alpha \mapsto \text{pbeta}(\alpha/(\alpha+\beta), \alpha+1, \beta)$ is increasing over the positive reals, with the common limit for $\alpha \to \infty$ expressible in terms of the Gamma distribution functions, and discuss implications for the distribution functions of the Gamma, Poisson and Binomial distributions.

Keywords: Beta distribution; Gamma distribution; monotonicity

1. Introduction

Write $\text{Gamma}(\alpha)$ and $\text{Beta}(\alpha, \beta)$ for, respectively, the Gamma distribution with shape parameter α and rate/scale parameter 1 and the Beta distribution with parameters α and β, and write $\text{pgamma}(\cdot, \alpha)$ and $\text{pbeta}(\cdot, \alpha, \beta)$ for the corresponding cumulative distribution functions.

If $X_\alpha \sim \text{Gamma}(\alpha)$, $\mathbb{E}(X_\alpha/\alpha) = 1$. Using the addition theorem for the Gamma distribution, as $\alpha \to \infty$, we have $X_\alpha/\alpha \to 1$ by the law of large numbers and $\mathbb{P}(X_\alpha/\alpha \le 1) = \text{pgamma}(\alpha, \alpha) \to 1/2$ by the central limit theorem. On the other hand, using integration by parts, for $\epsilon > 0$ we have

$$\mathbb{P}(X_\alpha/\alpha > \epsilon) = \frac{1}{\Gamma(\alpha)} \int_{\epsilon\alpha}^{\infty} t^{\alpha-1} e^{-t}\, dt = \frac{1}{\Gamma(\alpha+1)} \int_{\epsilon\alpha}^{\infty} t^{\alpha} e^{-t}\, dt - \frac{(\epsilon\alpha)^\alpha e^{-\epsilon\alpha}}{\Gamma(\alpha+1)}$$

so that as $\alpha \to 0+$

$$\mathbb{P}(X_\alpha/\alpha > \epsilon) \to \frac{1}{\Gamma(1)} \int_0^\infty e^{-x}\, dx - 1 = 0$$

and hence, in particular, $\mathbb{P}(X_\alpha/\alpha \le 1) = \text{pgamma}(\alpha, \alpha) \to 1$.

Write

$$\pi_\alpha = \mathbb{P}(X_\alpha/\alpha \le 1), \qquad X_\alpha \sim \text{Gamma}(\alpha).$$

Ref. [1] shows that $\alpha \mapsto \pi_\alpha = \text{pgamma}(\alpha, \alpha)$ decreases monotonically from 1 to 1/2 as α varies from 0 to ∞. In this paper, we show that, quite remarkably, monotonicity continues to hold if 1 is replaced by the normalized Gamma distributed random variable X_β/β independent of X_α/α. We also establish a second, related monotonicity result. These results are formulated and discussed in Section 2. Section 3 gives the proofs.

2. Results

Theorem 1. *For $\alpha, \beta > 0$, let $X_\alpha \sim \text{Gamma}(\alpha)$ be independent from $X_\beta \sim \text{Gamma}(\beta)$ and let $Y_{\alpha,\beta} \sim \text{Beta}(\alpha, \beta)$ so that $\mathbb{E}(Y_{\alpha,\beta}) = \alpha/(\alpha+\beta)$. Write*

$$p_{\alpha,\beta} = \mathbb{P}(X_\alpha/\alpha \le X_\beta/\beta).$$

Then

$$p_{\alpha,\beta} = \mathbb{P}(Y_{\alpha,\beta} \le \mathbb{E}(Y_{\alpha,\beta})) = \text{pbeta}\left(\frac{\alpha}{\alpha+\beta}, \alpha, \beta\right),$$

the function $\alpha \mapsto p_{\alpha,\beta}$ *is decreasing for* $\alpha > 0$, *with limits 1 for* $\alpha \to 0+$ *and* $1 - \text{pgamma}(\beta, \beta) < 1/2$ *for* $\alpha \to \infty$, *and the function* $\beta \mapsto p_{\alpha,\beta}$ *is increasing for* $\beta > 0$, *with limits 0 for* $\beta \to 0+$ *and* $\text{pgamma}(\alpha, \alpha) > 1/2$ *as* $\beta \to \infty$.

The above can also be formulated in terms of the Beta prime and F distributions, noting that trivially

$$p_{\alpha,\beta} = \mathbb{P}\left(\frac{X_\alpha}{X_\beta} \leq \frac{\alpha}{\beta}\right) = \mathbb{P}\left(\frac{X_\alpha/\alpha}{X_\beta/\beta} \leq 1\right)$$

where X_α/X_β has a Beta prime distribution with parameters α and β, and $(X_\alpha/\alpha)/(X_\beta/\beta)$ has an F distribution with parameters $\alpha/2$ and $\beta/2$. Note also that for $\beta \to \infty$, $X_\beta/\beta \to 1$ in probability and, thus, $p_{\alpha,\beta} \to \mathbb{P}(X_\alpha \leq \alpha) = \text{pgamma}(\alpha, \alpha)$, so Theorem 1 implies the result of [1].

Refs. [2,3] show that $\text{pbeta}(\alpha/(\alpha+\beta), \alpha+1, \beta) < 1/2$ for, respectively, all positive integers or all positive reals α, β. The following substantially improves these results:

Theorem 2. *Let* $\beta > 0$. *The function*

$$\alpha \mapsto \tilde{p}_{\alpha,\beta} = \text{pbeta}\left(\frac{\alpha}{\alpha+\beta}, \alpha+1, \beta\right)$$

is increasing for $\alpha > 0$, *with limits 0 for* $\alpha \to 0+$ *and* $1 - \text{pgamma}(\beta, \beta)$ *for* $\alpha \to \infty$.

If we write $\text{pbinom}(\cdot, n, p)$ for the cumulative distribution function of the Binomial distribution with parameters n and p, then for integer $0 \leq k \leq n$ we have

$$\text{pbinom}(k, n, p) = \text{pbeta}(1-p, n-k, k+1).$$

Using Theorem 1 with $\alpha = n - k$, $\beta = k + 1$ and $1 - p = \alpha/(\alpha+\beta) = (n-k)/(n+1)$, we obtain for integer $0 \leq k < n$

$$\text{pbinom}\left(k, n, \frac{k+1}{n+1}\right) \geq 1 - \text{pgamma}(k, k).$$

Similarly, using Theorem 2 with $\alpha + 1 = n - k$, $\beta = k + 1$ and $1 - p = \alpha/(\alpha+\beta) = (n-k-1)/n$, we obtain for integer $0 \leq k < n - 1$

$$\text{pbinom}\left(k, n, \frac{k+1}{n}\right) \leq 1 - \text{pgamma}(k, k).$$

If $X_{\alpha+1} \sim \text{Gamma}(\alpha+1)$ is independent from $X_\beta \sim \text{Gamma}(\beta)$, $X_{\alpha+1}/(X_{\alpha+1} + X_\beta) \sim \text{Beta}(\alpha+1, \beta)$, so that

$$\text{pbeta}\left(\frac{\alpha}{\alpha+\beta}, \alpha+1, \beta\right) = \mathbb{P}\left(\frac{X_{\alpha+1}}{X_{\alpha+1} + X_\beta} \leq \frac{\alpha}{\alpha+\beta}\right) = \mathbb{P}\left(X_{\alpha+1} \leq \alpha\frac{X_\beta}{\beta}\right).$$

For $\beta \to \infty$, $X_\beta/\beta \to 1$ in probability, so Theorem 2 yields the following:

Corollary 1. *The function* $\alpha \mapsto \text{pgamma}(\alpha, \alpha+1)$ *is increasing for* $\alpha > 0$, *with limits of 0 for* $\alpha \to 0+$ *and* $1/2$ *for* $\alpha \to \infty$.

In combination with [1] (or using Theorem 1 with $\beta \to \infty$), we, thus, find that the median m_α of $\text{Gamma}(\alpha)$ satisfies $\alpha - 1 < m_\alpha < \alpha$, where the lower bound is worse than the sharp lower bound $m_\alpha > \alpha - 1/3$ of [4].

If we write $\text{ppois}(\cdot,\lambda)$ for the cumulative distribution function of the Poisson distribution with parameter λ, then for the integer $n \geq 0$ we have

$$\text{ppois}(n,\lambda) = 1 - \text{pgamma}(\lambda, n+1).$$

From Corollary 1, we, thus, find that $n \mapsto \text{ppois}(n,n) = 1 - \text{pgamma}(n, n+1)$ is decreasing from 1 to 1/2 as n varies over the non-negative integers, nicely extending the bounds of [5] in the integer case. We note that $\lambda \mapsto \text{ppois}(\lambda,\lambda)$ is not monotone: it jumps at the positive integers, and for $n \leq \lambda < n+1$

$$\text{ppois}(\lambda,\lambda) = \text{ppois}(n,\lambda) = 1 - \text{pgamma}(\lambda, n+1)$$

which decreases from $\text{ppois}(n,n)$ to $\text{ppois}(n+1,n) = 1 - \text{pgamma}(n+1,n+1)$, where we just obtained that the former upper envelope sequence is decreasing in n, and based on the result of [1], the latter lower envelope sequence is increasing in n (with common limit 1/2 as $n \to \infty$).

Clearly, Theorem 2 is equivalent to

$$\alpha \mapsto \text{pbeta}\left(\frac{\alpha-1}{\alpha+\beta-1}, \alpha, \beta\right)$$

increasing for $\alpha > 1$ (it is zero for $0 < \alpha \leq 1$), where, in fact, $(\alpha-1)/(\alpha+\beta-1)$ is the *harmonic mean* of the Beta distribution with parameters α and β. Thus, if for $\alpha > \max(u,0)$ and $\beta > 0$, we write

$$p_{\alpha,\beta,u} = \text{pbeta}\left(\frac{\alpha-u}{\alpha+\beta-u}, \alpha, \beta\right),$$

and our results say that $\alpha \mapsto p_{\alpha,\beta,0}$ is decreasing, and $\alpha \mapsto p_{\alpha,\beta,1}$ is increasing, and we can ask about the monotonicity for other values of u. Numerical experiments suggest that for $\beta > 1$, $\alpha \mapsto p_{\alpha,\beta,u}$ is decreasing iff $u \leq 1/3$ and increasing iff $u \geq 0.5$, but we have thus far been unable to obtain rigorous monotonicity results for $u \notin \{0,1\}$. We also note also that for $u = 1$, we find that for $\alpha > 1$, the median $m_{\alpha,\beta}$ of the Beta distribution with parameters α and β satisfies $m_{\alpha,\beta} > (\alpha-1)/(\alpha+\beta-1)$, which for $\alpha < \beta$ is worse than the lower bound $m_{\alpha,\beta} > (\alpha-1)/(\alpha+\beta-2)$ of [6]. This suggests the importance of more generally investigating the monotonicity of $\alpha \mapsto p_{\alpha,\beta,u,v} = \text{pbeta}((\alpha-u)/(\alpha+\beta-v), \alpha, \beta)$. For $v = 2u$, this includes the bounds in [6] and the approximations suggested in [7], and it conveniently allows using $p_{\alpha,\beta,u,2u} = 1 - p_{\beta,\alpha,u,2u}$ to obtain monotonicity in β from the monotonicity in α.

3. Proofs

We first establish several lemmas. We write that

$$g_{\alpha,\beta} = \left.\frac{x^\alpha(1-x)^\beta}{\alpha B(\alpha,\beta)}\right|_{x=\frac{\alpha}{\alpha+\beta}} = \frac{\alpha^{\alpha-1}\beta^\beta}{B(\alpha,\beta)(\alpha+\beta)^{\alpha+\beta}}$$

Lemma 1. *Let $\alpha, \beta > 0$. Then,*

$$\text{pbeta}\left(\frac{\alpha}{\alpha+\beta}, \alpha, \beta\right) = \text{pbeta}\left(\frac{\alpha}{\alpha+\beta}, \alpha+1, \beta\right) + g_{\alpha,\beta}.$$

Proof. Immediate from Equation 8.17.20 (http://dlmf.nist.gov/8.17.E20, accessed on 28 October 2024) in [8]. □

Lemma 2. *Let $\beta > 0$. Then, $\alpha \mapsto g_{\alpha,\beta}$ is decreasing and positive for $\alpha > 0$.*

Proof. Positivity is trivial. As

$$g_{\alpha,\beta} = \frac{\beta^\beta}{\Gamma(\beta)} \frac{\Gamma(\alpha+\beta)}{\Gamma(\alpha)} \frac{\alpha^{\alpha-1}}{(\alpha+\beta)^{\alpha+\beta}},$$

we have

$$\frac{\partial \log(g_{\alpha,\beta})}{\partial \alpha} = \psi(\alpha+\beta) - \psi(\alpha) + \log(\alpha) - \frac{1}{\alpha} - \log(\alpha+\beta),$$

where $\psi(z) = (\log(\Gamma(z)))' = \Gamma'(z)/\Gamma(z)$ is the psi (or digamma) function (e.g., Equation 5.2.2 (https://dlmf.nist.gov/5.2.E2, accessed on 28 October 2024) in [8]). Using Equation 5.9.13 (http://dlmf.nist.gov/5.9.E13, accessed on 28 October 2024) in [8], for $\Re(z) > 0$, we find that

$$\psi(z) - \log(z) = \int_0^\infty \left(\frac{1}{t} - \frac{1}{1-e^{-t}}\right) e^{-zt}\, dt,$$

so that

$$\begin{aligned}
\frac{\partial \log(g_{\alpha,\beta})}{\partial \alpha} &= \int_0^\infty \left(\frac{1}{t} - \frac{1}{1-e^{-t}}\right)(e^{-(\alpha+\beta)t} - e^{-\alpha t})\, dt - \frac{1}{\alpha} \\
&= \int_0^\infty \left(\frac{1}{t} - \frac{1}{1-e^{-t}}\right)(e^{-\beta t} - 1)e^{-\alpha t}\, dt - \int_0^\infty e^{-\alpha t}\, dt \\
&= \int_0^\infty \left(\left(\frac{1}{t} - \frac{1}{1-e^{-t}}\right)(e^{-\beta t} - 1) - 1\right) e^{-\alpha t}\, dt \\
&= \int_0^\infty (k(t)(1-e^{-\beta t}) - 1)e^{-\alpha t}\, dt,
\end{aligned}$$

where

$$k(t) = \frac{1}{1-e^{-t}} - \frac{1}{t}$$

has the derivative

$$k'(t) = -\frac{e^{-t}}{(1-e^{-t})^2} + \frac{1}{t^2} = \frac{-t^2e^{-t} + (1-e^{-t})^2}{t^2(1-e^{-t})^2}$$

with

$$-t^2e^{-t} + (1-e^{-t})^2 = 1 - 2e^{-t} + e^{-2t} - t^2e^{-t} = e^{-t}(e^t - (2+t^2) + e^{-t}) > 0$$

for $t > 0$. Hence, for all $t > 0$, k is increasing, from which first $k(t) < k(\infty) = 1$ and then $k(t)(1-e^{-\beta t}) - 1 < 1 - 1 = 0$ are derived. This in turn shows that $\log(g_{\alpha,\beta})$ and, hence, $g_{\alpha,\beta}$ are decreasing for $\alpha > 0$. □

Lemma 3. *Let $\alpha, \beta > 0$. Then,*

$$\begin{aligned}
&\text{pbeta}\left(\frac{\alpha+1}{\alpha+\beta+1}, \alpha+1, \beta\right) - \text{pbeta}\left(\frac{\alpha}{\alpha+\beta}, \alpha+1, \beta\right) \\
&= \frac{1}{B(\alpha+1,\beta)} \int_0^1 \frac{(\alpha+v)^\alpha \beta^\beta}{(\alpha+\beta+v)^{\alpha+\beta+1}}\, dv \\
&= g_{\alpha+1,\beta} \int_0^1 \left(\frac{\alpha+v}{\alpha+1}\right)^\alpha \left(\frac{\alpha+\beta+1}{\alpha+\beta+v}\right)^{\alpha+\beta+1} dv \\
&= g_{\alpha,\beta} \int_0^1 \left(\frac{\alpha+v}{\alpha}\right)^\alpha \left(\frac{\alpha+\beta}{\alpha+\beta+v}\right)^{\alpha+\beta+1} dv.
\end{aligned}$$

Proof. We have

$$\begin{aligned}
&\text{pbeta}\left(\frac{\alpha+1}{\alpha+\beta+1},\alpha+1,\beta\right)-\text{pbeta}\left(\frac{\alpha}{\alpha+\beta},\alpha+1,\beta\right)\\
&= \frac{1}{B(\alpha+1,\beta)}\int_{\frac{\alpha}{\alpha+\beta}}^{\frac{\alpha+1}{\alpha+1+\beta}} t^{\alpha}(1-t)^{\beta-1}\,dt.
\end{aligned}$$

Substituting $t=u/(1+u)$ so that $1-t=1/(1+u)$ and $dt=du/(1+u)^2$ and then $u=(\alpha+v)/\beta$,

$$\begin{aligned}
\int_{\frac{\alpha}{\alpha+\beta}}^{\frac{\alpha+1}{\alpha+1+\beta}} t^{\alpha}(1-t)^{\beta-1}\,dt &= \int_{\frac{\alpha}{\beta}}^{\frac{\alpha+1}{\beta}} \frac{u^{\alpha}}{(1+u)^{\alpha+\beta+1}}\,du\\
&= \frac{1}{\beta}\int_0^1 \left(\frac{\alpha+v}{\beta}\right)^{\alpha}\left(\frac{\beta}{\beta+\alpha+v}\right)^{\alpha+\beta+1}\\
&= \int_0^1 \frac{(\alpha+v)^{\alpha}\beta^{\beta}}{(\alpha+\beta+v)^{\alpha+\beta+1}}\,dv
\end{aligned}$$

from which the first equality follows. The second is immediate, and the third obtained from

$$g_{\alpha,\beta}=\frac{\alpha^{\alpha}\beta^{\beta}}{(\alpha+\beta)^{\alpha+\beta}}\frac{1}{\alpha B(\alpha,\beta)}=\frac{\alpha^{\alpha}\beta^{\beta}}{(\alpha+\beta)^{\alpha+\beta+1}}\frac{1}{B(\alpha+1,\beta)}.$$

□

Write

$$h_{\alpha,\beta}=1-\int_0^1\left(\frac{\alpha+v}{\alpha}\right)^{\alpha}\left(\frac{\alpha+\beta}{\alpha+\beta+v}\right)^{\alpha+\beta+1}dv.$$

Lemma 4. *Let $\beta>0$. Then, $\alpha\mapsto h_{\alpha,\beta}$ is decreasing and positive for $\alpha>0$.*

Proof. We write

$$h_{\alpha,\beta}=1-\int_0^1 k_{\alpha,\beta}(v)\,dv,\qquad k_{\alpha,\beta}(v)=\left(\frac{\alpha+v}{\alpha}\right)^{\alpha}\left(\frac{\alpha+\beta}{\alpha+\beta+v}\right)^{\alpha+\beta+1}.$$

Then,

$$\log(k_{\alpha,\beta}(v))=\alpha\log\frac{\alpha+v}{\alpha}+(\alpha+\beta+1)\log\frac{\alpha+\beta}{\alpha+\beta+v}$$

and, hence,

$$\begin{aligned}
\frac{\partial\log(k_{\alpha,\beta}(v))}{\partial\alpha} &= \log\frac{\alpha+v}{\alpha}+\alpha\left(\frac{1}{\alpha+v}-\frac{1}{\alpha}\right)\\
&\quad+\log\frac{\alpha+\beta}{\alpha+\beta+v}+(\alpha+\beta+1)\left(\frac{1}{\alpha+\beta}-\frac{1}{\alpha+\beta+v}\right).
\end{aligned}$$

As a function of v, this has the derivative

$$\begin{aligned}
\frac{\partial}{\partial v}\frac{\partial\log(k_{\alpha,\beta}(v))}{\partial\alpha} &= \frac{1}{\alpha+v}-\frac{\alpha}{(\alpha+v)^2}-\frac{1}{\alpha+\beta+v}+\frac{\alpha+\beta+1}{(\alpha+\beta+v)^2}\\
&= \frac{v}{(\alpha+v)^2}+\frac{1-v}{(\alpha+\beta+v)^2}
\end{aligned}$$

which is positive for $0<v<1$. Hence, for $\alpha,\beta>0$ and $0<v<1$, so

$$\frac{\partial\log(k_{\alpha,\beta}(v))}{\partial\alpha}>\left.\frac{\partial\log(k_{\alpha,\beta}(v))}{\partial\alpha}\right|_{v=0}=0$$

from which we infer that for $\beta > 0$ and $0 < v < 1$, $\alpha \mapsto k_{\alpha,\beta}(v)$ is increasing for $\alpha > 0$, which in turn yields that $\alpha \mapsto h_{\alpha,\beta}$ is decreasing for $\alpha > 0$.

For $\alpha \to \infty$,

$$k_{\alpha,\beta}(v) = \frac{(1+v/\alpha)^{\alpha}}{(1+v/(\alpha+\beta))^{\alpha+\beta+1}} \to \frac{e^v}{e^v} = 1$$

and, hence, $h_{\alpha,\beta} \to h_{\infty,\beta} = 1 - \int_0^1 1\,dv = 0$. Thus, for all $\alpha > 0$, $h_{\alpha,\beta} > h_{\infty,\beta} = 0$, thus completing the proof. □

Lemma 5. *Let $\alpha, \beta > 0$. Then,*

$$p_{\alpha,\beta} = p_{\alpha+1,\beta} + g_{\alpha,\beta} h_{\alpha,\beta}$$

and

$$p_{\alpha,\beta} = p_{\infty,\beta} + \sum_{n=0}^{\infty} g_{\alpha+n,\beta} h_{\alpha+n,\beta}.$$

Proof. Using Lemmas 1 and 3,

$$\begin{aligned}
p_{\alpha,\beta} &= \text{pbeta}\left(\frac{\alpha}{\alpha+\beta}, \alpha, \beta\right) \\
&= \text{pbeta}\left(\frac{\alpha}{\alpha+\beta}, \alpha+1, \beta\right) + g_{\alpha,\beta} \\
&= \text{pbeta}\left(\frac{\alpha+1}{\alpha+\beta+1}, \alpha+1, \beta\right) + g_{\alpha,\beta} \\
&\quad -\left(\text{pbeta}\left(\frac{\alpha+1}{\alpha+\beta+1}, \alpha+1, \beta\right) - \text{pbeta}\left(\frac{\alpha}{\alpha+\beta}, \alpha+1, \beta\right)\right) \\
&= p_{\alpha+1,\beta} + g_{\alpha,\beta}\left(1 - \int_0^1 \left(\frac{\alpha+v}{\alpha}\right)^{\alpha} \left(\frac{\alpha+\beta}{\alpha+\beta+v}\right)^{\alpha+\beta+1} dv\right) \\
&= p_{\alpha+1,\beta} + g_{\alpha,\beta} h_{\alpha,\beta},
\end{aligned}$$

from which

$$p_{\alpha,\beta} = p_{\infty,\beta} + \sum_{n=0}^{\infty} (p_{\alpha+n,\beta} - p_{\alpha+n+1,\beta}) = p_{\infty,\beta} + \sum_{n=0}^{\infty} g_{\alpha+n,\beta} h_{\alpha+n,\beta}$$

as asserted. □

Proof of Theorem 1. As $x \mapsto t(x) = x/(1+x)$ increases monotonically from 0 to 1 as x varies from 0 to ∞, and $t(u/v) = u/(u+v)$,

$$p_{\alpha,\beta} = \mathbb{P}(t(X_\alpha/X_\beta) \leq t(\alpha/\beta)) = \mathbb{P}\left(\frac{X_\alpha}{X_\alpha + X_\beta} \leq \frac{\alpha}{\alpha+\beta}\right)$$

where $Y_{\alpha,\beta} = X_\alpha/(X_\alpha + X_\beta) \sim \text{Beta}(\alpha, \beta)$ has the mean $\mathbb{E}(Y_{\alpha,\beta}) = \alpha/(\alpha+\beta)$, so that $p_{\alpha,\beta} = \text{pbeta}(\alpha/(\alpha+\beta), \alpha, \beta)$.

Combining Lemmas 2, 4 and 5, we see that $\alpha \mapsto p_{\alpha,\beta}$ is decreasing for $\alpha > 0$. To determine the limits, remember that if $X_\alpha \sim \text{Gamma}(\alpha)$, then X_α/α goes to 0 in probability as $\alpha \to 0+$ and to 1 as $\alpha \to \infty$. Hence,

$$p_{\alpha,\beta} = \mathbb{P}\left(\frac{X_\alpha}{\alpha} \leq \frac{X_\beta}{\beta}\right)$$

goes to $\mathbb{P}(0 \leq X_\beta/\beta) = 1$ as $\alpha \to 0+$ and to $\mathbb{P}(1 \leq X_\beta/\beta) = 1 - \text{pgamma}(\beta, \beta)$ as $\alpha \to \infty$.

Finally, $p_{\beta,\alpha} = 1 - p_{\alpha,\beta}$, thus completing the proof. □

We write

$$\tilde{h}_{\alpha,\beta} = \int_0^1 \left(\frac{\alpha+v}{\alpha+1}\right)^{\alpha} \left(\frac{\alpha+\beta+1}{\alpha+\beta+v}\right)^{\alpha+\beta+1} dv - 1.$$

Lemma 6. *Let $\beta > 0$. Then, $\alpha \mapsto \tilde{h}_{\alpha,\beta}$ is decreasing and positive for $\alpha > 0$.*

Proof. This parallels the proof of Lemma 4. We write

$$\tilde{h}_{\alpha,\beta} = \int_0^1 \tilde{k}_{\alpha,\beta}(v)\, dv - 1, \qquad \tilde{k}_{\alpha,\beta}(v) = \left(\frac{\alpha+v}{\alpha+1}\right)^{\alpha} \left(\frac{\alpha+\beta+1}{\alpha+\beta+v}\right)^{\alpha+\beta+1}.$$

Then,

$$\log(\tilde{k}_{\alpha,\beta}(v)) = \alpha \log\frac{\alpha+v}{\alpha+1} + (\alpha+\beta+1)\log\frac{\alpha+\beta+1}{\alpha+\beta+v}$$

and, hence,

$$\begin{aligned} \frac{\partial \log(\tilde{k}_{\alpha,\beta}(v))}{\partial \alpha} &= \log\frac{\alpha+v}{\alpha+1} + \alpha\left(\frac{1}{\alpha+v} - \frac{1}{\alpha+1}\right) \\ &\quad + \log\frac{\alpha+\beta+1}{\alpha+\beta+v} + (\alpha+\beta+1)\left(\frac{1}{\alpha+\beta+1} - \frac{1}{\alpha+\beta+v}\right). \end{aligned}$$

As a function of v, this (again) has the derivative

$$\begin{aligned} \frac{\partial}{\partial v}\frac{\partial \log(\tilde{k}_{\alpha,\beta}(v))}{\partial \alpha} &= \frac{1}{\alpha+v} - \frac{\alpha}{(\alpha+v)^2} - \frac{1}{\alpha+\beta+v} + \frac{\alpha+\beta+1}{(\alpha+\beta+v)^2} \\ &= \frac{v}{(\alpha+v)^2} + \frac{1-v}{(\alpha+\beta+v)^2} \end{aligned}$$

which is positive for $0 < v < 1$. Hence, for $\alpha, \beta > 0$ and $0 < v < 1$,

$$\frac{\partial \log(\tilde{k}_{\alpha,\beta}(v))}{\partial \alpha} < \left.\frac{\partial \log(\tilde{k}_{\alpha,\beta}(v))}{\partial \alpha}\right|_{v=1} = 0$$

from which we infer that for $\beta > 0$ and $0 < v < 1$, $\alpha \mapsto \tilde{k}_{\alpha,\beta}(v)$ is decreasing for $\alpha > 0$, which in turn implies that $\alpha \mapsto \tilde{h}_{\alpha,\beta}$ is decreasing for $\alpha > 0$. Finally, for $\alpha \to \infty$,

$$\tilde{k}_{\alpha,\beta}(v) = \left(\frac{1+v/\alpha}{1+1/\alpha}\right)^{\alpha} \left(\frac{1+1/(\alpha+\beta)}{1+v/(\alpha+\beta)}\right)^{\alpha+\beta+1} \to \frac{e^v}{e}\frac{e}{e^v} = 1$$

and, hence, $\tilde{h}_{\alpha,\beta} \to \tilde{h}_{\infty,\beta} = \int_0^1 1\, dv - 1 = 0$. Thus, for all $\alpha > 0$, $\tilde{h}_{\alpha,\beta} > \tilde{h}_{\infty,\beta} = 0$, thus completing the proof. □

Lemma 7. *Let $\alpha, \beta > 0$. Then,*

$$\tilde{p}_{\alpha,\beta} = \tilde{p}_{\alpha+1,\beta} - g_{\alpha+1,\beta}\tilde{h}_{\alpha,\beta}$$

and

$$\tilde{p}_{\alpha,\beta} = \tilde{p}_{\infty,\beta} - \sum_{n=0}^{\infty} g_{\alpha+n+1,\beta}\tilde{h}_{\alpha+n,\beta}.$$

Proof. Using Lemma 1 (with $\alpha+1$ instead of α) and Lemma 3, we have

$$\begin{aligned}
\tilde{p}_{\alpha,\beta} &= \mathrm{pbeta}\left(\frac{\alpha}{\alpha+\beta}, \alpha+1, \beta\right) \\
&= \mathrm{pbeta}\left(\frac{\alpha+1}{\alpha+1+\beta}, \alpha+1, \beta\right) \\
&\quad -\left(\mathrm{pbeta}\left(\frac{\alpha+1}{\alpha+\beta+1}, \alpha+1, \beta\right) - \mathrm{pbeta}\left(\frac{\alpha}{\alpha+\beta}, \alpha+1, \beta\right)\right) \\
&= \mathrm{pbeta}\left(\frac{\alpha+1}{\alpha+1+\beta}, \alpha+2, \beta\right) + g_{\alpha+1,\beta} \\
&\quad - g_{\alpha+1,\beta} \int_0^1 \left(\frac{\alpha+v}{\alpha+1}\right)^{\alpha} \left(\frac{\alpha+\beta+1}{\alpha+\beta+v}\right)^{\alpha+\beta+1} dv \\
&= \tilde{p}_{\alpha+1,\beta} - g_{\alpha+1,\beta}\tilde{h}_{\alpha,\beta}.
\end{aligned}$$

The second assertion again follows by taking telescope sums. □

Proof of Theorem 2. Combining Lemmas 2, 6 and 7, we see that $\alpha \mapsto \tilde{p}_{\alpha,\beta}$ is increasing for $\alpha > 0$. The limits are immediate from (the proof of) Theorem 1. □

Funding: This research received no external funding.

Institutional Review Board Statement: Not applicable.

Data Availability Statement: The original contributions presented in the study are included in the article, further inquiries can be directed to the corresponding author.

Conflicts of Interest: The author declares no conflicts of interest.

References

1. Letac, G.; Paine, T. A Monotonic Function. *Am. Math. Mon.* **1992**, *99*, 468–472. [CrossRef]
2. Vietoris, L. Über gewisse die unvollständige Betafunktion betreffende Ungleichungen. *Sitzungsberichte Derösterreischischen Ak Wiss. Abt. II* **1982**, *191*, 85–95.
3. Raab, W. Die Ungleichungen von Vietoris. *Monatshefte Math.* **1984**, *98*, 311–322. [CrossRef]
4. Chen, J.; Rubin, H. Bounds for the Difference between Median and Mean of Gamma and Poisson Distributions. *Stat. Probab. L* **1986**, *4*, 281–283. [CrossRef]
5. Teicher, H. An Inequality on Poisson Probabilities. *Ann. Math. Stat.* **1955**, *26*, 147–149. [CrossRef]
6. Payton, M.E.; Young, L.J.; Young, J.H. Bounds for the Difference Between Median and Mean of Beta and Negative Binom Distributions. *Metrika* **1989**, *36*, 347–354. [CrossRef]
7. Kerman, J. A closed-form approximation for the median of the Beta distribution. *arXiv* **2011**, arXiv:1111.0433. [CrossRef]
8. Olver, F.W.J.; Daalhuis, A.B.O.; Lozier, D.W.; Schneider, B.I.; Boisvert, R.F.; Clark, C.W.; Miller, B.R.; Saunders, B.V.; Cohl, H. McClain, M.A. (Eds.) NIST Digital Library of Mathematical Functions. Release 1.2.2 of 15 September 2024. 2024. Available onli https://dlmf.nist.gov/ (accessed on 28 October 2024).

entropy

MDPI

Article

Occupation Times on the Legs of a Diffusion Spider

Paavo Salminen [1,*] and David Stenlund [2]

[1] Faculty of Science and Engineering, Åbo Akademi University, 20500 Åbo, Finland
[2] Department of Mathematics, University of British Columbia, Vancouver, BC V6T 1Z2, Canada; stenlund@math.ubc.ca
* Correspondence: paavo.salminen@abo.fi

Abstract: We study the joint moments of occupation times on the legs of a diffusion spider. Specifically, we give a recursive formula for the Laplace transform of the joint moments, which extends earlier results for a one-dimensional diffusion. For a Bessel spider, of which the Brownian spider is a special case, our approach yields an explicit formula for the joint moments of the occupation times.

Keywords: diffusions on graphs; Walsh's Brownian motion; Green's function; resolvent; Kac's moment formula; additive functional; moment generating function

MSC: 60J60; 60J55; 60J65; 05A10

1. Introduction

When trying to understand and quantify the behavior of a stochastic process, we are often faced with analyzing various functionals of the process. Such functionals include first passage times to subsets of the state space, maximum (minimum) value up to random/fixed times, and occupation times in subsets. The first question is, of course, whether it is possible to find the distribution of the functional. Unfortunately, this is often not possible, or the expression is too complicated to have any practical value. In some cases, the Laplace transform of the distribution is more tractable for further studies than the distribution itself. In addition, the moments of the distribution often determine the distribution uniquely via a series expansion. Hence, being able to calculate the moments is a good contribution in many respects. In this paper, we study the moments of occupation time functionals for a family of stochastic processes that we call diffusion spiders. We proceed now to explain intuitively what lies behind this notion, to give references to earlier works, and to indicate some applications.

The process known as Walsh Brownian motion was introduced by J.B. Walsh in 1978 as an extension of the skew Brownian motion. The Walsh Brownian motion lives in $\mathbb{R}^2$, best expressed using polar coordinates. When away from the origin, the angular coordinate stays constant (so the process moves along a line), while the radial distance follows a positive excursion from 0 of a standard Brownian motion. Intuitively and roughly speaking, every time the process reaches the origin, a new angle is randomly selected according to some distribution on $[0, 2\pi)$. This process was brilliantly described by Walsh in the following way [1]:

> It is a diffusion which, when away from the origin, is a Brownian motion along a ray, but which has what might be called a roundhouse singularity at the origin: when the process enters it, it, like Stephen Leacock's hero, immediately rides off in all directions at once.

The construction of the Walsh Brownian motion was described in more detail by Barlow, Pitman, and Yor [2]. We also refer to Salisbury [3] and Yano [4].

If the angle is selected according to a discrete distribution, then there are at most countably many rays on which the diffusion lives. The state space of the process then corresponds to a star graph with edges of infinite length, and we call such a graph a spider. Thus, the Walsh Brownian motion can in this case be seen as an early example of a diffusion on a graph, and this process is called a Brownian spider. An example of a spider with five legs is given in Figure 1.

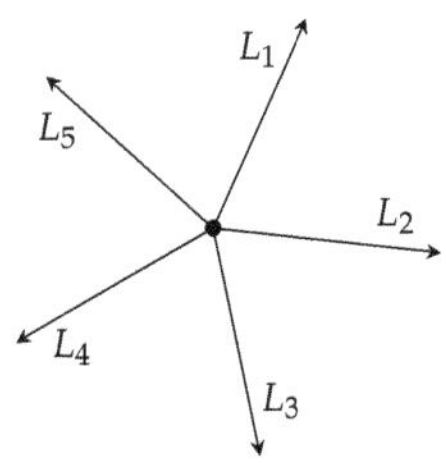

Figure 1. The graph of a diffusion spider with five legs.

To make the diffusion more general, we can relax the requirement that the radial distance follows a Brownian motion and replace it with excursions from 0 of any regular reflected non-negative recurrent one-dimensional diffusion. In this paper, such a process is simply called a diffusion spider, which can also be seen as an abbreviation for "diffusion process on a spider". The focus of this paper is on the occupation times on the legs of a diffusion spider, that is, the amount of time that the process is located on the different legs up to a given (fixed or random) time. If the underlying diffusion is not recurrent, we could in principle still study occupation times on the legs of the spider, but the problem loses much of its interest if the process at some point is located on a single leg without ever returning to the origin. For this reason, we only consider recurrent diffusions here.

Diffusions on graphs have been subjected to intensive research at least since the pioneering work by Freidlin and Wentzell [5]. We refer to Weber [6] for earlier references, but also for a study in the direction of our paper. In addition to [1,2,7] concerning diffusions on spiders, we recall, in particular, the papers by Papanicolaou, Papageorgiou, and Lepipas [8], Vakeroudis and Yor [9], Fitzsimmons and Kuter [10], Yano [4], Csáki, Csörgő, Földes and Révész [11,12], Ernst [13], Karatzas and Yan [14], Bayraktar and Zhang [15], Lempa, Mordecki and Salminen [16], and Bednarz, Ernst and Osękowski [17].

For results on occupation times and other earlier references, see [4] where the joint law of the occupation times on legs of a diffusion spider (there called a "multiray diffusion") is analyzed via a double Laplace transform formula generalizing the results in [7] for a spider with excursions following a Bessel process. We also refer to [4] for a formula for the density of the joint law. Refs. [8,9] consider the occupation times for a Brownian spider, and [12] focus on limit theorems for local and occupation times for the Brownian spider. One could consider other stochastic processes on a spider as well, such as random walks [11,12] or continuous-time random walks. We leave the treatment of these interesting topics for eventual future work; however, in this paper, we focus on diffusion spiders, since the methods we apply for finding moment formulas do not lend themselves to a similar treatment of discrete or jump processes. A brief overview of the work by Révész et al. on random walks of spiders and Brownian spiders is given in [18].

As mentioned above, a skew diffusion can be seen as a special case of a diffusion spider. Namely, a one-dimensional diffusion which is skew at 0 corresponds to a spider with two legs (the positive and negative half-lines), which moves like its ordinary counterpart away from zero, but whenever it hits 0, it has a certain (skewed) probability of continuing to the positive side next. Due to this close relation, some applications of diffusion spiders can be anticipated by looking at applications of skew diffusions. The skew Brownian motion, in particular, has been used in models for a large number of phenomena, such as population dynamics over a boundary, ecosystems in rivers, pollutants diffusing in rock layers, shock acceleration of charged particles, and brain imaging; references are given by Lejay [19] and Ramirez et al. [20]. See Appuhamillage et al. [21] for results on the joint distribution of occupation and local times and applications in the dispersion of a solute concentration across an interface. Exact simulations of skew Brownian motion are discussed by Lejay and Pichot [22], statistical aspects by Lejay, Mordecki, and Torres [23], and applications in financial mathematics by Alvarez and Salminen [24], Rosello [25], and Hussain et al. [26]. Furthermore, we refer to Dassios and Zhang [27] for results on hitting times of Brownian spiders and, in particular, applications in the banking business. Finally, for an application of the Brownian spider in queueing theory, see Atar and Cohen [28].

This paper is structured as follows: In the next section, some key results from the theory of linear diffusions are presented, which are crucial in order to introduce and understand the notion of a diffusion spider briefly given in this section. We recall the explicit form of the Green function (resolvent density) derived in [16]. From this expression, we can immediately deduce some regularity properties of the Green function that are important in the subsequent analysis. The basic mathematical tool of the paper is an extension of Kac's moment formula discussed in Section 3. The first main result, i.e., a recursive formula for the joint moments of the occupation times on the legs of a diffusion spider, is given in Theorem 3, Section 4. This can be seen as an extension of our previous results for one-dimensional diffusions in [29]. In Section 4, we also present a new formula for the joint Laplace transform of the occupation times, see Theorem 4, and connect this to earlier results by Barlow et al. [7] and Yano [4]. In Section 5, some examples are discussed, and we solve (see Theorem 5) the recursive equation for the joint moments for a Bessel spider—of which the Brownian spider is a special case. This is our third main result. At the end of Section 5, we also briefly return to the original Walsh Brownian motion. The proofs of the main results are given in the Appendices A–E at the end of the paper.

2. Preliminaries

2.1. Linear Diffusions

To make the paper more self-contained, we first recall the basic facts from the theory of linear diffusions needed to introduce the concept of a diffusion spider. Let $X = (X_t)_{t\geq 0}$ be a linear diffusion living on $\mathbb{R}_+ = [0, +\infty)$. Let $\mathbf{P}_x$ denote the probability measure associated with X when initiated at $x \geq 0$. For $y \geq 0$ introduce the first the hitting time via

$$H_y := \inf\{t \geq 0 : X_t = y\}.$$

It is assumed that X is regular and recurrent. Hence, for all $x \geq 0$ and $y \geq 0$ it holds that

$$\mathbf{P}_x(H_y < \infty) = 1.$$

Moreover, we suppose that 0 is a reflecting boundary and $+\infty$ is a natural boundary (for the boundary classification for linear diffusions, see [30,31]). The $\mathbf{P}_x$-distribution of H_y is characterized for $\lambda > 0$ via the Laplace transform

$$\mathbf{E}_x\left(\mathrm{e}^{-\lambda H_y}\right) = \begin{cases} \dfrac{\varphi_\lambda(x)}{\varphi_\lambda(y)}, & x \geq y, \\ \dfrac{\psi_\lambda(x)}{\psi_\lambda(y)}, & x \leq y, \end{cases} \tag{1}$$

where $\mathbf{E}_x$ refers to the expectation operator associated with X and φ_λ (ψ_λ) is a positive, continuous and decreasing (increasing) solution of the generalized differential equation

$$\mathcal{G}u := \frac{d}{dm}\frac{d}{dS}u = \lambda u, \quad \lambda > 0. \tag{2}$$

Here, S and m denote the scale function (strictly increasing and continuous) and the speed measure, respectively, associated with X. Under our assumptions, m is a positive measure. To fix ideas, we also assume that m does not have atoms and that φ_λ and ψ_λ are differentiable with respect to S. Recall that φ_λ and ψ_λ are unique solutions—up to multiplicative constants—of Equation (2) with the stated properties and satisfying the associated boundary conditions. Notice also that $\mathcal{G}$, when operating in an appropriate function space, constitutes the infinitesimal generator of X. We also introduce the diffusion X^∂ with the same speed and scale as X but for which 0 is a killing boundary. For X^∂ there exist functions φ_λ^∂ and ψ_λ^∂ describing the distribution of H_y for X^∂ similarly as is conducted in (1) for X.

Recall that

$$\psi^\partial(0) = 0, \quad \frac{d\psi}{dS}(0+) = 0, \quad \varphi^\partial \equiv \varphi, \tag{3}$$

where the notation is shortened by omitting the subindex λ. Moreover, we normalize, as in [16],

$$S(0) = 0, \quad \psi(0) = \varphi(0) = \varphi^\partial(0) = 1, \quad \text{and} \quad \frac{d\psi^\partial}{dS}(0+) = 1. \tag{4}$$

As is well known, X has a transition density p with respect to m, i.e., for a Borel subset A of $\mathbb{R}_+$,

$$\mathbf{P}_x(X_t \in A) = \int_A p(t;x,y)\, m(dy),$$

and the Green function (resolvent density) is given by

$$\begin{aligned} g_\lambda(x,y) &:= \int_0^\infty \mathrm{e}^{-\lambda t}\, p(t;x,y)\, dt \\ &= \begin{cases} w_\lambda^{-1}\psi(y)\varphi(x), & 0 \leq y \leq x, \\ w_\lambda^{-1}\psi(x)\varphi(y), & 0 \leq x \leq y, \end{cases} \end{aligned} \tag{5}$$

with the Wronskian

$$w_\lambda = \frac{d\psi}{dS}(x)\varphi(x) - \frac{d\varphi}{dS}(x)\psi(x) = -\frac{d\varphi}{dS}(0+).$$

For later use, recall that a diffusion X with starting point $X_0 = 0$ is called self-similar if for any $a > 0$ there exists $b > 0$ such that

$$(X_{at})_{t\geq 0} \overset{(d)}{=} (bX_t)_{t\geq 0}.$$

Perhaps the most well-known example of a self-similar diffusion is a standard Brownian motion starting in 0, for which the above identity holds with $b = \sqrt{a}$.

2.2. Diffusion Spider

Let $\Gamma \subset \mathbb{R}^2$ be a star graph with one vertex at the origin of $\mathbb{R}^2$ and R edges of infinite length meeting in the vertex (see Figure 1 for an example). Here, such a graph is called a spider. The edges $L_1, \ldots, L_R$ of the graph are known as the "rays" or—as hereafter called—the "legs" of the spider. The ordered pair (x, i) describes the point on Γ located on leg L_i $(i = 1, \ldots, R)$ at the distance $x \geq 0$ to the origin. We take the origin to be common to all legs, i.e.,

$$(0,1) = (0,2) = \cdots = (0,R),$$

so for simplicity we just write $\mathbf{0}$ for the origin.

Let X be the linear diffusion introduced above. On the graph Γ we consider a stochastic process $\mathbf{X} := (\mathbf{X}_t)_{t\geq 0}$ using the notation

$$\mathbf{X}_t := (X_t, \rho_t),$$

where $\rho_t \in \{1, 2, \ldots, R\}$ indicates the leg on which $\mathbf{X}_t$ is located at time t and X_t is the distance of $\mathbf{X}_t$ to the origin at time t measured along the leg L_{ρ_t}. On each leg L_i, the process $\mathbf{X}$ behaves like the diffusion X until it hits $\mathbf{0}$. The process $\mathbf{X}$ is called a (homogeneous) diffusion spider. We could allow different diffusions on the different legs (the inhomogeneous case), but do not perform so in this paper. As part of the definition of the process, there are positive real numbers β_i, $i = 1, \ldots, R$, such that $\sum_{i=1}^{R} \beta_i = 1$. When $\mathbf{X}$ hits $\mathbf{0}$, it continues, roughly speaking, with probability β_i onto leg L_i. We do not here discuss the rigorous construction of the process, which can be performed, e.g., applying excursion theory; for this and other approaches, see the references given in the introduction. Notations $\mathbf{P}_{(x,i)}$ and $\mathbf{E}_{(x,i)}$ are used for the probability measure and expectation, respectively, when the diffusion spider starts at point (x, i), that is, on leg number i and at a distance x from the origin. As mentioned above, we write $\mathbf{P}_\mathbf{0}$ and $\mathbf{E}_\mathbf{0}$ without specifying a leg when the starting point is the origin.

For the diffusion spider $\mathbf{X}$, we introduce its Green kernel (also called the resolvent kernel) via

$$\mathbf{G}_\lambda u(x,i) := \int_0^\infty e^{-\lambda t} \mathbf{E}_{(x,i)}(u(\mathbf{X}_t))\, dt,$$

where $(x, i) \in \Gamma$, $\lambda > 0$ and $u\colon \Gamma \to \mathbb{R}$ is a bounded measurable function. Moreover, define

$$\begin{aligned} \mathbf{m}(dx,i) &:= \beta_i m(dx), \quad i = 1, \ldots, R, \qquad \mathbf{m}(\{\mathbf{0}\}) := 0, \\ \mathbf{S}(dx,i) &:= \frac{1}{\beta_i} S(x). \end{aligned} \tag{6}$$

We call $\mathbf{m}$ and $\mathbf{S}$ the speed measure and the scale function, respectively, of $\mathbf{X}$. Clearly, on every leg L_i of the diffusion spider,

$$\frac{d}{d\mathbf{m}} \frac{d}{d\mathbf{S}} = \frac{d}{dm} \frac{d}{dS}.$$

Let $H_0 = \inf\{t \geq 0 : \mathbf{X}_t = \mathbf{0}\}$ be the first hitting time of $\mathbf{0}$ for the diffusion spider $\mathbf{X}$. Since on every leg of the diffusion spider we have, loosely speaking, the same one-dimensional diffusion, for every $i = 1, 2, \ldots, R$ and $x > 0$,

$$\mathbf{E}_{(x,i)}(e^{-\lambda H_0}) = \mathbf{E}_x(e^{-\lambda H_0}) = \varphi_\lambda(x). \tag{7}$$

The following theorem, proved in [16], states an explicit expression for the resolvent density of $\mathbf{X}$.

Theorem 1. *The Green kernel of the diffusion spider* $\mathbf{X}$ *has a density* $\mathbf{g}_\lambda$ *with respect to the speed measure* $\mathbf{m}$*, which is given for* $x \geq 0$ *and* $y \geq 0$ *by*

$$\mathbf{g}_\lambda((x,i),(y,j)) = \begin{cases} \varphi(y)\tilde{\psi}(x,i), & x \leq y,\ i = j, \\ \varphi(x)\tilde{\psi}(y,i), & y \leq x,\ i = j, \\ c_\lambda^{-1}\,\varphi(y)\varphi(x), & i \neq j, \end{cases} \tag{8}$$

where

$$\tilde{\psi}(x,i) := \frac{1}{\beta_i}\psi^\partial(x) + \frac{1}{c_\lambda}\varphi(x) \tag{9}$$

and

$$c_\lambda := -\frac{d}{dS}\varphi(0+) > 0. \tag{10}$$

From the properties of the functions ψ^∂ and φ, we immediately have the following result.

Corollary 1. *The resolvent density (the Green function)* $\mathbf{g}_\lambda$ *given in* (8) *is continuous on* Γ*, and for every i and j,*

$$\lim_{(x,i)\to\mathbf{0}} \mathbf{g}_\lambda((x,i),(y,j)) = \mathbf{g}_\lambda(\mathbf{0},(y,j)) = \frac{1}{c_\lambda}\varphi(y) = g_\lambda(0,y). \tag{11}$$

3. Kac's Moment Formula

The tool that we will use to obtain the recursive expression for the joint moments is an extended variant of the Kac moment formula. Let Y be a regular diffusion taking values on an interval E. In spite of some conflict with our earlier notation, here we also let m, p, and $\mathbf{E}_x$ ($x \in E$) denote the speed measure, the transition density and the expectation operator, respectively, associated with Y. Moreover, let $V : E \mapsto \mathbb{R}$ be a measurable and bounded function and define for $t > 0$ the additive functional

$$A_t(V) := \int_0^t V(Y_s)\,\mathrm{d}s.$$

The moment formula by M. Kac for integral functionals, see [32], i.e.,

$$\mathbf{E}_x((A_t(V))^n) = n\int_E m(\mathrm{d}y)\int_0^t p(s;x,y)V(y)\mathbf{E}_y((A_{t-s}(V))^{n-1})\,\mathrm{d}s,$$

is here extended into the following formula for the expected value of a product of powers of different functionals.

Proposition 1. *Let* $V_1,\ldots,V_N$ *be measurable and bounded functions on E. For* $t > 0$, $x \in E$ *and* $n_1,\ldots,n_N \in \{1,2,\ldots\}$,

$$\mathbf{E}_x\left(\prod_{k=1}^N (A_t(V_k))^{n_k}\right) = \sum_{k=1}^N n_k \int_E m(\mathrm{d}y)\int_0^t p(s;x,y)V_k(y)\mathbf{E}_y\left(\frac{\prod_{i=1}^N (A_{t-s}(V_i))^{n_i}}{A_{t-s}(V_k)}\right)\mathrm{d}s. \tag{12}$$

Proof. See Appendix A. □

The Formula in (12) is instrumental in the derivation of the results in Theorems 3 and 4 presented in Section 4.2.

4. Main Results

Let $(\mathbf{X}_t)_{t\geq 0}$ be a diffusion spider with $R \geq 2$ legs meeting in the point $\mathbf{0}$, and let

$$A_t^{(i)} := \int_0^t \mathbb{1}_{L_i}(X_s)\,\mathrm{d}s$$

be the occupation time on leg number i up to time t. Note that if the underlying diffusion X is self-similar, it follows for any i and any fixed $t \geq 0$ that

$$A_t^{(i)} \overset{(\mathrm{d})}{=} tA_1^{(i)},$$

meaning that for any such diffusion spider, we can equally well consider the occupation time up to time 1 instead of a general (fixed) time t.

Figure 2 shows the radial distance from $\mathbf{0}$ as a function of time in a sample path of a Brownian spider with five legs. The excursions from $\mathbf{0}$ are colored to specify which leg the process is located on.

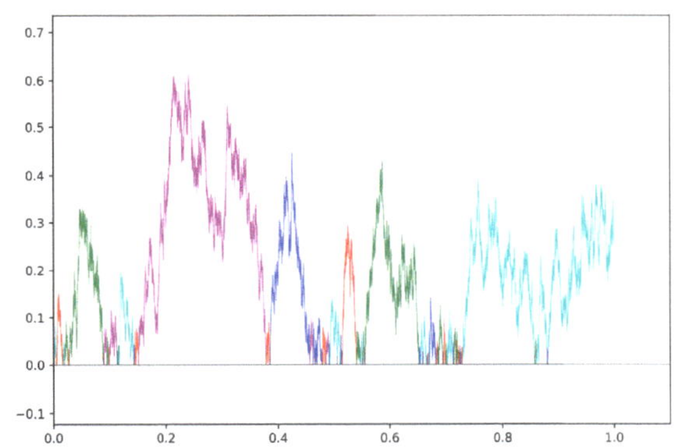

Figure 2. Sample path of the radial distance in a Brownian spider with five legs up to time 1. The five different colors indicate on which leg of the spider the process is located at any given time.

In this section we present formulas for recursively finding the moments of occupation times on the legs of a diffusion spider. In the first and shorter subsection we recapitulate the result for moments of a single occupation time, which is presented in our earlier paper [29]. In the second subsection this result is extended to joint moments of multiple occupation times.

4.1. Moments of the Occupation Time on a Single Leg

As pointed out in Section 6.4 of [29], the occupation time on a single leg L_i of a (homogeneous) diffusion spider has the same law as the occupation time on the positive half-line of a one-dimensional skew diffusion process with the state space $\mathbb{R}$ and with the skewness parameter given by β_i. Namely, the spider is mapped onto $\mathbb{R}$ so that the leg L_i corresponds to the positive half-line $[0, \infty)$, while all other legs are grouped together into a single second leg with parameter $\sum_{k\neq i} \beta_k = 1 - \beta_i$, which then is taken to be the negative half-line $(-\infty, 0]$. When considering the occupation time on the leg L_i; therefore, we can equally well consider the occupation time on $[0, \infty)$ of a one-dimensional diffusion.

The following results are shown in the previous paper [29], although here it is slightly modified to comply with the notation for diffusion spiders introduced in Section 2. In particular, note the differences mentioned in Remark 1.

Theorem 2. *The Laplace transform of the first moment of $A_t^{(i)}$ is given by*

$$\mathcal{L}_t\left\{ \mathbf{E}_0\left(A_t^{(i)}\right) \right\}(\lambda) = \frac{1}{\lambda}\int_0^\infty \mathbf{g}_\lambda(\mathbf{0},(y,i))\beta_i\, m(\mathrm{d}y) \tag{13}$$

and for the higher moments, $n \geq 2$, recursively by

$$\mathcal{L}_t\left\{ \mathbf{E}_0\left((A_t^{(i)})^n\right) \right\}(\lambda) = \sum_{k=1}^{n} \frac{n! D_k^{(i)}(\lambda)}{(n-k)!\lambda^k} \mathcal{L}_t\left\{ \mathbf{E}_0\left((A_t^{(i)})^{n-k}\right) \right\}(\lambda) + \frac{n!}{\lambda^{n-1}} \mathcal{L}_t\left\{ \mathbf{E}_0(A_t^{(i)}) \right\}(\lambda) - \frac{n!}{\lambda^{n+1}} \sum_{k=1}^{n} D_k^{(j)}(\lambda), \tag{14}$$

where $\mathcal{L}_t$ denotes the Laplace transform with respect to t of the function in curly brackets, λ is the Laplace parameter, and

$$D_k^{(i)}(\lambda) := \frac{\lambda^k}{(k-1)!}\int_0^\infty \mathbf{g}_\lambda(\mathbf{0},(y,i))\mathbf{E}_{(y,i)}(H_\mathbf{0}^{k-1}\mathrm{e}^{-\lambda H_\mathbf{0}})\beta_i\, m(\mathrm{d}y). \tag{15}$$

Furthermore, if X is self-similar, then for any $\lambda > 0$,

$$\mathbf{E}_0\left((A_1^{(i)})^n\right) = \mathbf{E}_0\left(A_1^{(i)}\right) - \sum_{k=1}^{n} D_k^{(i)}(\lambda)\left(1 - \mathbf{E}_0\left((A_1^{(i)})^{n-k}\right)\right), \tag{16}$$

and, in particular, $D_k^{(i)}(\lambda)$ does not depend on λ for any $i = 1,\ldots,R$ and $k = 1,2,\ldots$.

The proof is given in [29] (Theorem 2) with some minor notational differences.

Remark 1. *Note the following:*

1. *The one-dimensional diffusion X on $\mathbb{R}$ with speed measure m, in the setting of the other paper [29], here really corresponds to a two-legged diffusion spider $\mathbf{X}$ with speed measure $\mathbf{m}$, which is why $m(dx)$ has been replaced by $\beta_i m(dx)$ in* (13) *and* (15)*, in accordance with* (6).
2. *There is a sign change in the factor $D_k^{(i)}(\lambda)$ as defined in* (15) *compared to the corresponding expression in [29].*
3. *The variable λ is not at all present on the left hand side of* (16)*, and (using induction) we conclude that the factors $D_k^{(i)}(\lambda)$ cannot depend on λ either. Thus, the value $\lambda > 0$ can be chosen arbitrarily. As a side note, this is the reason why a factor λ^k is included in the expression for $D_k^{(i)}(\lambda)$ in* (15).

4.2. Joint Moments

The result in the previous section (from [29]) is here extended to a recursive formula for the Laplace transforms of the joint moments of the occupation times on multiple legs of a diffusion spider. For self-similar spiders we have a recursive formula directly for the joint moments, as in the case of the occupation time on one leg, cf. (16) in Theorem 2.

Theorem 3. *For $r \in \{2,\ldots,R\}$ and $n_1,\ldots,n_r \geq 1$,*

$$\mathcal{L}_t\left\{ \mathbf{E}_0\left(\prod_{i=1}^{r}(A_t^{(i)})^{n_i}\right) \right\}(\lambda) = \sum_{i=1}^{r}\sum_{k=1}^{n_i} \frac{n_i! D_k^{(i)}(\lambda)}{(n_i-k)!\lambda^k} \mathcal{L}_t\left\{ \mathbf{E}_0\left(\frac{\prod_{j=1}^{r}(A_t^{(j)})^{n_j}}{(A_t^{(i)})^k}\right) \right\}(\lambda), \tag{17}$$

where $D_k^{(i)}$ *is defined in* (15). *If X is self-similar, then for any* $\lambda > 0$,

$$\mathbf{E}_0\left(\prod_{i=1}^{r}(A_1^{(i)})^{n_i}\right) = \sum_{i=1}^{r}\sum_{k=1}^{n_i} \frac{\binom{n_i}{k}}{\binom{n_1+\ldots+n_r}{k}} D_k^{(i)}(\lambda)\mathbf{E}_0\left(\frac{\prod_{j=1}^{r}(A_1^{(j)})^{n_j}}{(A_1^{(i)})^k}\right). \tag{18}$$

Proof. See Appendix B. □

Remark 2. *Despite the similarity, Theorem 2 does not follow by letting* $r = 1$ *in Theorem 3. On the right-hand sides of equations* (14) *and* (16) *are not only the respective parts corresponding to* (17) *and* (18) *with* $r = 1$, *but also some additional terms. This difference seems to originate from the fact that up to the first hitting time of* $\mathbf{0}$, *the occupation time on the starting leg is equal to the elapsed time (and, hence, positive), while the occupation time on any other leg is zero. Therefore, any product of occupation times on more than one leg is also zero up to time* H_0, *as can be seen in* (A2), *and even though we let the starting point tend to* $\mathbf{0}$ *when deriving the aforementioned theorems, there remains still a component which is nonzero in the case of a single leg but zero for the joint moments. With this in mind, Theorem 3 should not be seen as a replacement of Theorem 2 but as a complement to it.*

The result in Theorem 3 tells us that if we know the Green kernel of the diffusion spider **X**, we can recursively compute any joint moments of the occupation times on a number of legs. Recall also from (7) that for $y > 0$

$$\mathbf{E}_{(y,i)}\left(H_0^k \mathrm{e}^{-\lambda H_0}\right) = \mathbf{E}_y\left(H_0^k \mathrm{e}^{-\lambda H_0}\right) = (-1)^k \frac{\mathrm{d}^k}{\mathrm{d}\lambda^k}\varphi_\lambda(y),$$

i.e., we have all the ingredients needed to calculate the factors $D_k^{(i)}$ using the integral expression in (15).

The generalized version of Kac's moment formula in Proposition 1 is now used to derive a moment generating function of the occupation times on the legs of a diffusion spider up to an exponential time T.

Theorem 4. *Let* T *be exponentially distributed with mean* $1/\lambda$, $\lambda > 0$, *and independent of* **X**. *Then, for any* $z_1, \ldots, z_R \geq 0$,

$$\mathbf{E}_0\left(\exp\left(-\sum_{i=1}^{R} z_i A_T^{(i)}\right)\right) = \frac{1 - \sum_{j=1}^{R} \frac{\lambda z_j}{\lambda + z_j} \int_0^\infty \mathbf{g}_\lambda(\mathbf{0},(y,j))\left(1 - \mathbf{E}_{(y,j)}(\mathrm{e}^{-(\lambda+z_j)H_0})\right)\beta_j\, m(\mathrm{d}y)}{1 + \sum_{j=1}^{R} z_j \int_0^\infty \mathbf{g}_\lambda(\mathbf{0},(y,j))\mathbf{E}_{(y,j)}(\mathrm{e}^{-(\lambda+z_j)H_0})\beta_j\, m(\mathrm{d}y)}. \tag{19}$$

Proof. See Appendix C. □

Formula (21) in the next corollary is due to Yano [4] (Theorem 3.5); see also Theorem 4 in Barlow, Pitman, and Yor [7], where the formula is presented for Bessel spiders (more on them in Section 5.1). We prove here that (20) is equivalent to our formula (19). For a Bessel spider, c_λ is as given in (22), and notice that this formula shows that the inverse of the local time at 0 of the underlying reflecting Bessel process is a stable subordinator.

Corollary 2. *For* $r \in \{1,2,\ldots,R\}$ *and* $z_i > 0$, $i = 1,2,\ldots,r$,

$$\mathbf{E}_0\left(\exp\Big(-\sum_{i=1}^{r} z_i A_T^{(i)}\Big)\right) = \frac{1-\sum_{j=1}^{r}\beta_j + \sum_{j=1}^{r}\frac{\lambda\,\beta_j}{\lambda+z_j}\frac{c_{\lambda+z_j}}{c_\lambda}}{1-\sum_{j=1}^{r}\beta_j + \sum_{j=1}^{r}\beta_j\frac{c_{\lambda+z_j}}{c_\lambda}}, \tag{20}$$

where (cf. (10))

$$c_\lambda := -\frac{d}{dS}\varphi_\lambda(0+) > 0.$$

In particular, for $z_i > 0$, $i = 1,2,\ldots,R$,

$$\mathbf{E}_0\left(\exp\Big(-\sum_{i=1}^{R} z_i A_T^{(i)}\Big)\right) = \frac{1}{\sum_{j=1}^{R}\beta_j\, c_{\lambda+z_j}}\sum_{j=1}^{R}\frac{\lambda\,\beta_j\, c_{\lambda+z_j}}{\lambda+z_j}. \tag{21}$$

Proof. See Appendix D. □

5. Examples

In this section we highlight our results by analyzing a few different diffusion spiders, first and foremost Bessel spiders. For the Brownian spider, which is an important special case of Bessel spiders, it is possible to pursue the formulas further, and this evaluation is presented in a subsection of its own. Finally, we make some comments concerning occupation times for Walsh Brownian motion.

5.1. Bessel Spider

A Bessel process of dimension n and parameter $\nu := n/2 - 1$, where n is a positive integer, corresponds to the Euclidean norm of an n-dimensional Brownian motion. The n-dimensional Bessel process has the generator

$$\mathcal{G}f = \frac{1}{2}\frac{d^2 f}{dx^2} + \frac{n-1}{2x}\frac{df}{dx}, \quad x > 0,$$

which makes sense not only for integers n but any real values and, hence, any real parameter ν. We define the Bessel spider as a diffusion spider that behaves like a Bessel process with parameter $\nu \in (-1,0)$ (i.e., dimension $2+2\nu$) on each leg and has the corresponding excursion probabilities $\beta_i > 0$, $i = 1,2,\ldots R$, such that $\beta_1 + \cdots + \beta_R = 1$. The restriction on ν to $(-1,0)$ is so that the process is recurrent and hits 0; see [31] (p. 77). We now let $\mathbf{X}$ be a Bessel spider with $R \geq 2$ legs and apply the result in Theorem 3.

The Bessel spider has the self-similar property, which means that the recurrence equation in (18) applies. Recall that this recurrence hinges on the factors $D_k^{(i)}$ given in (15). For the purpose of finding $\mathbf{g}_\lambda(\mathbf{0},(y,i))$, that is, where the point y is on a particular leg L_i, we follow the procedure leading to Theorem 1. For the reflected Bessel diffusion on $[0,+\infty)$, we have from [31] (p. 137) that

$$m(dx) = 2x^{2\nu+1}dx, \qquad S(x) = -\frac{1}{2\nu}x^{-2\nu}, \qquad \varphi_\lambda(x) = x^{-\nu}K_\nu(x\sqrt{2\lambda}),$$

where K_ν is a modified Bessel function of the second kind. Then

$$c_\lambda := -\frac{d}{dS}\varphi(0+) = \left(\frac{2}{\sqrt{2\lambda}}\right)^{\nu}\Gamma(\nu+1) = 2^{\nu/2}\Gamma(\nu+1)\,\lambda^{-\nu/2} \tag{22}$$

and, hence,

$$\mathbf{g}_\lambda(\mathbf{0},(y,i)) = \frac{1}{\Gamma(\nu+1)}\left(\frac{\sqrt{2\lambda}}{2}\right)^{\nu} y^{-\nu}K_\nu(y\sqrt{2\lambda}).$$

Note that $\mathbf{g}_\lambda(\mathbf{0},(y,i))$ is the same for all i. Similarly, the hitting time H_0 when starting in $y \in L_i$ corresponds precisely to the hitting time of zero in the reflected Bessel process. The values of $D_k^{(i)}$ are calculated as in [29] (Proof of Theorem 3), but note that a different normalization is used for m and S in that paper. This way, we get for any $\lambda > 0$ that

$$D_k^{(i)}(\lambda) = -\beta_i\binom{\nu+k-1}{k} = -\frac{\beta_i}{k!}\sum_{j=1}^{k}\begin{bmatrix}k\\j\end{bmatrix}\nu^j, \tag{23}$$

where $\left[{n \atop k}\right]$ are unsigned Stirling numbers of the first kind. In the rest of this section, we will drop λ and only write $D_k^{(i)}$, as its value does not depend on λ.

As explained in Section 4.1, when only considering the occupation time on a single leg L_i, we can directly use the earlier obtained results for skew two-sided Bessel processes. Hence, by [29] (Theorem 4), the nth moment of the occupation time on L_i up to time 1 is given by

$$\mathbf{E}_0\left((A_1^{(i)})^n\right) = \sum_{l=1}^{n}\sum_{k=1}^{l}(-1)^{k-1}\frac{\Gamma(k)}{\Gamma(n)}\begin{bmatrix}n\\l\end{bmatrix}\begin{Bmatrix}l\\k\end{Bmatrix}\nu^{l-1}\beta_i^k, \tag{24}$$

where $\left\{{n \atop k}\right\}$ are Stirling numbers of the second kind.

Using the recurrence equation in Theorem 3, the result in (24) is here extended to an explicit formula for the joint moments of the occupation times on multiple legs in a Bessel spider with $R \geq 2$ legs. With the numbering of legs being arbitrary, it should be clear that the formula—although written for the first r legs of the spider—holds when considering the occupation times on any number r of the R legs. Contrary to the recursive formula in Theorem 3 (see Remark 2), this formula also holds when $r = 1$.

Theorem 5. *For any $r \in \{1,\dots,R\}$ and $n_1,\dots,n_r \geq 1$,*

$$\mathbf{E}_0\left(\prod_{i=1}^{r}(A_1^{(i)})^{n_i}\right) = \sum_{1\leq k_1\leq l_1\leq n_1}\cdots\sum_{1\leq k_r\leq l_r\leq n_r}(-1)^{K-1}\frac{\Gamma(K)}{\Gamma(N)}\nu^{L-1}\prod_{j=1}^{r}\begin{bmatrix}n_j\\l_j\end{bmatrix}\begin{Bmatrix}l_j\\k_j\end{Bmatrix}\beta_j^{k_j}, \tag{25}$$

where $N = n_1+\cdots+n_r$, $K = k_1+\cdots+k_r$ and $L = l_1+\cdots+l_r$.

A proof of the theorem is given in Appendix E. For a particularly simple instance of the theorem above, consider the joint first moment of the occupation times on r legs in the Bessel spider.

Corollary 3. *For any $r \in \{1,\dots,R\}$,*

$$\mathbf{E}_0\left(A_1^{(1)}A_1^{(2)}\cdots A_1^{(r)}\right) = (-\nu)^{r-1}\beta_1\beta_2\cdots\beta_r. \tag{26}$$

Proof. Immediate from (25) with $n_1 = \cdots = n_r = 1$. □

The first few moments of the occupation times up to time t on one or two legs of a Bessel spider are given in Table 1. Recall that since the Bessel spider is self-similar, the (joint) moments of the occupation times on the legs up to a fixed time t satisfy

$$\mathbf{E}_0\left((A_t^{(i)})^{n_1}(A_t^{(j)})^{n_2}\right) = t^{n_1+n_2}\mathbf{E}_0\left((A_1^{(i)})^{n_1}(A_1^{(j)})^{n_2}\right).$$

Using this, the moments are found directly from Theorem 5. The variance, covariance, and correlation coefficients are also included in the table. Note, as expected, that the correlation coefficient is always negative and does not depend on the time t or the Bessel parameter ν. If the spider has only two legs, so that $\beta_1 = 1 - \beta_2$, the process is always located on either of the legs and the correlation coefficient of the occupation times on the legs is then equal to -1.

Table 1. Some moments and descriptive statistics for the occupation times on the legs of a Bessel spider.

Moment/Statistic	Value
$\mathbf{E}_0\left(A_t^{(i)}\right)$	$t\beta_i$
$\mathbf{E}_0\left(\left(A_t^{(i)}\right)^2\right)$	$t^2\beta_i(1+\nu-\nu\beta_i)$
$\mathbf{E}_0\left(A_t^{(i)}A_t^{(j)}\right)$	$-t^2\nu\beta_i\beta_j$
$\mathrm{Var}\left(A_t^{(i)}\right)$	$t^2(1+\nu)\beta_i(1-\beta_i)$
$\mathrm{Cov}\left(A_t^{(i)}, A_t^{(j)}\right),\ i \neq j$	$-t^2(1+\nu)\beta_i\beta_j$
$\mathrm{Corr}\left(A_t^{(i)}, A_t^{(j)}\right),\ i \neq j$	$-\sqrt{\frac{\beta_i\beta_j}{(1-\beta_i)(1-\beta_j)}}$

5.2. Brownian Spider

The special case of a Bessel spider with the parameter $\nu = -\frac{1}{2}$ is the Brownian spider mentioned in the introduction, also known as Walsh Brownian motion on a finite number of legs. In this case, the result in Theorem 5 has the following, somewhat simpler expression.

Theorem 6. *Let* $\mathbf{X}$ *be a Brownian spider and let* $A_1^{(i)}$ *be the occupation time on leg* L_i *up to time 1. For any* $r \in \{1, \ldots, R\}$ *and* $n_1, \ldots, n_r \geq 1$,

$$\mathbf{E}_0\left(\prod_{i=1}^{r}(A_1^{(i)})^{n_i}\right) = \sum_{k_1=1}^{n_1} \cdots \sum_{k_r=1}^{n_r} 2^{-(2N-K-1)} \frac{\Gamma(K)}{\Gamma(N)} \prod_{j=1}^{r} \frac{\Gamma(2n_j - k_j)\,\beta_j^{k_j}}{\Gamma(k_j)\Gamma(n_j - k_j + 1)}, \tag{27}$$

where $N = n_1 + \cdots + n_r$ *and* $K = k_1 + \cdots + k_r$.

Proof. The result follows from (25) and the identity

$$\sum_{i=k}^{n} \begin{bmatrix} n \\ i \end{bmatrix} \begin{Bmatrix} i \\ k \end{Bmatrix} (-2)^{n-i} = (-1)^{n-k} \frac{(2n-k-1)!}{2^{n-k}(k-1)!(n-k)!} =: b(n,k),$$

where $b(n,k)$ is a (signed) Bessel number of the first kind. For proofs of this identity and some related ones, see [33,34]. □

5.3. Walsh Brownian Motion

Finally, we briefly return to the Walsh Brownian motion in its original form. As the state space can be the entire $\mathbb{R}^2$ and is not restricted to a spider graph with a fixed number of legs, in this section we follow Walsh's terminology and talk about "rays" rather than "legs", although it should be clear that the meaning is the same. Here, the diffusion behaves like a Brownian motion on each ray, and when it reaches the origin, the direction θ of the next ray is selected according to some given distribution on $[0, 2\pi)$. As we have already studied the case when this distribution is discrete, i.e., the number of rays is at most countable, we now consider a continuous distribution.

The diffusion will, almost surely, choose a new direction every time it reaches $\mathbf{0}$, so that it visits no ray more than once. Furthermore, the probability of visiting a particular ray (i.e., a ray whose angle is a fixed value) is zero. For this reason, it is not meaningful to consider the occupation times on specific rays in this case. Rather, we can consider the occupation times within sectors of the $\mathbb{R}^2$ plane. Let $0 = \theta_0 < \theta_1 < \theta_2 < \cdots < \theta_R = 2\pi$ be fixed angles and let S_i consist of all points with angle in $[\theta_{i-1}, \theta_i)$, so that $\mathbb{R}^2$ is partitioned into R non-overlapping sectors $S_1, S_2, \ldots, S_R$. If $\Theta(X_t)$ denotes the angle of the ray on which the diffusion X is located at time t, then

$$A_t^{(S_i)} = \int_0^t \mathbb{1}_{[\theta_{i-1},\theta_i)}(\Theta(X_s))\,\mathrm{d}s$$

is the occupation time of the diffusion within sector S_i up to time t. This is illustrated in Figure 3, which contains a plot of a simulated Walsh Brownian motion. Each line corresponds to an excursion along a ray from the origin, and the length of each line is proportional to the maximal height of that excursion. The $\mathbb{R}^2$ plane has been divided into five separate sectors of equal size, each with its own color, and we may consider the occupation time of the process in these sectors.

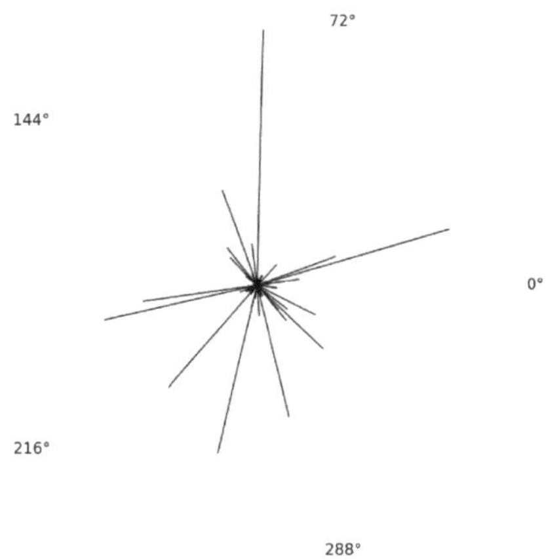

Figure 3. Plot of excursions from the origin of a simulated Walsh Brownian motion.

With respect to the occupation time on a sector, the outcome is the same as if all rays within the sector were combined and mapped onto a single ray. Therefore, the occupation times of a Walsh Brownian motion in the sectors $S_1, \ldots, S_R$ correspond precisely to the occupation times on the R legs of a Brownian spider. Thus, the result in Theorem 6 applies for the occupation times on sectors of a Walsh Brownian motion, with β_i being equal to the probability of selecting an angle within sector S_i when at the origin. Naturally, if the diffusion behaves like a Bessel process with parameter $\nu \in (-1, 0)$ on each ray (this could, perhaps, be called a "Walsh Bessel process"), then Theorem 5 applies instead.

Author Contributions: Conceptualization, P.S.; methodology, P.S. and D.S.; formal analysis, P.S. and D.S.; writing—original draft preparation, D.S.; writing—review and editing, P.S and D.S. All authors have read and agreed to the published version of the manuscript.

Funding: This research was in part funded through personal grants to D.S. from the Magnus Ehrnrooth Foundation and the Swedish Cultural Foundation in Finland.

Institutional Review Board Statement: Not applicable.

Data Availability Statement: No new data were created or analyzed in this study. Data sharing is not applicable to this article.

Conflicts of Interest: The authors declare no conflicts of interest.

Appendix A

Proof of Proposition 1. We prove the statement for $N = 2$, as the proof is analogous for any $N > 2$. Restating the equation above with $N = 2$, what we want to prove is that

$$\begin{aligned}\mathbf{E}_x(A_t(V_1))^{n_1}A_t(V_2))^{n_2}) =& n_1\int_E m(\mathrm{d}y)\int_0^t p(s;x,y)V_1(y)\mathbf{E}_y\Big(A_{t-s}(V_1))^{n_1-1}A_{t-s}(V_2))^{n_2}\Big)\,\mathrm{d}s\\ &+n_2\int_E m(\mathrm{d}y)\int_0^t p(u;x,y)V_2(y)\mathbf{E}_y\Big(A_{t-u}(V_1))^{n_1}A_{t-u}(V_2))^{n_2-1}\Big)\,\mathrm{d}u.\end{aligned}$$

Expanding the powers of $A_t(V_1)$ and $A_t(V_2)$ on the left hand side, we get

$$\begin{aligned}&\mathbf{E}_x(A_t(V_1))^{n_1}A_t(V_2))^{n_2})\\ &=\mathbf{E}_x\left(\int_0^t \mathrm{d}s_1\cdots\int_0^t \mathrm{d}s_{n_1}\int_0^t \mathrm{d}u_1\cdots\int_0^t \mathrm{d}u_{n_2}\,V_1(Y_{s_1})\cdots V_1(Y_{s_{n_1}})\cdot V_2(Y_{u_1})\cdots V_2(Y_{u_{n_2}})\right)\\ &=n_1\mathbf{E}_x\left(\int_0^t \mathrm{d}s_1V_1(Y_{s_1})\int_{s_1}^t \mathrm{d}s_2\cdots\int_{s_1}^t \mathrm{d}u_{n_2}\,V_1(Y_{s_2})\cdots V_2(Y_{u_{n_2}})\right)\\ &\quad+n_2\mathbf{E}_x\left(\int_0^t \mathrm{d}u_{n_2}V_2(Y_{u_{n_2}})\int_{u_{n_2}}^t \mathrm{d}s_1\cdots\int_{u_{n_2}}^t \mathrm{d}u_{n_2-1}\,V_1(Y_{s_1})\cdots V_2(Y_{u_{n_2-1}})\right)\\ &=n_1\int_0^t \mathrm{d}s_1\mathbf{E}_x\left(V_1(Y_{s_1})\int_0^{t-s_1}\mathrm{d}s_2\cdots\int_0^{t-s_1}\mathrm{d}u_{n_2}\,V_1(Y_{s_1+s_2})\cdots V_2(Y_{s_1+u_{n_2}})\right)\\ &\quad+n_2\int_0^t \mathrm{d}u_{n_2}\mathbf{E}_x\left(V_2(Y_{u_{n_2}})\int_0^{t-u_{n_2}}\mathrm{d}s_1\cdots\int_0^{t-u_{n_2}}\mathrm{d}u_{n_2-1}\,V_1(Y_{u_{n_2}+s_1})\cdots V_2(Y_{u_{n_2}+u_{n_2-1}})\right)\\ &=n_1\int_0^t \mathrm{d}s_1\int_E m(\mathrm{d}y)p(s_1;x,y)V_1(y)\mathbf{E}_y\Big(A_{t-s_1}(V_1))^{n_1-1}A_{t-s_1}(V_2))^{n_2}\Big)\\ &\quad+n_2\int_0^t \mathrm{d}u_{n_2}\int_E m(\mathrm{d}y)p(u_{n_2};x,y)V_2(y)\mathbf{E}_y\Big(A_{t-u_{n_2}}(V_1))^{n_1}A_{t-u_{n_2}}(V_2))^{n_2-1}\Big),\end{aligned}$$

where we have used the symmetry of the integrand in the second step and the strong Markov property in the final step. After a change of the order of the integration, justified by Fubini's theorem, the desired result follows. □

Remark A1. *In the proof above, it is assumed that all values $n_1,\dots,n_N$ are strictly positive integers. However,* (12) *may hold even if some (but not all) of these values are zero. Note that the factor n_k in the terms on the right hand side ensures that any term with $n_k = 0$ will not contribute, as long as the integral in that term is convergent. Suppose that for any starting point $Y_0 = y$ of the underlying diffusion for which $V_k(y) \neq 0$, it almost surely holds that $A_t(V_k) > 0$ when $t > 0$, and $|A_t(V_k)| \geq |A_t(V_i)|, \forall i = 1,\dots,N$ when $t \to 0$. Then, the denominator $A_{t-s}(V_k)$ inside the expected value is nonzero except possibly when $s \to t$, in which case all factors in the numerator (and there is at least one) tend to zero as well, and at least as "fast". The first condition holds, for instance, if V_k is non-negative everywhere and continuous in y, as the diffusion Y is assumed to be regular. Observe that one choice of functions V_k that satisfies both these conditions is to take the indicator functions on the legs of a spider, i.e., $V_k = \mathbb{1}_{L_k}$, which is the case of interest in this paper. Technically, the point* **0** *should be excluded from the indicator functions for the conditions to hold also when* **0** *is the starting point, but assuming that* **0** *is not a sticky point (as we perform in this paper), that will not make a difference.*

Appendix B

Proof of Theorem 3. We first remark that the expression on the right hand side of (17) is well defined since $\mathbf{P}_0\left(A_t^{(i)} > 0\right) = 1$ for all $t > 0$ and $i = 1, 2, \ldots, R$. The procedure below closely follows the proof of Theorem 2 in [29], with the main difference being that instead of the original Kac's moment formula we use the generalized version given in Proposition 1. Proving the result for $r = 2$ should be sufficient, since the method is the same for any higher values of r (you only need to include more terms of similar form).

With $r = 2$, the claimed identity (17) can be written as

$$\begin{aligned}\mathcal{L}_t\left\{\mathbf{E}_0\left((A_t^{(1)})^{n_1}(A_t^{(2)})^{n_2}\right)\right\}(\lambda) &= \sum_{k=1}^{n_1}\frac{n_1!D_k^{(1)}(\lambda)}{(n_1-k)!\lambda^k}\mathcal{L}_t\left\{\mathbf{E}_0\left((A_t^{(1)})^{n_1-k}(A_t^{(2)})^{n_2}\right)\right\}(\lambda)\\ &+ \sum_{k=1}^{n_2}\frac{n_2!D_k^{(2)}(\lambda)}{(n_2-k)!\lambda^k}\mathcal{L}_t\left\{\mathbf{E}_0\left((A_t^{(1)})^{n_1}(A_t^{(2)})^{n_2-k}\right)\right\}(\lambda).\end{aligned} \tag{A1}$$

Note that the numbering of the diffusion spider legs is arbitrary, so any two legs could be considered, even though they are here numbered 1 and 2.

Assume first that the diffusion starts on one of the legs at a distance x from the origin. Without the loss of generality, we will write that it starts on the first leg L_1. Before the diffusion hits $\mathbf{0}$ for the first time, the occupation time on the starting leg L_1 equals the entire elapsed time, while the occupation time on any other leg stays zero. Thus, applying the strong Markov property at the first hitting time of $\mathbf{0}$, we have

$$A_t^{(1)} = \begin{cases} H_0 + A_{t-H_0}^{(1)} \circ \theta_{H_0}, & H_0 < t, \\ t, & H_0 \geq t, \end{cases}$$

while for any other leg,

$$A_t^{(k)} = \begin{cases} A_{t-H_0}^{(k)} \circ \theta_{H_0}, & H_0 < t, \\ 0, & H_0 \geq t, \end{cases} \quad (k > 1).$$

where θ_t is the usual shift operator and the use of the composition $\circ$ should here be understood as

$$A_t^{(i)} \circ \theta_u := \int_0^t \mathbb{1}_{L_i}((X_s \circ \theta_u)(\omega))\,\mathrm{d}s = \int_0^t \mathbb{1}_{L_i}(X_{u+s})\,\mathrm{d}s.$$

From this we obtain, for any $n_1, n_2 \geq 1$,

$$(A_t^{(1)})^{n_1}(A_t^{(2)})^{n_2} = \begin{cases} \sum_{k=0}^{n_1}\binom{n_1}{k}H_0^k(A_{t-H_0}^{(1)} \circ \theta_{H_0})^{n_1-k}(A_{t-H_0}^{(2)} \circ \theta_{H_0})^{n_2}, & H_0 < t, \\ 0, & H_0 \geq t, \end{cases} \tag{A2}$$

and

$$\mathbf{E}_{(x,1)}\left((A_t^{(1)})^{n_1}(A_t^{(2)})^{n_2}\right) = \sum_{k=0}^{n_1}\binom{n_1}{k}\int_0^t \mathbf{E}_0\left((A_{t-s}^{(1)})^{n_1-k}(A_{t-s}^{(2)})^{n_2}\right)s^k f(x,1;s)\,\mathrm{d}s,$$

where $f(x,1;t)$ denotes the $\mathbf{P}_{(x,1)}$-density of H_0. Taking the Laplace transform with respect to t, we first recall that

$$\mathcal{L}_t\{f(x,1;t)\}(\lambda) = \int_0^\infty \mathrm{e}^{-\lambda t}\mathbf{P}_x(H_0 \in \mathrm{d}t) = \mathbf{E}_{(x,1)}\left(\mathrm{e}^{-\lambda H_0}\right),$$

and

$$\mathcal{L}_t\{t^k f(x,1;t)\}(\lambda) = (-1)^k \frac{\mathrm{d}^k}{\mathrm{d}\lambda^k}\mathcal{L}_t\{f(x,1;t)\}(\lambda) = \mathbf{E}_{(x,1)}\big(H_0^k \mathrm{e}^{-\lambda H_0}\big),$$

so that we obtain, using the formula for the Laplace transform of a convolution,

$$\mathcal{L}_t\Big\{\mathbf{E}_{(x,1)}\Big((A_t^{(1)})^{n_1}(A_t^{(2)})^{n_2}\Big)\Big\}(\lambda) = \sum_{k=0}^{n_1}\binom{n_1}{k}\mathbf{E}_{(x,1)}\big(H_0^k \mathrm{e}^{-\lambda H_0}\big)\mathcal{L}_t\Big\{\mathbf{E}_{\mathbf{0}}\Big((A_t^{(1)})^{n_1-k}(A_t^{(2)})^{n_2}\Big)\Big\}(\lambda). \quad \text{(A}$$

On the right hand side of the equation, the starting point $(x,1)$ is only part of the expression involving the hitting time H_0, while the Laplace transform of the joint moments instead has the starting point $\mathbf{0}$. The equation above is now used together with Kac's moment formula to obtain a recursive formula for (the Laplace transform of) the joint moments of the occupation times on the different legs. Proposition 1 yields

$$\begin{aligned}\mathcal{L}_t\Big\{\mathbf{E}_{(x,1)}\Big((A_t^{(1)})^{n_1}(A_t^{(2)})^{n_2}\Big)\Big\}(\lambda) &= n_1\int_0^\infty \mathrm{g}_\lambda((x,1),(y,1))\mathcal{L}_t\Big\{\mathbf{E}_{(y,1)}\Big((A_t^{(1)})^{n_1-1}(A_t^{(2)})^{n_2}\Big)\Big\}(\lambda)\,\beta_1\, m(\mathrm{d}y)\\ &+ n_2\int_0^\infty \mathrm{g}_\lambda((x,1),(y,2))\mathcal{L}_t\Big\{\mathbf{E}_{(y,2)}\Big((A_t^{(1)})^{n_1}(A_t^{(2)})^{n_2-1}\Big)\Big\}(\lambda)\,\beta_2\, m(\mathrm{d}y),\end{aligned}$$

and inserting the expression in (A3) on both sides gives

$$\begin{aligned}&\sum_{k=0}^{n_1}\binom{n_1}{k}\mathbf{E}_{(x,1)}\big(H_0^k \mathrm{e}^{-\lambda H_0}\big)\mathcal{L}_t\Big\{\mathbf{E}_{\mathbf{0}}\Big((A_t^{(1)})^{n_1-k}(A_t^{(2)})^{n_2}\Big)\Big\}(\lambda)\\ &= n_1\sum_{k=0}^{n_1-1}\binom{n_1-1}{k}\mathcal{L}_t\Big\{\mathbf{E}_{\mathbf{0}}\Big((A_t^{(1)})^{n_1-k-1}(A_t^{(2)})^{n_2}\Big)\Big\}(\lambda)\int_0^\infty \mathrm{g}_\lambda((x,1),(y,1))\mathbf{E}_{(y,1)}\big(H_0^k \mathrm{e}^{-\lambda H_0}\big)\,\beta_1\, m(\mathrm{d}y)\\ &+ n_2\sum_{k=0}^{n_2-1}\binom{n_2-1}{k}\mathcal{L}_t\Big\{\mathbf{E}_{\mathbf{0}}\Big((A_t^{(1)})^{n_1}(A_t^{(2)})^{n_2-k-1}\Big)\Big\}(\lambda)\int_0^\infty \mathrm{g}_\lambda((x,1),(y,2))\mathbf{E}_{(y,2)}\big(H_0^k \mathrm{e}^{-\lambda H_0}\big)\,\beta_2\, m(\mathrm{d}y).\end{aligned}$$

Note that the second integral is taken over points $(y,2)$ that lie on the second leg L_2, which is why in that case the expression in (A3) is inserted with the roles of n_1 and n_2 interchanged. We now let $x \to 0$ on both sides of the equation above. For this, recall from [29] (Lemma 1) that

$$\lim_{x\to 0}\mathbf{E}_{(x,1)}\big(H_0^k \mathrm{e}^{-\lambda H_0}\big) = \begin{cases}1, & k=0,\\ 0, & k\geq 1,\end{cases}$$

and by Corollary 1 we may take the limit inside the integrals to obtain

$$\begin{aligned}&\mathcal{L}_t\Big\{\mathbf{E}_{\mathbf{0}}\Big((A_t^{(1)})^{n_1}(A_t^{(2)})^{n_2}\Big)\Big\}(\lambda)\\ &= \sum_{k=1}^{n_1}\frac{n_1!}{(n_1-k)!}\mathcal{L}_t\Big\{\mathbf{E}_{\mathbf{0}}\Big((A_t^{(1)})^{n_1-k}(A_t^{(2)})^{n_2}\Big)\Big\}(\lambda)\frac{1}{(k-1)!}\int_0^\infty \mathrm{g}_\lambda(\mathbf{0},(y,1))\mathbf{E}_{(y,1)}\big(H_0^{k-1}\mathrm{e}^{-\lambda H_0}\big)\,\beta_1\, m(\mathrm{d}y)\\ &+ \sum_{k=1}^{n_2}\frac{n_2!}{(n_2-k)!}\mathcal{L}_t\Big\{\mathbf{E}_{\mathbf{0}}\Big((A_t^{(1)})^{n_1}(A_t^{(2)})^{n_2-k}\Big)\Big\}(\lambda)\frac{1}{(k-1)!}\int_0^\infty \mathrm{g}_\lambda(\mathbf{0},(y,2))\mathbf{E}_{(y,2)}\big(H_0^{k-1}\mathrm{e}^{-\lambda H_0}\big)\,\beta_2\, m(\mathrm{d}y),\end{aligned}$$

where also the summation index is changed. This is equivalent to (A1) when introducing $D_k^{(i)}(\lambda)$ as defined in (15), and this proves the first part of the theorem.

For a self-similar spider,

$$(A_t^{(1)})^{n_1}(A_t^{(2)})^{n_2} \overset{(\mathrm{d})}{=} t^{n_1+n_2}(A_1^{(1)})^{n_1}(A_1^{(2)})^{n_2},$$

and, in this case,

$$\mathcal{L}_t\Big\{\mathbf{E}_0\Big((A_t^{(1)})^{n_1}(A_t^{(2)})^{n_2}\Big)\Big\}(\lambda)=\frac{(n_1+n_2)!}{\lambda^{n_1+n_2+1}}\mathbf{E}_0\Big((A_1^{(1)})^{n_1}(A_1^{(2)})^{n_2}\Big).$$

Hence, for self-similar spiders, the expression in (A1) simplifies to

$$\begin{aligned}\mathbf{E}_0\Big((A_1^{(1)})^{n_1}(A_1^{(2)})^{n_2}\Big)&=\sum_{k=1}^{n_1}\frac{\binom{n_1}{k}}{\binom{n_1+n_2}{k}}D_k^{(1)}(\lambda)\mathbf{E}_0\Big((A_1^{(1)})^{n_1-k}(A_1^{(2)})^{n_2}\Big)\\&\quad+\sum_{k=1}^{n_2}\frac{\binom{n_2}{k}}{\binom{n_1+n_2}{k}}D_k^{(2)}(\lambda)\mathbf{E}_0\Big((A_1^{(1)})^{n_1}(A_1^{(2)})^{n_2-k}\Big).\end{aligned}\tag{A4}$$

This proves the second part of the theorem for $r=2$, and the proof is easily extended for higher r. □

Appendix C

Proof of Theorem 4. If the diffusion spider starts in the point (x,j), that is, on a particular leg L_j, then up to the time H_0 the occupation time on the leg L_j is equal to the time elapsed, while the occupation time on any other leg is zero. Hence, for any $i\in\{1,\ldots,R\}$,

$$A_t^{(i)}=\begin{cases}H_0\,\mathbb{1}_{\{i=j\}}+A_{t-H_0}^{(i)}\circ\theta_{H_0}, & H_0<t,\\ t\,\mathbb{1}_{\{i=j\}}, & H_0\geq t.\end{cases}$$

To prove the theorem, we first consider the left hand side of (19) with a general starting point (x,j) instead of $\mathbf{0}$ and split the analysis into the two events whether the diffusion spider hits $\mathbf{0}$ before the exponential time T or not. This gives the two parts

$$\begin{aligned}\mathbf{E}_{(x,j)}\bigg(\exp\Big(-\sum_{i=1}^{R}z_iA_T^{(i)}\Big);H_0\geq T\bigg)&=\mathbf{E}_{(x,j)}\Big(\mathrm{e}^{-z_jT};H_0\geq T\Big)\\&=\frac{\lambda}{\lambda+z_j}\Big(1-\mathbf{E}_{(x,j)}\Big(\mathrm{e}^{-(\lambda+z_j)H_0}\Big)\Big)\end{aligned}$$

and

$$\begin{aligned}\mathbf{E}_{(x,j)}\bigg(\exp\Big(-\sum_{i=1}^{R}z_iA_T^{(i)}\Big);H_0<T\bigg)&=\mathbf{E}_{(x,j)}\Big(\mathrm{e}^{-z_jH_0};H_0<T\Big)\mathbf{E}_0\bigg(\exp\Big(-\sum_{i=1}^{R}z_iA_T^{(i)}\Big)\bigg)\\&=\mathbf{E}_{(x,j)}\Big(\mathrm{e}^{-(\lambda+z_j)H_0}\Big)\mathbf{E}_0\bigg(\exp\Big(-\sum_{i=1}^{R}z_iA_T^{(i)}\Big)\bigg),\end{aligned}$$

where in the second part we have used the strong Markov property to restart the process when it first hits $\mathbf{0}$, as well as the memoryless property of the exponential distribution. Combining both parts gives

$$\mathbf{E}_{(x,j)}\bigg(\exp\Big(-\sum_{i=1}^{R}z_iA_T^{(i)}\Big)\bigg)=\frac{\lambda}{\lambda+z_j}+\bigg(\mathbf{E}_0\bigg(\exp\Big(-\sum_{i=1}^{R}z_iA_T^{(i)}\Big)\bigg)-\frac{\lambda}{\lambda+z_j}\bigg)\mathbf{E}_{(x,j)}\Big(\mathrm{e}^{-(\lambda+z_j)H_0}\Big).\tag{A5}$$

The significance of this expression is that on the right hand side the dependency on the starting position (x,j) is contained only in a function of the first hitting time H_0, while the moment generating function of the occupation times has the starting point $\mathbf{0}$ instead.

As the left hand side of (A5) can be written

$$\mathbf{E}_{(x,j)}\left(\exp\left(-\sum_{i=1}^{R} z_i A_T^{(i)}\right)\right) = \int_0^\infty \mathbf{E}_{(x,j)}\left(\exp\left(-\sum_{i=1}^{R} z_i A_t^{(i)}\right)\right)\lambda \mathrm{e}^{-\lambda t}\,\mathrm{d}t, \tag{A6}$$

we will, for the moment, consider the expression with a fixed time t rather than the exponential time T. Expanding as a sum of joint moments, we obtain

$$\begin{aligned}
\mathbf{E}_{(x,j)}\left(\exp\left(-\sum_{i=1}^{R} z_i A_t^{(i)}\right)\right) &= \sum_{N=0}^{\infty}\frac{(-1)^N}{N!}\mathbf{E}_{(x,j)}\left(\left(\sum_{i=1}^{R} z_i A_t^{(i)}\right)^N\right) \\
&= \sum_{N=0}^{\infty}\frac{(-1)^N}{N!}\mathbf{E}_{(x,j)}\left(\sum_{\substack{n_1,\dots,n_R\geq 0\\ n_1+\dots+n_R=N}}\frac{N!}{n_1!n_2!\cdots n_R!}\prod_{i=1}^{R}(z_i A_t^{(i)})^{n_i}\right) \\
&= \sum_{N=0}^{\infty}\sum_{\substack{n_1,\dots,n_R\geq 0\\ n_1+\dots+n_R=N}}\left(\prod_{l=1}^{R}\frac{(-z_l)^{n_l}}{n_l!}\right)\mathbf{E}_{(x,j)}\left(\prod_{i=1}^{R}(A_t^{(i)})^{n_i}\right).
\end{aligned} \tag{A7}$$

The generalized Kac's moment Formula (12) with the functions $V_k(x) = \mathbb{1}_{L_k}(x)$ (and formulated for the spider) becomes

$$\mathbf{E}_{(x,j)}\left(\prod_{i=1}^{R}(A_t^{(i)})^{n_i}\right) = \sum_{i=1}^{R} n_i \int_0^\infty \beta_i m(\mathrm{d}y)\int_0^t \mathbf{p}(s;(x,j),(y,i))\mathbf{E}_{(y,i)}\left(\frac{\prod_{k=1}^{R}(A_{t-s}^{(k)})^{n_k}}{A_{t-s}^{(i)}}\right)\mathrm{d}s, \tag{A8}$$

where $\mathbf{p}(s;(x,j),(y,i))$ denotes the transition density of the spider. Next, Equation (A8) is inserted in (A7), bearing in mind that by Remark A1 this can be performed even when some of the values $n_1,\dots,n_R$ are zero. The exception is the term for $N=0$, since at least one of the n_i has to be strictly positive, so this term (which evaluates to 1) is separated from the rest of the sum. This yields

$$\begin{aligned}
&\mathbf{E}_{(x,j)}\left(\exp\left(-\sum_{i=1}^{R} z_i A_t^{(i)}\right)\right) \\
&= 1 + \sum_{N=1}^{\infty}\sum_{\substack{n_1,\dots,n_R\geq 0\\ n_1+\dots+n_R=N}}\left(\prod_{l=1}^{R}\frac{(-z_l)^{n_l}}{n_l!}\right)\sum_{i=1}^{R} n_i\int_0^\infty \beta_i\, m(\mathrm{d}y)\int_0^t \mathbf{p}(s;(x,j),(y,i))\mathbf{E}_{(y,i)}\left(\frac{\prod_{k=1}^{R}(A_{t-s}^{(k)})^{n_k}}{A_{t-s}^{(i)}}\right)\mathrm{d}s \\
&= 1 + \sum_{i=1}^{R}\int_0^\infty \beta_i\, m(\mathrm{d}y)\int_0^t \mathbf{p}(s;(x,j),(y,i))\sum_{N=0}^{\infty}\sum_{\substack{n_1,\dots,n_R\geq 0\\ n_1+\dots+n_R=N}}(-z_i)\left(\prod_{l=1}^{R}\frac{(-z_l)^{n_l}}{n_l!}\right)\mathbf{E}_{(y,i)}\left(\prod_{k=1}^{R}(A_{t-s}^{(k)})^{n_k}\right)\mathrm{d}s \\
&= 1 - \sum_{i=1}^{R} z_i\int_0^\infty \beta_i\, m(\mathrm{d}y)\int_0^t \mathbf{p}(s;(x,j),(y,i))\mathbf{E}_{(y,i)}\left(\exp\left(-\sum_{i=1}^{R} z_i A_{t-s}^{(i)}\right)\right)\mathrm{d}s.
\end{aligned}$$

Note that the summation indices N and n_i have both been shifted by one in the third step and that in the last step (A7) has been applied again. From (A6) and the above, we obtain

$$\begin{aligned}
\mathbf{E}_{(x,j)}\left(\exp\Big(-\sum_{i=1}^{R} z_i A_T^{(i)}\Big)\right) &= \lambda\,\mathcal{L}_t\left\{\mathbf{E}_{(x,j)}\left(\exp\Big(-\sum_{i=1}^{R} z_i A_t^{(i)}\Big)\right)\right\}(\lambda)\\
&= \frac{\lambda}{\lambda} - \lambda\sum_{i=1}^{R} z_i \int_0^\infty \mathcal{L}_t\left\{\int_0^t \mathbf{p}(s;(x,j),(y,i))\mathbf{E}_{(y,i)}\left(\exp\Big(-\sum_{i=1}^{R} z_i A_{t-s}^{(i)}\Big)\right) \mathrm{d}s\right\}(\lambda)\,\beta_i\, m(\mathrm{d}y)\\
&= 1 - \lambda\sum_{i=1}^{R} z_i \int_0^\infty \mathbf{g}_\lambda((x,j),(y,i))\mathcal{L}_t\left\{\mathbf{E}_{(y,i)}\left(\exp\Big(-\sum_{i=1}^{R} z_i A_t^{(i)}\Big)\right)\right\}(\lambda)\,\beta_i\, m(\mathrm{d}y)\\
&= 1 - \sum_{i=1}^{R} z_i \int_0^\infty \mathbf{g}_\lambda((x,j),(y,i))\mathbf{E}_{(y,i)}\left(\exp\Big(-\sum_{i=1}^{R} z_i A_T^{(i)}\Big)\right)\beta_i\, m(\mathrm{d}y). \qquad \text{(A9)}
\end{aligned}$$

We now insert (A5) into the right hand side of (A9) and let $x \to 0$ on both sides. This gives

$$\begin{aligned}
\mathbf{E}_0\left(\exp\Big(-\sum_{i=1}^{R} z_i A_T^{(i)}\Big)\right) = 1 &- \sum_{i=1}^{R} z_i \int_0^\infty \mathbf{g}_\lambda(\mathbf{0},(y,i))\frac{\lambda}{\lambda+z_i}\left(1-\mathbf{E}_{(y,i)}\left(\mathrm{e}^{-(\lambda+z_i)H_0}\right)\right)\beta_i\, m(\mathrm{d}y)\\
&- \mathbf{E}_0\left(\exp\Big(-\sum_{i=1}^{R} z_i A_T^{(i)}\Big)\right)\sum_{i=1}^{R} z_i \int_0^\infty \mathbf{g}_\lambda(\mathbf{0},(y,i))\mathbf{E}_{(y,i)}\left(\mathrm{e}^{-(\lambda+z_i)H_0}\right)\beta_i\, m(\mathrm{d}y),
\end{aligned}$$

which, when solved for the left hand side expression, results in the claimed formula (19). □

Appendix D

Proof of Corollary 2. Recall from (11) that

$$\mathbf{g}_\lambda(\mathbf{0},(y,j)) = \frac{1}{c_\lambda}\,\varphi_\lambda(y)$$

and from (7)

$$\mathbf{E}_{(y,j)}(\mathrm{e}^{-(\lambda+z_j)H_0}) = \varphi_{\lambda+z_j}(y).$$

Hence, (19) can be rewritten

$$\mathbf{E}_0\left(\exp\Big(-\sum_{i=1}^{r} z_i A_T^{(i)}\Big)\right) = \frac{1-\displaystyle\sum_{j=1}^{r}\frac{\lambda\,\beta_j\, z_j}{c_\lambda\,(\lambda+z_j)}\left(\int_0^\infty \varphi_\lambda(y)\,m(\mathrm{d}y) - \int_0^\infty \varphi_\lambda(y)\varphi_{\lambda+z_j}(y)\,m(\mathrm{d}y)\right)}{1+\displaystyle\sum_{j=1}^{r}\frac{\beta_j\, z_j}{c_\lambda}\int_0^\infty \varphi_\lambda(y)\varphi_{\lambda+z_j}(y)\,m(\mathrm{d}y)}.$$

For the integrals, we have (cf. [29], proof of Corollary 1)

$$\begin{aligned}
\lambda\int_0^\infty \varphi_\lambda(y)\,m(\mathrm{d}y) &= c_\lambda,\\
z_j\int_0^\infty \varphi_\lambda(y)\varphi_{\lambda+z_j}(y)\,m(\mathrm{d}y) &= -c_\lambda + c_{\lambda+z_j}
\end{aligned}$$

by which the previous equation becomes

$$\mathbf{E}_0\left(\exp\Big(-\sum_{i=1}^{r} z_i A_T^{(i)}\Big)\right) = \frac{1-\displaystyle\sum_{j=1}^{r}\left(\frac{\lambda\,\beta_j\, z_j}{\lambda+z_j}\right)\left(\frac{1}{\lambda}+\frac{1}{z_j}\right)+\sum_{j=1}^{r}\frac{\lambda\,\beta_j}{\lambda+z_j}\frac{c_{\lambda+z_j}}{c_\lambda}}{1-\displaystyle\sum_{j=1}^{r}\beta_j+\sum_{j=1}^{r}\beta_j\frac{c_{\lambda+z_j}}{c_\lambda}}$$

from which (20) easily follows, and (21) is immediate since $\sum_{j=1}^{R}\beta_j = 1$. □

Appendix E

Proof of Theorem 5. The known Equation (24) coincides with (25) where $r = 1$, showing that the theorem holds in that particular case. As in the proof of Theorem 3, we here prove the statement for $r = 2$, say the two legs L_1 and L_2 in the Bessel spider. This will be enough to demonstrate the procedure, which can then readily be repeated for a larger value of r with more tedious but hardly more difficult work.

To begin with, we repeat the statement in (25) for $r = 2$:

$$\mathbf{E}_0\Big((A_1^{(1)})^{n_1}(A_1^{(2)})^{n_2}\Big) = \sum_{l_1=1}^{n_1}\sum_{k_1=1}^{l_1}\sum_{l_2=1}^{n_2}\sum_{k_2=1}^{l_2}(-1)^{k_1+k_2-1}\frac{\Gamma(k_1+k_2)}{\Gamma(n_1+n_2)}\begin{bmatrix}n_1\\l_1\end{bmatrix}\begin{Bmatrix}l_1\\k_1\end{Bmatrix}\begin{bmatrix}n_2\\l_2\end{bmatrix}\begin{Bmatrix}l_2\\k_2\end{Bmatrix}\nu^{l_1+l_2-1}\beta_1^{k_1}\beta_2^{k_2}. \quad \text{(A10)}$$

We prove this statement by induction using the recurrence in (18) and the known moment formula (24) for the occupation time on a single leg. For the simplest case $n_1 = n_2 = 1$, we see from (18) that

$$\mathbf{E}_0\Big(A_1^{(1)}A_1^{(2)}\Big) = \frac{1}{2}D_1^{(1)}\mathbf{E}_0\Big(A_1^{(2)}\Big) + \frac{1}{2}D_1^{(2)}\mathbf{E}_0\Big(A_1^{(1)}\Big) = -\beta_1\beta_2\nu,$$

since $D_1^{(i)} = -\beta_i\nu$ and $\mathbf{E}_0(A_1^{(i)}) = \beta_i$. Thus, (A10) holds in this case. Assume now that (A10) holds whenever $\{1 \le n_1 \le a-1, 1 \le n_2 \le b\}$ or $\{1 \le n_1 \le a, 1 \le n_2 \le b-1\}$ for some integers $a, b \ge 1$. We proceed to show that then (A10) holds also for $n_1 = a, n_2 = b$.

First, we apply the recurrence Equation (18) to obtain

$$\begin{aligned}\mathbf{E}_0\Big((A_1^{(1)})^a(A_1^{(2)})^b\Big) &= \frac{D_a^{(1)}}{\binom{a+b}{a}}\mathbf{E}_0\Big((A_1^{(2)})^b\Big) + \sum_{i=1}^{a-1}\frac{\binom{a}{i}}{\binom{a+b}{i}}D_i^{(1)}\mathbf{E}_0\Big((A_1^{(1)})^{a-i}(A_1^{(2)})^b\Big)\\ &+ \frac{D_b^{(2)}}{\binom{a+b}{b}}\mathbf{E}_0\Big((A_1^{(1)})^a\Big) + \sum_{i=1}^{b-1}\frac{\binom{b}{i}}{\binom{a+b}{i}}D_i^{(2)}\mathbf{E}_0\Big((A_1^{(1)})^a(A_1^{(2)})^{b-i}\Big). \quad \text{(A11)}\end{aligned}$$

Here, we have separated the terms with moments of the occupation time on only one leg, for which (24) applies, and the terms with joint moments of the occupation times on both legs, for which we can apply the induction assumption. In the first case, we insert the expressions in (23) and (24) to obtain

$$\begin{aligned}&\frac{D_a^{(1)}}{\binom{a+b}{a}}\mathbf{E}_0\Big((A_1^{(2)})^b\Big)\\ &= \frac{1}{\binom{a+b}{a}}\left(-\frac{\beta_1}{a!}\sum_{l_1=1}^{a}\begin{bmatrix}a\\l_1\end{bmatrix}\nu^{l_1}\right)\sum_{l_2=1}^{b}\sum_{k_2=1}^{l_2}(-1)^{k_2-1}\frac{\Gamma(k_2)}{\Gamma(b)}\begin{bmatrix}b\\l_2\end{bmatrix}\begin{Bmatrix}l_2\\k_2\end{Bmatrix}\nu^{l_2-1}\beta_2^{k_2}\\ &= b\sum_{l_1=1}^{a}\sum_{k_1=1}^{1}\sum_{l_2=1}^{b}\sum_{k_2=1}^{l_2}(-1)^{k_1+k_2-1}\frac{\Gamma(k_1+k_2-1)}{\Gamma(a+b+1)}\begin{bmatrix}a\\l_1\end{bmatrix}\begin{Bmatrix}l_1\\k_1\end{Bmatrix}\begin{bmatrix}b\\l_2\end{bmatrix}\begin{Bmatrix}l_2\\k_2\end{Bmatrix}\nu^{l_1+l_2-1}\beta_1^{k_1}\beta_2^{k_2}. \quad \text{(A12)}\end{aligned}$$

Note that the variable k_1 only takes the value 1 here, but it is nevertheless added so that the expression above resembles the form of (A10) more closely. Next, we turn to the following term in (A11), assuming for the moment that $a > 1$ so that the sum is not empty. Inserting (23) and the induction assumption, we obtain

$$\sum_{i=1}^{a-1}\frac{\binom{a}{i}}{\binom{a+b}{i}}D_i^{(1)}\mathbf{E}_0\left((A_1^{(1)})^{a-i}(A_1^{(2)})^b\right)=\sum_{i=1}^{a-1}\frac{\binom{a}{i}}{\binom{a+b}{b+i}}D_{a-i}^{(1)}\mathbf{E}_0\left((A_1^{(1)})^{i}(A_1^{(2)})^b\right)$$

$$=\sum_{i=1}^{a-1}\frac{\binom{a}{i}}{\binom{a+b}{b+i}}\left(-\frac{\beta_1}{(a-i)!}\sum_{j=1}^{a-i}\begin{bmatrix}a-i\\j\end{bmatrix}\nu^j\right)\sum_{\substack{1\le k_1\le l_1\le i,\\1\le k_2\le l_2\le b}}(-1)^{k_1+k_2-1}\frac{\Gamma(k_1+k_2)}{\Gamma(b+i)}\begin{bmatrix}i\\l_1\end{bmatrix}\begin{bmatrix}b\\l_2\end{bmatrix}\begin{Bmatrix}l_1\\k_1\end{Bmatrix}\begin{Bmatrix}l_2\\k_2\end{Bmatrix}\nu^{l_1+l_2-1}\beta_1^{k_1}\beta_2^{k_2}$$

$$=\sum_{\substack{1\le k_1\le l_1\le i\le j\le a-1,\\1\le k_2\le l_2\le b}}(-1)^{k_1+k_2}\nu^{a+l_1+l_2-j-1}\beta_1^{k_1+1}\beta_2^{k_2}\frac{(b+i)\Gamma(k_1+k_2)}{\Gamma(a+b+1)}\binom{a}{i}\begin{bmatrix}i\\l_1\end{bmatrix}\begin{bmatrix}b\\l_2\end{bmatrix}\begin{Bmatrix}l_1\\k_1\end{Bmatrix}\begin{Bmatrix}l_2\\k_2\end{Bmatrix}\begin{bmatrix}a-i\\a-j\end{bmatrix}$$

$$=\sum_{\substack{1\le k_1\le j\le a-1,\\1\le k_2\le l_2\le b}}(-1)^{k_1+k_2}\nu^{l_2+j}\beta_1^{k_1+1}\beta_2^{k_2}\frac{\Gamma(k_1+k_2)}{\Gamma(a+b+1)}\begin{bmatrix}b\\l_2\end{bmatrix}\begin{Bmatrix}l_2\\k_2\end{Bmatrix}\left(\sum_{l_1=k_1}^{j}\begin{Bmatrix}l_1\\k_1\end{Bmatrix}\sum_{i=l_1}^{a+l_1-j-1}(b+i)\binom{a}{i}\begin{bmatrix}i\\l_1\end{bmatrix}\begin{bmatrix}a-i\\j-l_1+1\end{bmatrix}\right),\quad\text{(A13)}$$

where, in the last step, we have changed the order of summation according to the pattern

$$\sum_{k=1}^{n}\sum_{l=k}^{n}\sum_{i=l}^{n}\sum_{j=i}^{n}f(i,j,k,l)=\sum_{k=1}^{n}\sum_{l=k}^{n}\sum_{i=l}^{n}\sum_{j=l}^{n+l-i}f(i,n+l-j,k,l)$$
$$=\sum_{k=1}^{n}\sum_{j=k}^{n}\sum_{l=k}^{j}\sum_{i=l}^{n+l-j}f(i,n+l-j,k,l).$$

To simplify the expression further, we use the two closely related identities

$$\sum_{i=k}^{n-m}\begin{bmatrix}i\\k\end{bmatrix}\begin{bmatrix}n-i\\m\end{bmatrix}\binom{n}{i}=\binom{k+m}{k}\begin{bmatrix}n\\k+m\end{bmatrix}$$

and

$$\sum_{i=k}^{n-m}\begin{bmatrix}i+1\\k+1\end{bmatrix}\begin{bmatrix}n-i\\m\end{bmatrix}\binom{n}{i}=\binom{k+m}{k}\begin{bmatrix}n+1\\k+m+1\end{bmatrix},$$

the first of which is well known [35] and is also utilized in the proof of the latter (see Lemma 2 in [29]). Applying these identities, we know that the innermost sum in (A13) is equal to

$$\sum_{i=l_1}^{a+l_1-j-1}(b+i)\binom{a}{i}\begin{bmatrix}i\\l_1\end{bmatrix}\begin{bmatrix}a-i\\j-l_1+1\end{bmatrix}$$
$$=b\sum_{i=l_1}^{a-(j-l_1+1)}\binom{a}{i}\begin{bmatrix}i\\l_1\end{bmatrix}\begin{bmatrix}a-i\\j-l_1+1\end{bmatrix}+a\sum_{i=l_1}^{a-(j-l_1+1)}\binom{a-1}{i-1}\begin{bmatrix}i\\l_1\end{bmatrix}\begin{bmatrix}a-i\\j-l_1+1\end{bmatrix}$$
$$=b\binom{j+1}{l_1}\begin{bmatrix}a\\j+1\end{bmatrix}+a\binom{j}{l_1-1}\begin{bmatrix}a\\j+1\end{bmatrix}$$
$$=\begin{bmatrix}a\\j+1\end{bmatrix}\left(b\binom{j}{l_1}+(a+b)\binom{j}{l_1-1}\right).$$

The expression inside the parenthesis in (A13) becomes

$$\begin{aligned}
&\sum_{l_1=k_1}^{j} \left\{ {l_1 \atop k_1} \right\} \sum_{i=l_1}^{a+l_1-j-1} (b+i) \binom{a}{i} \left[{i \atop l_1} \right] \left[{a-i \atop j-l_1+1} \right] \\
&= \left[{a \atop j+1} \right] \left(b \sum_{l_1=k_1}^{j} \left\{ {l_1 \atop k_1} \right\} \binom{j}{l_1} + (a+b) \sum_{l_1=k_1}^{j} \left\{ {l_1 \atop k_1} \right\} \binom{j}{l_1-1} \right) \\
&= \left[{a \atop j+1} \right] \left\{ {j+1 \atop k_1+1} \right\} (b+(a+b)k_1),
\end{aligned}$$

where the second step follows by the identities

$$\sum_{i=k}^{n} \left\{ {i \atop k} \right\} \binom{n}{i} = \left\{ {n+1 \atop k+1} \right\}, \quad \sum_{i=k}^{n} \left\{ {i \atop k} \right\} \binom{n}{i-1} = k \left\{ {n+1 \atop k+1} \right\},$$

see Equation (6.15) in [35] and the proof of Theorem 4 in [29], respectively. Inserting this into (A13) gives

$$\begin{aligned}
&\sum_{i=1}^{a-1} \frac{\binom{a}{i}}{\binom{a+b}{i}} D_i^{(1)} \mathbf{E}_0\left((A_1^{(1)})^{a-i} (A_1^{(2)})^b \right) \\
&= \sum_{\substack{1 \le k_1 \le j \le a-1, \\ 1 \le k_2 \le l_2 \le b}} (-1)^{k_1+k_2} \nu^{l_2+j} \beta_1^{k_1+1} \beta_2^{k_2} \frac{\Gamma(k_1+k_2)}{\Gamma(a+b+1)} \left[{b \atop l_2} \right] \left\{ {l_2 \atop k_2} \right\} \left[{a \atop j+1} \right] \left\{ {j+1 \atop k_1+1} \right\} (b+(a+b)k_1) \\
&= \sum_{\substack{2 \le k_1 \le j \le a, \\ 1 \le k_2 \le l_2 \le b}} (-1)^{k_1+k_2-1} \nu^{l_2+j-1} \beta_1^{k_1} \beta_2^{k_2} \frac{\Gamma(k_1+k_2-1)}{\Gamma(a+b+1)} \left[{a \atop j} \right] \left\{ {j \atop k_1} \right\} \left[{b \atop l_2} \right] \left\{ {l_2 \atop k_2} \right\} (b+(a+b)(k_1-1)).
\end{aligned}$$

When this is combined with (A12), replacing the summation index j with l_1 in the process, the result is

$$\begin{aligned}
&\frac{D_a^{(1)}}{\binom{a+b}{a}} \mathbf{E}_0\left((A_1^{(2)})^b \right) + \sum_{i=1}^{a-1} \frac{\binom{a}{i}}{\binom{a+b}{i}} D_i^{(1)} \mathbf{E}_0\left((A_1^{(1)})^{a-i} (A_1^{(2)})^b \right) \\
&= \sum_{\substack{1 \le k_1 \le l_1 \le a, \\ 1 \le k_2 \le l_2 \le b}} (-1)^{k_1+k_2-1} \frac{\Gamma(k_1+k_2-1)}{\Gamma(a+b+1)} \left[{a \atop l_1} \right] \left\{ {l_1 \atop k_1} \right\} \left[{b \atop l_2} \right] \left\{ {l_2 \atop k_2} \right\} \nu^{l_1+l_2-1} \beta_1^{k_1} \beta_2^{k_2} (b+(a+b)(k_1-1)).
\end{aligned}$$

Note that this coincides with (A12) when $a = 1$, so the temporary assumption $a > 1$ is not necessary for this expression to hold. This is half the right hand side of (A11). We obtain the other half simply by interchanging the roles of a and b in the expression above (renaming the summation indices accordingly). Thus, adding all the terms together, we get

$$\begin{aligned}
&\mathbf{E}_0\left((A_1^{(1)})^a (A_1^{(2)})^b \right) \\
&= \sum_{\substack{1 \le k_1 \le l_1 \le a, \\ 1 \le k_2 \le l_2 \le b}} (-1)^{k_1+k_2-1} \frac{\Gamma(k_1+k_2-1)}{\Gamma(a+b+1)} \left[{a \atop l_1} \right] \left\{ {l_1 \atop k_1} \right\} \left[{b \atop l_2} \right] \left\{ {l_2 \atop k_2} \right\} \nu^{l_1+l_2-1} \beta_1^{k_1} \beta_2^{k_2} \cdot \\
&\qquad \left(b + (a+b)(k_1-1) + a + (a+b)(k_2-1) \right) \\
&= \sum_{\substack{1 \le k_1 \le l_1 \le a, \\ 1 \le k_2 \le l_2 \le b}} (-1)^{k_1+k_2-1} \frac{\Gamma(k_1+k_2)}{\Gamma(a+b)} \left[{a \atop l_1} \right] \left\{ {l_1 \atop k_1} \right\} \left[{b \atop l_2} \right] \left\{ {l_2 \atop k_2} \right\} \nu^{l_1+l_2-1} \beta_1^{k_1} \beta_2^{k_2},
\end{aligned}$$

which proves that (A10) indeed holds for $n_1 = a, n_2 = b$. By induction, it holds for any $n_1, n_2 \ge 1$, and the theorem is thereby proved when $r = 2$. As mentioned in the beginning of the proof, the same method can be repeated for increasingly larger values of r as well. However, due to the long expressions we include only the proof given above and trust that the reader can recognize how it generalizes to (25) for higher r. □

References

Walsh, J.B. A diffusion with a discontinuous local time. In *Temps locaux*; Société Mathématique de France: Marseille, France, 1978; Volume 52–53, pp. 37–45.

Barlow, M.; Pitman, J.; Yor, M. On Walsh's Brownian motions. In *Séminaire de Probabilités, XXIII*; Lecture Notes in Mathematics; Springer: Berlin/Heidelberg, Germany, 1989; Volume 1372, pp. 275–293. [CrossRef]

Salisbury, T.S. Construction of right processes from excursions. *Probab. Theory Related Fields* **1986**, *73*, 351–367. [CrossRef]

Yano, Y. On the joint law of the occupation times for a diffusion process on multiray. *J. Theoret. Probab.* **2017**, *30*, 490–509. [CrossRef]

Freidlin, M.I.; Wentzell, A.D. Diffusion processes on graphs and the averaging principle. *Ann. Probab.* **1993**, *21*, 2215–2245. [CrossRef]

Weber, M. On occupation time functionals for diffusion processes and birth-and-death processes on graphs. *Ann. Appl. Probab.* **2001**, *11*, 544–567. [CrossRef]

Barlow, M.; Pitman, J.; Yor, M. Une extension multidimensionnelle de la loi de l'arc sinus. In *Séminaire de Probabilités, XXIII*; Lecture Notes in Mathematics; Springer: Berlin/Heidelberg, Germany, 1989; Volume 1372, pp. 294–314. [CrossRef]

Papanicolaou, V.; Papageorgiou, E.; Lepipas, D. Random motion on simple graphs. *Methodol. Comput. Appl. Probab.* **2012**, *14*, 285–297. [CrossRef]

Vakeroudis, S.; Yor, M. A scaling proof for Walsh's Brownian motion extended arc-sine law. *Electron. Commun. Probab.* **2012**, *17*, 63. [CrossRef]

Fitzsimmons, P.J.; Kuter, K.E. Harmonic functions on Walsh's Brownian motion. *Stoch. Process. Appl.* **2014**, *124*, 2228–2248. [CrossRef]

Csáki, E.; Csörgő, M.; Földes, A.; Révész, P. Some limit theorems for heights of random walks on a spider. *J. Theoret. Probab.* **2016**, *29*, 1685–1709. [CrossRef]

Csáki, E.; Csörgő, M.; Földes, A.; Révész, P. Limit theorems for local and occupation times of random walks and Brownian motion on a spider. *J. Theoret. Probab.* **2019**, *32*, 330–352. [CrossRef]

Ernst, P. Exercising control when confronted by a (Brownian) spider. *Oper. Res. Lett.* **2016**, *44*, 487–490. [CrossRef]

Karatzas, I.; Yan, M. Semimartingales on rays, Walsh diffusions, and related problems of control and stopping. *Stoch. Process. Appl.* **2019**, *129*, 1921–1963. [CrossRef]

Bayraktar, E.; Zhang, X. Embedding of Walsh Brownian motion. *Stoch. Process. Appl.* **2021**, *134*, 1–28. [CrossRef]

Lempa, J.; Mordecki, E.; Salminen, P. Diffusion spiders: Green kernel, excessive functions and optimal stopping. *Stoch. Process. Appl.* **2024**, *167*, 104229. [CrossRef]

Bednarz, E.; Ernst, P.A.; Osękowski, A. On the diameter of the stopped spider process. *Math. Oper. Res.* **2024**, *49*, 346–365. [CrossRef]

Csáki, E.; Földes, A. In memoriam Pál Révész (1934–2022). *Period. Math. Hungar.* **2024**, *89*, 201–229. [CrossRef]

Lejay, A. On the constructions of the skew Brownian motion. *Probab. Surv.* **2006**, *3*, 413–446. [CrossRef]

Ramirez, J.M.; Thomann, E.A.; Waymire, E.C. Advection-dispersion across interfaces. *Statist. Sci.* **2013**, *28*, 487–509. [CrossRef]

Appuhamillage, T.; Bokil, V.; Thomann, E.; Waymire, E.; Wood, B. Occupation and local times for skew Brownian motion with applications to dispersion across an interface. *Ann. Appl. Probab.* **2011**, *21*, 183–214. [CrossRef]

Lejay, A.; Pichot, G. Simulating diffusion processes in discontinuous media: Numerical scheme with constant time step. *J. Comput. Phys.* **2012**, *231*, 7299–7314. [CrossRef]

Lejay, A.; Mordecki, E.; Torres, S. Is a Brownian motion skew? *Scand. J. Statist.* **2014**, *41*, 346–364. [CrossRef]

Alvarez, L.; Salminen, P. Timing in the presence of directional predictability: Optimal stopping of skew Brownian motion. *Math. Meth. Oper. Res.* **2017**, *86*, 377–400. [CrossRef]

Rossello, D. Arbitrage in skew Brownian motion models. *Insur. Math. Econom.* **2012**, *50*, 50–56. [CrossRef]

Hussain, J.; Soomro, M.A.; Dahri, S.A.; Memon, K.N.; Bano, M.; Awwad, F.A.; Ismail, E.A.A.; Ahmad, H. A study of maximizing skew Brownian motion with applications to option pricing. *J. Radiat. Res. Appl. Sci.* **2024**, *17*, 100732. [CrossRef]

Dassios, M.; Zhang, J. First Hitting Time of Brownian Motion on Simple Graph with Skew Semiaxes. *Methodol. Comput. Appl. Probab.* **2022**, *24*, 1805–1831. [CrossRef]

Atar, R.; Cohen, A. Serve the shortest queue and Walsh Brownian motion. *Ann. Appl. Probab.* **2019**, *29*, 613–651. [CrossRef]

Salminen, P.; Stenlund, D. On occupation times of one-dimensional diffusions. *J. Theoret. Probab.* **2021**, *34*, 975–1011. [CrossRef]

Itô, K.; McKean, H.P., Jr. *Diffusion Processes and Their Sample Paths*; Springer: Berlin/Heidelberg, Germany, 1974.

31. Borodin, A.N.; Salminen, P. *Handbook of Brownian Motion—Facts and Formulae*, 2nd ed.; Probability and Its Applications; Birkhäus Verlag: Basel, Switzerland, 2015. [CrossRef]
32. Kac, M. On some connections between probability theory and differential and integral equations. In Proceedings of the Secor Berkeley Symposium on Mathematical Statistics and Probability, Berkeley/Los Angeles, CA, USA, 31 July–12 August 19 University of California Press: Berkeley, LA, USA, 1951; pp. 189–215.
33. Stenlund, D. On the connection between Stirling numbers and Bessel numbers. *Electron. J. Combin.* **2022**, *29*, P1.40. [CrossRef
34. Yang, S.L.; Qiao, Z.K. The Bessel numbers and Bessel matrices. *J. Math. Res. Expo.* **2011**, *31*, 627–636. [CrossRef]
35. Graham, R.L.; Knuth, D.E.; Patashnik, O. *Concrete Mathematics*, 2nd ed.; Addison-Wesley Publishing Company: Reading, M USA, 1994.

entropy

MDPI

·ticle

Simple Wide Range Approximation of Symmetric Binomial Distribution

ımás Szabados

Department of Stochastics, Institute of Mathematics, Budapest University of Technology and Economics, Muegyetem rkp. 3, H ep, 5 em, 1521 Budapest, Hungary; szabados@math.bme.hu; Tel.: +36-30-390-0660

Abstract: The paper gives a wide range, uniform, local approximation of symmetric binomial distribution. The result clearly shows how one has to modify the classical de Moivre–Laplace normal approximation in order to give an estimate at the tail as well as to minimize the relative error.

Keywords: wide range; approximation; binomial distribution

MSC: 60E15; 60F05

The topic of this paper is a wide range, uniform, local approximation of symmetric binomial distribution, an extension of the classical de Moivre–Laplace theorem in the symmetric case [1] (Ch. VII) [2]. In other words, I would like to approximate individual binomial probabilities not only in a classical neighborhood of the center, but at the tail as well. The result clearly shows how one has to modify the normal approximation in order to give a wide range estimate to minimize the relative error. The method will be somewhat similar to the ones applied by [3–5] or in the proof of Tusnády's lemma, see, e.g., [6]; however, my task is much simpler than those. This simplification makes the proof short, transparent and natural. Moreover, the result is non-asymptotic, that is, it gives explicit, nearly optimal, upper and lower bounds for the relative error with a finite n. Thus, I hope that it can be used in both applications and teaching.

Let $(X_r)_{r\geq 1}$ be a sequence of independent, identically distributed random steps with $\mathbb{P}(X_r = \pm 1) = \frac{1}{2}$ and $S_\ell = \sum_{r=1}^{\ell} X_r$ $(\ell \geq 1)$, $S_0 = 0$, be the corresponding simple, symmetric random walk. Then

$$\mathbb{P}(S_\ell = j) = \binom{\ell}{\frac{\ell+j}{2}} 2^{-\ell} \qquad (|j| \leq \ell). \tag{1}$$

Here, we use the convention that the above binomial coefficient is zero whenever $\ell + j$ is not divisible by 2. Since $\mathbb{P}(S_\ell = j) = \mathbb{P}(S_\ell = -j)$ for any j, it is enough to consider only the case $j \geq 0$ whenever it is convenient.

First we consider the case when $\ell = 2n$, even. Let us introduce the notation

$$a_{k,n} := \mathbb{P}(S_{2n} = 2k) = \binom{2n}{n+k} 2^{-2n} \qquad (|k| \leq n).$$

Also, introduce the notation

$$b_{k,n} := n\left\{ \left(1 + \frac{k+\frac{1}{2}}{n}\right) \log\left(1 + \frac{k}{n}\right) + \left(1 - \frac{k-\frac{1}{2}}{n}\right) \log\left(1 - \frac{k}{n}\right) \right\} \tag{2}$$

when $n \geq 1$ and $|k| < n$, and

$$b_{\pm n,n} := \left(2n + \frac{1}{2}\right)\log 2 - \frac{1}{2}\log(2\pi n) \qquad (n \geq 1). \tag{3}$$

Theorem 1. *(a) For any $n \geq 1$ and $|k| \leq n$, we have*

$$a_{k,n} \leq \frac{1}{\sqrt{\pi n}} e^{-b_{k,n}}. \tag{4}$$

(b) For any $n \geq 1$ and $|k| \leq rn$, $r \in (0,1)$, we have

$$a_{k,n} > \frac{1}{\sqrt{\pi n}} e^{-b_{k,n}} \exp\left(-\frac{1}{7n} - \frac{r^4}{3(1-r^2)^2\, n}\right). \tag{5}$$

(c) In accordance with the classical de Moivre–Laplace normal approximation, for $n \geq 3$ and $|k| \leq n^{\frac{2}{3}}$ one has

$$1 - 2n^{-\frac{1}{3}} < \frac{a_{k,n}}{\frac{1}{\sqrt{\pi n}} e^{-\frac{k^2}{n}}} < 1 + 2n^{-\frac{1}{3}}. \tag{6}$$

Proof. As usual, the first step is to estimate the central term

$$a_{0,n} = \binom{2n}{n} 2^{-2n} = \frac{(2n)!}{(n!)^2} 2^{-2n}.$$

By Stirling's formula, see, e.g., [1] (p. 54), we have:

$$\sqrt{2\pi n}\left(\frac{n}{e}\right)^n e^{\frac{1}{12n+1}} < n! < \sqrt{2\pi n}\left(\frac{n}{e}\right)^n e^{\frac{1}{12n}} \qquad (n \geq 1). \tag{7}$$

Thus, after simplification we obtain

$$\frac{1}{\sqrt{\pi n}} e^{-\frac{1}{7n}} < a_{0,n} < \frac{1}{\sqrt{\pi n}} e^{-\frac{1}{9n}} \qquad (n \geq 1). \tag{8}$$

Second, also by the standard way, for $1 \leq k \leq n$,

$$a_{k,n} = a_{0,n} \frac{n(n-1)\cdots(n-k+1)}{(n+1)(n+2)\cdots(n+k)} = a_{0,n} \frac{\left(1-\frac{1}{n}\right)\left(1-\frac{2}{n}\right)\cdots\left(1-\frac{k-1}{n}\right)}{\left(1+\frac{1}{n}\right)\left(1+\frac{2}{n}\right)\cdots\left(1+\frac{k}{n}\right)}.$$

So it follows that

$$\begin{aligned} \log a_{k,n} &= \log a_{0,n} - \log\left(1+\tfrac{k}{n}\right) - 2\sum_{j=1}^{k-1} \tfrac{1}{2}\log\frac{1+\frac{j}{n}}{1-\frac{j}{n}} \\ &= \log a_{0,n} - \log\left(1+\tfrac{k}{n}\right) - 2\sum_{j=1}^{k-1} \tanh^{-1}\left(\tfrac{j}{n}\right). \end{aligned} \tag{9}$$

To approximate the sum here, let us introduce the integral

$$I(x) := \int_0^x \tanh^{-1}(t)\, dt = \frac{1}{2}(1+x)\log(1+x) + \frac{1}{2}(1-x)\log(1-x) \tag{10}$$

for $|x| < 1$, and its approximation by a trapezoidal sum

$$T_{k,n} := \frac{1}{n}\left\{\frac{1}{2}\tanh^{-1}(0) + \sum_{j=1}^{k-1}\tanh^{-1}\left(\frac{j}{n}\right) + \frac{1}{2}\tanh^{-1}\left(\frac{k}{n}\right)\right\}, \tag{11}$$

where $0 \le k < n$. It is well-known that the error of the trapezoidal formula for a function $f \in C^2([a,b])$ is

$$T_n(f) - \int_a^b f(t)\,\mathrm{d}t = \frac{(b-a)^3}{12n^2} f''(x), \qquad x \in [a,b].$$

Since $(\tanh^{-1})''(x) = 2x(1-x^2)^{-2}$, we obtain that

$$0 \le T_{k,n} - I\left(\frac{k}{n}\right) \le \frac{r^4}{6(1-r^2)^2\,n^2}, \quad \text{when} \quad 0 \le k \le rn, \quad r \in (0,1). \tag{12}$$

Let us combine Formulas (8)–(12):

$$\log a_{k,n} = \log a_{0,n} - 2nT_{k,n} - \frac{1}{2}\log\left(1+\frac{k}{n}\right) - \frac{1}{2}\log\left(1-\frac{k}{n}\right),$$

thus

$$\log\frac{1}{\sqrt{\pi n}} - b_{k,n} - \frac{1}{7n} - \frac{r^4}{3(1-r^2)^2\,n} < \log a_{k,n} < \log\frac{1}{\sqrt{\pi n}} - b_{k,n} - \frac{1}{9n}, \tag{13}$$

where $0 \le k \le rn$ and

$$b_{k,n} = 2nI\left(\frac{k}{n}\right) + \frac{1}{2}\log\left(1-\frac{k^2}{n^2}\right). \tag{14}$$

Clearly, (14) is the same as (2). Thus, (13) proves (a) and (b) of the theorem.

Let us see now, using Taylor expansions, a series expansion of $b_{k,n}$ when $|k| < n$. First, for $|x| < 1$,

$$I(x) = \frac{x^2}{1\cdot 2} + \frac{x^4}{3\cdot 4} + \frac{x^6}{5\cdot 6} + \frac{x^8}{7\cdot 8} + \cdots.$$

Second, also for $|x| < 1$,

$$\log(1-x^2) = -x^2 - \frac{x^4}{2} - \frac{x^6}{3} - \frac{x^8}{4} - \cdots.$$

So by (14), for $|k| < n$ we have a convergent series for $b_{k,n}$:

$$\begin{aligned} b_{k,n} &= \tfrac{k^2}{n}\left(1-\tfrac{1}{2n}\right) + \tfrac{k^4}{2n^3}\left(\tfrac{1}{3}-\tfrac{1}{2n}\right) + \tfrac{k^6}{3n^5}\left(\tfrac{1}{5}-\tfrac{1}{2n}\right) + \cdots \\ &= \sum_{j=1}^{\infty}\left(\tfrac{k}{n}\right)^{2j}\tfrac{1}{j}\left(\tfrac{n}{2j-1}-\tfrac{1}{2}\right). \end{aligned} \tag{15}$$

By (15), for $n \ge 3$ and $|k| \le n^{\frac{2}{3}}$ we obtain that

$$\begin{aligned} \left|b_{k,n} - \tfrac{k^2}{n}\right| &\le \tfrac{n^{-\frac{2}{3}}}{2} + \sum_{j=2}^{\infty} n^{-\frac{2}{3}j}\tfrac{1}{j}\left(\tfrac{n}{2j-1}+\tfrac{1}{2}\right) \\ &\le \tfrac{n^{-\frac{2}{3}}}{2} + \tfrac{n}{2}\left(\tfrac{1}{3}+\tfrac{1}{6}\right)\sum_{j=2}^{\infty} n^{-\frac{2}{3}j} \le n^{-\frac{1}{3}}. \end{aligned}$$

Thus, by (4), for $n \ge 3$ and $|k| \le n^{\frac{2}{3}}$,

$$a_{k,n} \le \frac{1}{\sqrt{\pi n}} e^{-\frac{k^2}{n}} e^{n^{-1/3}} < \frac{1}{\sqrt{\pi n}} e^{-\frac{k^2}{n}}\left(1+2n^{-\frac{1}{3}}\right). \tag{16}$$

Similarly, by (5), for $n \geq 3$ and $|k| \leq n^{\frac{2}{3}}$,

$$\begin{aligned} a_{k,n} &> \tfrac{1}{\sqrt{\pi n}} e^{-\frac{k^2}{n}} \exp\left(-\tfrac{1}{7n} - \tfrac{n^{-\frac{7}{3}}}{3(1-n^{-\frac{2}{3}})^2} - n^{-\frac{1}{3}}\right) \\ &\geq \tfrac{1}{\sqrt{\pi n}} e^{-\frac{k^2}{n}} e^{-1.21 n^{-1/3}} > \tfrac{1}{\sqrt{\pi n}} e^{-\frac{k^2}{n}} \left(1 - 2n^{-1/3}\right). \end{aligned} \tag{17}$$

(16) and (17) together prove (c) of the theorem. □

The main moral of Theorem 1 is that the exponent k^2/n in the exponent of the normal approximation is only a first approximation of the series (15). In (c), the bound $|k| \leq n^{\frac{2}{3}}$ was chosen somewhat arbitrarily. It is clear from the series (15) that the bound should be $o(n^{\frac{3}{4}})$. The above given bound was picked because it seemed to be satisfactory for usual applications with large deviation and gave a nice relative error bound $2n^{-\frac{1}{3}}$.

It is not difficult to extend the previous results to the odd-valued case of the symmetric binomial probabilities

$$a^*_{k,n} := \mathbb{P}(S_{2n-1} = 2k - 1) = \binom{2n-1}{n+k-1} 2^{-2n+1} \qquad (-n+1 \leq k \leq n).$$

Define

$$b^*_{k,n} := n\left\{\left(1 + \frac{k - \frac{1}{2}}{n}\right)\log\left(1 + \frac{k}{n}\right) + \left(1 - \frac{k - \frac{1}{2}}{n}\right)\log\left(1 - \frac{k}{n}\right)\right\} \tag{18}$$

for $n \geq 1$ and $|k| < n$, and

$$b^*_{n,n} := \left(2n - \frac{1}{2}\right)\log 2 - \frac{1}{2}\log(2\pi n) \qquad (n \geq 1). \tag{19}$$

Theorem 2. *(a) For any $n \geq 1$ and $-n+1 \leq k \leq n$, we have*

$$a^*_{k,n} < \frac{1}{\sqrt{\pi n}} e^{-b^*_{k,n}} \exp\left(\frac{2}{3n}\right). \tag{20}$$

(b) For any $n \geq 1$ and $|k| \leq rn$, $r \in (0,1)$, we have

$$a^*_{k,n} > \frac{1}{\sqrt{\pi n}} e^{-b^*_{k,n}} \exp\left(-\frac{1}{n} - \frac{r^4}{3(1-r^2)^2\, n}\right). \tag{21}$$

(c) In accordance with the classical de Moivre–Laplace normal approximation, for $n \geq 4$ and $|k| \leq n^{\frac{2}{3}}$ one has

$$1 - 3n^{-\frac{1}{3}} < \frac{a^*_{k,n}}{\frac{1}{\sqrt{\pi n}} e^{-\frac{k^2}{n}}} < 1 + 6n^{-\frac{1}{3}}. \tag{22}$$

Proof. Since this proof is very similar to the previous one, several details are omitted. First, by Stirling's Formula (7), after simplifications we obtain that

$$\frac{1}{\sqrt{\pi n}} e^{-\frac{1}{n}} < a^*_{0,n} < \frac{1}{\sqrt{\pi n}} e^{\frac{2}{3n}} \qquad (n \geq 1). \tag{23}$$

Second, similarly to (13), for $n \geq 1$ and $|k| \leq rn$, $r \in (0,1)$, we obtain that

$$\log \frac{1}{\sqrt{\pi n}} - b^*_{k,n} - \frac{1}{n} - \frac{r^4}{3(1-r^2)^2\, n} < \log a^*_{k,n} < \log \frac{1}{\sqrt{\pi n}} - b^*_{k,n} + \frac{2}{3n}, \tag{24}$$

where

$$b^*_{k,n} := 2nI\left(\frac{k}{n}\right) - \tanh^{-1}\left(\frac{k}{n}\right) = \sum_{j=1}^{\infty}\left(\frac{k}{n}\right)^{2j-1}\frac{1}{2j-1}\left(\frac{k}{j}-1\right). \quad (25)$$

(25) clearly agrees with (18). (24) proves (a) and (b).

By the series in (25), for $n \geq 4$ and $|k| \leq n^{\frac{2}{3}}$ we obtain that

$$\left|b^*_{k,n} - \frac{k^2}{n}\right| < 2n^{-\frac{1}{3}}.$$

This and (24) imply (c). □

Funding: This research received no external funding.

Institutional Review Board Statement: Not applicable.

Data Availability Statement: No new data were created or analyzed in this study. Data sharing is not applicable to this article.

Conflicts of Interest: The author declares no conflicts of interest.

References

Feller, W. *An Introduction to Probability Theory and Its Applications*, 3rd ed.; Wiley: New York, NY, USA, 1968; Volume I.
Révész, P. *Random Walk in Random and Non-Random Environments*, 2nd ed.; World Scientific: Singapore, 2005.
Feller, W. On the normal approximation to the binomial distribution. *Ann. Math. Statist.* **1945**, *16*, 319–329. [CrossRef]
Littlewood, J.E. On the probability in the tail of a binomial distribution. *Adv. Appl. Prob.* **1969**, *1*, 43–72. [CrossRef]
McKay, B.D. On Littlewood's estimate for the binomial distribution. *Adv. Appl. Prob.* **1989**, *21*, 475–478. [CrossRef]
Massart, P. Tusnady's lemma, 24 years later. *Ann. I. H. Poincaré—PR* **2002**, *38*, 991–1007. [CrossRef]

entropy

Article

Random Walks and Lorentz Processes

Domokos Szász

Department of Stochastics, Budapest University of Technology and Economics, H-1111 Budapest, Hungary; szasz@math.bme.hu

Abstract: Random walks and Lorentz processes serve as fundamental models for Brownian motion. The study of random walks is a favorite object of probability theory, whereas that of Lorentz processes belongs to the theory of hyperbolic dynamical systems. Here we first present an example where the method based on the probabilistic approach led to new results for the Lorentz process: concretely, the recurrence of the planar periodic Lorentz process with a finite horizon. Afterwards, an unsolved problem—related to a 1981 question of Sinai on locally perturbed periodic Lorentz processes—is formulated as an analogous problem in the language of random walks.

Keywords: random walk; Lorentz process; recurrence

1. Introduction

According to Pólya's classical theorem [1], the simple symmetric random walk (SSRW) on $\mathbb{Z}^d$ is recurrent if $d = 1, 2$; otherwise, it is transient. Since the one- and two-dimensional Lorentz processes with a periodic configuration of scatterers share a number of stochastic properties with those of SSRWs, it had also been expected that the analogues of Pólya's theorem also hold for them. Indeed, in $d = 2$, the recurrence of the periodic finite-horizon Lorentz process (FHLP) was settled by ergodic theoretic methods independently by K. Schmidt [2] and J.-P. Conze [3]. For the same case, in 2004, with T. Varjú, we succeeded in giving a probabilistic–dynamical proof in [4]. The recurrence of the infinite-horizon Lorentz process (IHLP) in the plane was open until 2007, when the method of [4] could be extended to the infinite-horizon case (see [5]). It is worth mentioning that in the infinite-horizon case, the limit law of the Lorentz process belongs to the non-standard domain of attraction of the normal law, in contrast with the finite-horizon case where convergence to the normal law (and to the Wiener process) holds with the diffusive scaling.

Sinai asked in 1981 whether probabilistic properties of the Lorentz process remain valid if one changes the scatterer configuration in a bounded domain. For convergence to the Gaussian law (and to the Wiener process) and, moreover, for the local limit theorem (LLT) and for recurrence, we gave an affirmative answer in [6]. It is worth mentioning that—in our probabilistic approach and for our purposes solely—the recurrence property can be positioned above the limit theorem (with diffusive or over-diffusive scaling) and even over the LLT, see Section 5. Of course, other properties are also very important, such as the speed of correlation decay, almost sure invariance principle, etc. (cf. [7]).

However, as to Sinai's 1981 question, nothing is known in the infinite-horizon case. Since the study of random walks might be much instructive for the behavior of Lorentz processes—in Section 5—we formulate some problems for random walks with unbounded jumps that are most interesting in themselves. Before the closing section, this paper contains a survey of results known for recurrence properties of RWs and of Lorentz processes.

2. Random Walks and Lorentz Processes

2.1. Random Walks

Definition 1 (random walk).

1. *Let* $\{X_n \in \mathbb{Z}^d | n \geq 0\}$ *be independent random variables, and for* $n \geq 0$*, denote*

$$S_n = \sum_{j=1}^{n} X_j.$$

Then the Markov chain $S_0, S_1, S_2, \ldots, S_n, \ldots$ *is called a* random walk.

2. *The random walk is called* symmetric *if the* X_n*s are symmetric random variables.*
3. *The random walk is* simple *if* $|X_n| = 1$ *holds* $\forall n \geq 0$.
4. *The probabilities*

$$P(X_{n+1} = k | S_n)$$

are called the transition (or jump) probabilities *of the random walk.*

5. *The random walk is called* translation-invariant *(or classical or homogeneous) if its transition probabilities are translation-invariant.*

As to basic notions and properties of random walks, we refer to the monographs [8–10].

Definition 2 (locally perturbed random walk). *Assume* $a > 0$*. If—possibly outside an origo-centered cube* Q_a *of size* a*—the translation probabilities of a random walk* $S_0, S_1, S_2, \ldots, S_n, \ldots$ *are translation-invariant, then we say that the random walk is a* locally perturbed random walk *(LPRW) (more precisely an* a*-*locally perturbed random walk*). For simplicity, we assume that all transition probabilities are bounded away from* 0.

2.2. Sinai Billiards and Lorentz Processes

2.2.1. Sinai Billiards

As far as notations go, we mainly follow [11] for planar billiards and [12] for multidimensional ones.

Billiards are defined in Euclidean domains bounded by a finite number of smooth boundary pieces. For our purpose, a *billiard* is a dynamical system describing the motion of a point particle in a connected, compact domain $\mathcal{Q} \subset \mathbb{T}^d = \mathbb{R}^d / \mathbb{Z}^d$. In general, the boundary $\partial\mathcal{Q}$ of the domain is assumed to be piecewise C^3-smooth, i.e., there are no corner points; if $0 < J < \infty$ is the number of such pieces, we can write $\partial\mathcal{Q} = \cup_{1 \leq \alpha \leq J} \partial\mathcal{Q}_\alpha$. Connected components of $\mathbb{T}^d \setminus \mathcal{Q}$ are called *scatterers* and are assumed to be strictly convex. Motion is uniform inside $\mathcal{Q}$, and specular reflections take place at the boundary $\partial\mathcal{Q}$; in other words, a particle propagates freely until it collides with a scatterer, where it is reflected elastically, i.e., following the classical rule that the angle of incidence be equal to the angle of reflection.

Definition 3 (Sinai billiard). *A billiard with strictly convex scatterers is called a* Sinai billiard.

Remark 1. *The above notion of a Sinai billiard is more general than its original one where it was supposed that* $d = 2$, $J = 1$*, and* $\mathcal{Q}_1$ *was a circle.*

Since the absolute value of the velocity is a first integral of motion, the phase space of our billiard is defined as the product of the set of spatial configurations by the $(d-1)$-sphere, $\mathcal{M} = \mathcal{Q} \times \mathbb{S}_{d-1}$, which is to say that every phase point $x \in \mathcal{M}$ is of the form $x = (q, v)$, with $q \in \mathcal{Q}$ and $v \in \mathbb{R}^d$ with norm $|v| = 1$. According to the reflection rule, $\mathcal{M}$ is subject to identification of incoming and outgoing phase points at the boundary $\partial\mathcal{M} = \partial\mathcal{Q} \times \mathbb{S}_{d-1}$. The billiard dynamics on $\mathcal{M}$ is called the *billiard flow* and denoted by $S^t : t \in (-\infty, \infty)$, where $S^t : \mathcal{M} \to \mathcal{M}$. The set of points defined by the trajectory going through $x \in \mathcal{M}$ is denoted as $S^{\mathbb{R}}x$. The smooth, invariant probability measure of the billiard flow, μ on $\mathcal{M}$, also called the Liouville measure, is essentially the product of

Lebesgue measures on the respective spaces, i.e., $\mathrm{d}\mu = \text{const.}\, \mathrm{d}q\, \mathrm{d}v$, where the constant is $(\operatorname{vol} \mathcal{Q} \operatorname{vol} \mathbb{S}_{d-1})^{-1}$.

The appearance of collision–free orbits is a distinctive feature of some billiards which are said to have infinite horizons.

Definition 4 (infinite and finite horizons)**.**

1. *Denote by $\mathcal{M}_{free} \subset \mathcal{M}$ the subset of collision-free orbits, i.e.,*

$$\mathcal{M}_{free} = \{x \in \mathcal{M} \,:\, S^{\mathbb{R}}x \cap \partial\mathcal{M} = \emptyset\}\,.$$

2. *The billiard has a* finite horizon *if $\mathcal{M}_{free} = \emptyset$. Otherwise it has an* infinite horizon.

2.2.2. Lorentz Processes

The Lorentz process was introduced in 1905 by H. A. Lorentz [13] for the study of a dilute electron gas in a metal. While Lorentz considered the motion of a collection of independent pointlike particles moving uniformly among immovable metallic ions modeled by elastic spheres, we consider here the uniform motion of a single pointlike particle in a fixed array of strictly convex scatterers with which it interacts via elastic collisions.

Thus defined, the *Lorentz process* is the billiard dynamics of a point particle on a billiard table $\mathcal{Q} = \mathbb{R}^d \setminus \cup_{\alpha=1}^{\infty} O_\alpha$, where the scatterers O_α, $1 \le \alpha \le \infty$, are strictly convex with C^3-smooth boundaries. Generally speaking, it could happen that $\mathcal{Q}$ has several connected components. For simplicity, however, we assume that the scatterers are disjoint and that $\mathcal{Q}$ is unbounded and connected. The phase space of this process is then given according to the above definition, namely, $\mathcal{M} = \mathcal{Q} \times \mathbb{S}_{d-1}$.

It should finally be noted that, under this assumption, the Liouville measure $\mathrm{d}\mu = \mathrm{d}q\, \mathrm{d}v$, while invariant, is infinite. If, however, there exists a regular lattice of rank d for which we have that for every point z of this lattice, $\mathcal{Q} + z = \mathcal{Q}$, then we say that the corresponding Lorentz process is *periodic*. In this case, the Liouville measure is finite (more exactly, its factor with respect to the lattice is finite). (For simplicity, the lattice of periodicity will be taken as $\mathbb{Z}^d$.)

Definition 5 (periodic Lorentz process)**.** *The Lorentz process is called* periodic *if the configuration $\{O_\alpha | 1 \le \alpha < \infty\}$ of its scatterers is $\mathbb{Z}^d$-periodic.*

Figure 1 shows examples of trajectories (red lines) in periodic Lorentz processes (for the finite- vs. the infinite-horizon cases, respectively, cf. Definition 4).

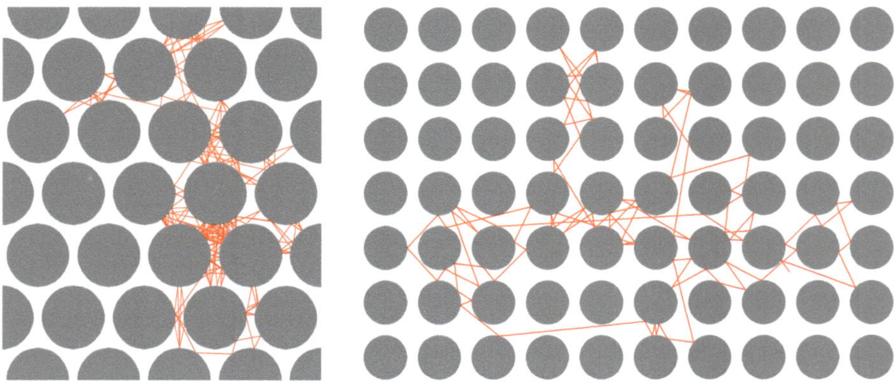

(**a**) Finite horizon. (**b**) Infinite horizon.

Figure 1. Periodic Lorentz process.

Definition 6 (locally perturbed (periodic) Lorentz process). *If one changes arbitrarily the scatterer configuration of a periodic Lorentz process in a bounded domain, then we talk about a* locally perturbed Lorentz process (LPLP). *This process has a* finite or an infinite horizon *if the original periodic Lorentz process had a finite or an infinite horizon, respectively.*

2.2.3. Recurrence of Stochastic Processes

Definition 7 (recurrence). *A stochastic process in $\mathbf{Z}^d$ or in $\mathbf{R}^d$ ($d \geq 1$) is* recurrent *if for any bounded subset of $\mathbf{Z}^d$ (or of $\mathbf{R}^d$) it is true that the process returns to the subset infinitely often with probability* 1.

3. Recurrence of Periodic Random Walks and Lorentz Processes in the Plane

In this section, we restrict ourselves to the case when—on the one hand—the transition probabilities of the random walk are translation-invariant and—on the other hand—the Lorentz process is periodic.

3.1. Random Walks

Start with the classical theorem of Pólya.

Theorem 1 ([1]). *The SSRW is recurrent if $d = 1, 2$, and otherwise it is transient.*

For more general random walks, we refer to results of Chung-Ornstein and Breiman.

Theorem 2 ([14,15]).
1. *Assume $(S_0, S_1, S_2, \dots)$ is a translation-invariant RW on $\mathbb{Z}$. If $\mathbf{E}X_1 = 0$, then the RW is recurrent.*
2. *Assume $(S_0, S_1, S_2, \dots)$ is a translation-invariant RW on $\mathbb{Z}^2$. If $\mathbf{E}X_1 = 0$ and $\mathbf{E}|X_n|^2 < \infty$, then the RW is recurrent.*

3.2. Lorentz Processes

Based on the analogy with random walks, for periodic Lorentz processes, the exact analogue of Pólya's theorem known for random walks had been expected.

3.2.1. Finite Horizon

The first positive result was obtained in [16], where a slightly weaker form of recurrence was demonstrated: the process almost surely returns infinitely often to a moderately (actually logarithmically) increasing sequence of domains. The authors used a probabilistic method combined with the dynamical tools of Markov approximations. (The weaker form of recurrence was the consequence of the weaker form of their local limit theorem based on the weaker CLT of [17].)

An original approach appeared in 1998–99, when, independently, Schmidt [2] and Conze [3] were, indeed, able to deduce recurrence from the global central limit theorem (CLT) of [18] by adding (abstract) ergodic theoretic ideas.

Theorem 3 ([2,3]). *The planar Lorentz process with a finite horizon is almost surely recurrent.*

Their approach seems, however, to be essentially restricted to the planar finite-horizon case.

3.2.2. Infinite Horizon

For attacking the infinite-horizon case, the authors of [4] returned to the probabilistic approach via the local limit theorem and first gave a new proof of the theorems of Conze and Schmidt. Finally, in [5], they could prove a local limit theorem for the Lorentz process in the infinite-horizon case that already implied recurrence in this case, too.

Theorem 4 ([5]). *The planar Lorentz process with an infinite horizon is almost surely recurrent.*

4. Recurrence Properties of Locally Perturbed Planar Lorentz Processes

4.1. Finite-Horizon Case

Answering Sinai's 1981 question, we could prove the following:

Theorem 5 ([6]). *The locally perturbed planar Lorentz process with a finite horizon is almost surely recurrent.*

We note that the proof of the above theorem uses delicate recurrence properties of the periodic Lorentz process (cf. [7]), being interesting in themselves. Actually, they are analogues of several properties of classical random walks.

4.2. Infinite-Horizon Case

Conjecture 1. *The locally perturbed planar Lorentz process with an infinite horizon is almost surely recurrent.*

5. Recurrence Properties of Symmetric vs. Locally Perturbed Random Walks with Unbounded Jumps

For understanding the difficulties in proving Conjecture 1, it should be instructive to answer the analogous question for LPRWs with unbounded jumps.

For LPRWs with bounded jumps, the first result related to Sinai's question was given in the paper [19].

5.1. Reminder of Some Results of [19]

We recall a simple example of its main theorem.

Definition 8. *Let $\{S_n|n \geq 0\}$ be a simple RW on $\mathbb{Z}^2$ such that for $i = 1, 2$*

$$P(X_{n+1} = \pm e_i | S_n) = \begin{cases} \frac{1}{4} & \text{if } S_n \neq (0,0) \\ \text{arbitrary} & \text{if } S_n = (0,0) \end{cases}$$

where $e_1 = (1, 0)$ and $e_2 = (0, 1)$.

Let, moreover,

$$U_n(t) := n^{-1/2} S_{[nt]} \qquad t \in [0, 1]$$

Theorem 6 ([19]). *As $n \to \infty$*

$$U_n(t) \Rightarrow W(t)$$

weakly in $C[0, 1]$, where W is the standard planar Wiener process.

Remark 2.

1. *By applying the methods of [7,19], one can easily see the following:*
    (a) *For $U_n(1)$, the global CLT holds;*
    (b) *For $U_n(1)$, the local CLT also holds;*
    (c) *As a consequence of the later one, the RW of Definition 8 is recurrent.*
2. *In fact, Theorem 6 is the special case of a more general theorem of [19], whose statement roughly says that if one has a CLT for a translation-invariant RW, then changing the jump probabilities in a bounded domain does not change the statement of the CLT. The methods of [7] also imply the truth of the local limit theorem and recurrence in this generality.*

5.2. A Locally Perturbed RW with Unbounded Jumps

Following the bounded jumps case, for the unbounded jumps case we will also start with a simple example:

Definition 9. *Let $\{S_n | n \geq 0\}$ be an RW (with unbounded jumps) such that for $i = 1, 2$ one has*

$$\begin{cases} P(X_{n+1} = \pm e_i | S_n = (0,0)) & = 1/4 \\ P(X_{n+1} = \pm n e_i | S_n \neq (0,0)) & = const. \frac{1}{|n|^3} \end{cases}$$

Let us explain why we suggest first the study of exactly this example. The simplest example of a periodic Lorentz process is the following: all scatterers are circles of radius R with $R_{\min} < R < \frac{1}{2}$. This condition ensures that all elements of $\mathcal{M}_{\text{free}}$ are parallel to one of the axes. In this case, the long jumps of the Lorentz process are almost parallel to one of the axes, and the distribution of their lengths is asymptotically $const. \frac{1}{|n|^3}$ and thus belongs to the non-standard domain of attraction of the normal law (cf. [5,20–22]).

The unperturbed RW corresponding to the previous example belongs to the non-standard domain of attraction of the normal law with $\sqrt{n \log n}$ scaling. Denote

$$V_n(t) := (n \log n)^{-1/2} S_{[nt]} \qquad t \in [0,1]$$

A special case of the main result of the work [23] is the following:

Theorem 7 ([23])**.** *As $n \to \infty$*

$$V_n(t) \Rightarrow CW(t)$$

weakly in $C[0,1]$, where W is the standard planar Wiener process and $C > 0$.

Conjecture 2. *In the setup of this theorem, the following hold:*

1. *The local version of the limit law for $V_n(1)$ is also true;*
2. *The RW defined in Definition 9 is recurrent.*

6. Strongly Perturbed RWs

For locally perturbed random walks, it was sort of expected that a local perturbation should not change the limiting behavior of the RW whether the jumps are bounded or unbounded, whatever difficulties the proofs of these statements would bring up. However, under what kind of extended perturbations the classical limiting behavior of the random walk survives is intriguing. Before a precise formulation of this question, let us introduce notations.

Definition 10 (strongly perturbed random walks)**.** *Assume $\{0 < a_n | n \geq 1\}$ are such that $\lim_{n\to\infty} a_n = \infty$. The sequence $S_0^{a_n}, S_1^{a_n}, S_2^{a_n}, \ldots, S_n^{a_n}, \ldots$ of a_n-locally perturbed random walks is called strongly a_n-perturbed.*

Question 1. *For a sequence $\{a_n | \lim_{n\to\infty} a_n = \infty\}$, denote*

$$Z_n(t) := n^{-1/2} S_{[nt]}^{a_n} \qquad t \in [0,1],$$

where the jump probabilities of the translation-invariant random walk are as in Definition 8.

1. *Find a sequence $\{a_n | \lim_{n\to\infty} a_n = \infty\}$ and a strongly a_n-locally perturbed sequence of random walks (cf. Definition 2) with bounded jumps such that*

$$Z_n(t) \Rightarrow W(t) \tag{1}$$

   weakly in $C[0,1]$.
2. *Can you prove Equation (1) for any sequences of a_n with $a_n = o(n^{1/2})$?*

Question 2. *For a sequence* $\{a_n |\, \lim_{n\to\infty} a_n = \infty\}$*, denote*

$$Y_n(t) := (n \log n)^{-1/2} S^{a_n}_{[nt]} \qquad t \in [0,1]$$

where the jump probabilities of the translation-invariant random walk are as in Definition 9.

1. *Find a sequence* $\{a_n |\, \lim_{n\to\infty} a_n = \infty\}$ *and a strongly* a_n*-locally perturbed sequence of random walks with unbounded jumps such that*

$$Y_n(t) \Rightarrow W(t) \tag{2}$$

weakly in $C[0,1]$.

2. *Can you prove Equation (2) for any sequences of* a_n *with* $a_n = o((n \log n)^{1/2})$*?*

Funding: This research was funded by NKFIH Research Fund grant number K142169.

Data Availability Statement: The original contributions presented in the study are included in the article, further inquiries can be directed to the corresponding author.

Acknowledgments: The author expresses the gratitude to István Berkes for their precious advice. I am also grateful to the referees for their useful remarks. The author thanks the Erwin Schrödinger International Institute for Mathematics and Physics since the questions raised in this paper were initiated during the workshop Rare Events in Dynamical Systems (18 March 2024–22 March 2024).

Conflicts of Interest: The authors declare no conflict of interest.

References

1. Pólya, G. Über eine Aufgabe der Wahrscheinlichkeitsrechnung betreffend die Irrfahrt im Straßennetz. *Math. Ann.* **19** *84*, 149–160. [CrossRef]
2. Schmidt, K. On joint recurrence. *C. R. Acad. Sci. Paris Sér. I Math.* **1998**, *327*, 837–842. [CrossRef]
3. Conze, J.P. Sur un critère de récurrence en dimension 2 pour les marches stationnaires, applications. *Ergod. Theory Dynam. Sy* **1999**, *19*, 1233–1245. [CrossRef]
4. Szász, D.; Varjú, T. Local limit theorem for the Lorentz process and its recurrence in the plane. *Ergod. Theory Dyn. Syst.* **20** *24*, 257–278. [CrossRef]
5. Szász, D.; Varjú, T. Limit laws and recurrence for the planar Lorentz process with infinite horizon. *J. Stat. Phys.* **2007**, *129*, 59– [CrossRef]
6. Dolgopyat, D.; Szász, D.; Varjú, T. Limit theorems for locally perturbed planar Lorentz processes. *Duke Math. J.* **2009**, *148*, 459–4 [CrossRef]
7. Dolgopyat, D.; Szász, D.; Varjú, T. Recurrence properties of planar Lorentz process. *Duke Math. J.* **2008**, *142*, 241–281. [CrossR
8. Spitzer, F. *Principles of Random Walk*, 2nd ed.; Graduate Texts in Mathematics; Springer: New York, NY, USA; Berlin/Heidelbe Germany, 1976; Volume 34, pp. xiii+408.
9. Révész, P. *Random Walk in Random and Non-Random Environments*, 3rd ed.; World Scientific Publishing Co. Pte. Ltd.: Hackensa NJ, USA, 2013; pp. xviii+402. [CrossRef]
10. Telcs, A. *The Art of Random Walks;* Lecture Notes in Mathematics; Springer: Berlin/Heidelberg, Germany, 2006; Volume 18 pp. viii+195.
11. Chernov, N.; Markarian, R. *Chaotic Billiards;* Mathematical Surveys and Monographs; American Mathematical Society: Providen RI, USA, 2006; Volume 127, pp. xii+316. [CrossRef]
12. Bálint, P.; Chernov, N.; Szász, D.; Tóth, I.P. Geometry of multi-dimensional dispersing billiards. *Asterisque* **2003**, *286*, 119–150.
13. Lorentz, H.A. The motion of electrons in metallic bodies i. *K. Ned. Akad. Van Wet. Proc.* **1905**, *7*, 438–453.
14. Chung, K.L.; Ornstein, D. On the recurrence of sums of random variables. *Bull. Amer. Math. Soc.* **1962**, *68*, 30–32. [CrossRef]
15. Breiman, L. *Probability;* Classics in Applied Mathematics; Society for Industrial and Applied Mathematics (SIAM): Philadelph PA, USA, 1992; Volume 7, pp. xiv+421. [CrossRef]
16. Krámli, A.; Szász, D. The problem of recurrence for Lorentz processes. *Comm. Math. Phys.* **1985**, *98*, 539–552. [CrossRef]
17. Bunimovich, L.A.; Sinai, Y.G. Statistical properties of Lorentz gas with periodic configuration of scatterers. *Comm. Math. Ph* **1981**, *78*, 479–497. [CrossRef]
18. Bunimovich, L.A.; Sinai, Y.G.; Chernov, N.I. Statistical properties of two-dimensional hyperbolic billiards. *Uspekhi Mat. Na* **1991**, *46*, 43–92, 192. [CrossRef]
19. Szász, D.; Telcs, A. Random walk in an inhomogeneous medium with local impurities. *J. Statist. Phys.* **1981**, *26*, 527–5 [CrossRef]

9. Bleher, P.M. Statistical properties of two-dimensional periodic Lorentz gas with infinite horizon. *J. Statist. Phys.* **1992**, *66*, 315–373. [CrossRef]
1. Dettmann, C.P. New Horizons in Multidimensional Diffusion: The Lorentz Gas and the Riemann Hypothesis. *J. Stat. Phys.* **2012**, *146*, 181–204. [CrossRef]
2. Nándori, P.; Szász, D.; Varjú, T. Tail asymptotics of free path lengths for the periodic Lorentz process: On Dettmann's geometric conjectures. *Comm. Math. Phys.* **2014**, *331*, 111–137. [CrossRef]
3. Paulin, D.; Szász, D. Locally perturbed random walks with unbounded jumps. *J. Stat. Phys.* **2010**, *141*, 1116–1130. [CrossRef]

entropy

Article

On the Komlós–Révész SLLN for Ψ-Mixing Sequences

Zbigniew S. Szewczak

Faculty of Mathematics and Computer Science, Nicolaus Copernicus University, ul. Chopina 12/18, 87-100 Toruń, Poland; zssz@mat.umk.pl

Abstract: The Komlós–Révész strong law of large numbers (SLLN) is proved for ψ-mixing sequences without a rate assumption.

Keywords: strong laws; Komlós–Révész law; ψ-mixing; dependent Cramér model

MSC: 60F15; 11N05

1. Introduction and Result

Let $\{X_k\}_{k\in\mathbb{N}}$, $\mathbb{N} = \{1,2,3,\ldots\}$, be a sequence of random variables defined on a probability space $(\Omega, \mathcal{F}, P)$ and $\|X\|_p^p = E(|X|^p)$. It was proved by Komlós and Révész in [1] that for centered, independent random variables X_k,

$$\frac{\sum_{k=1}^{n} \|X_k\|_2^{-2} X_k}{\sum_{k=1}^{n} \|X_k\|_2^{-2}} \to_n 0, \qquad \text{a.s.} \tag{1}$$

provided that $\sum_{k=1}^{\infty} \|X_k\|_2^{-2}$ diverges (see also [2], p. 75 and Ex. 13 on p. 137 in [3]). If $E(X_k) = m$, $k \geq 1$, then we have strong consistency:

$$\frac{\sum_{k=1}^{n} \|X_k - m\|_2^{-2} X_k}{\sum_{k=1}^{n} \|X_k - m\|_2^{-2}} \to_n m, \qquad \text{a.s.}$$

and it was proved that this estimator has minimal variance. Nevertheless, as observed in the preface of [4], *"For many phenomena in the real world, the observations are not independent..."*, so the question on (1) is intriguing when there is a lack of independence. In [5], the Komlós–Révész theorem is investigated for pairwise independence by the method of subsequences. For martingale difference sequences in L^p, $p \in (1,2]$, by the Doob theorem (see Th. 2 on p. 246 in [3]), it is obtained in [6]. In [7], the case $p \in (0,1)$ and $p > 2$ is also discussed for negatively dependent and mixing sequences. In the latter, some rate on mixing is assumed, so this paper aims to remove this restriction.

Let σ-fields $\mathcal{A}, \mathcal{B}$ satisfy $\mathcal{A}, \mathcal{B} \subset \mathcal{F}$. Recall the following strong measure of dependence:

$$\psi(\mathcal{A}, \mathcal{B}) = \sup \left|\frac{P(B \cap A)}{P(B) \cdot P(A)} - 1\right|; \; P(B) \cdot P(A) > 0, \; A \in \mathcal{A}, B \in \mathcal{B}.$$

It is well known that (see p. 124 in Vol. I, [4])

$$\psi_m = \sup_{J\geq 1} \psi(\mathcal{F}_1^J, \mathcal{F}_{J+m}^{\infty}) = \sup_{J\geq 1} \sup \frac{\| E(g|\mathcal{F}_1^J) - E(g) \|_\infty}{\| g \|_1},$$

where $\mathcal{F}_k^m$ denotes σ–field generated by $X_k, X_{k+1}, \ldots, X_m$, $m \in \mathbb{Z}$ and the inner sup is taken over $g \in L^1_{\text{real}}(\mathcal{F}_{J+m}^{\infty})$. We say that $\{X_k\}$ is ψ-mixing if $\lim_{m\to\infty} \psi_m = 0$. It is worth noticing that

Kesten and O'Brien and Bradley gave examples of ψ–mixing sequences with an arbitrary rate of mixing (see Ch. 3 and Ch. 26 in [4]).

The following is the main result in this paper.

Theorem 1. *Suppose* $\{X_k\}$ *is* ψ*–mixing. Let* $\{a_k\}$ *be a sequence satisfying* $0 < a_k^{p-1} E|X_k|^p \leq C < \infty$ *for* $k \in \mathbb{N}$.
(i) If $0 < p < 1$ *and* $\sum_{k=1}^{\infty} a_k$ *converges, then*

$$\frac{\sum_{k=1}^{n} a_k X_k}{\sum_{k=n}^{\infty} a_k} \to_n 0, \qquad \text{a.s.} \tag{2}$$

(ii) If $1 < p \leq 2$ *and* $E(X_k) = 0$, $\sup_n (\sum_{k=1}^{n} a_k)^{-1} \sum_{k=1}^{n} a_k E|X_k| < \infty$ *and* $\sum_{k=1}^{\infty} a_k$ *diverges, then*

$$\frac{\sum_{k=1}^{n} a_k X_k}{\sum_{k=1}^{n} a_k} \to_n 0, \qquad \text{a.s.} \tag{3}$$

(iii) If $p > 2$ *and* $E(X_k) = 0$, $\sup_n (\sum_{k=1}^{n} a_k)^{-1} \sum_{k=1}^{n} a_k E|X_k| < \infty$ *and* $\sum_{k=1}^{\infty} a_k$ *diverges and* $0 < a_k E|X_k|^2 \leq C < \infty$ *for* $k \in \mathbb{N}$*, then (3) holds.*

Remark 1. *(a) It follows from the proof that in case (i),* ψ*–mixing is not required.*
(b) In fact, $\sup_n (\sum_{k=1}^{n} a_k)^{-1} \sum_{k=1}^{n} a_k E|X_k| < \infty$ *if* $\sup_k E|X_k| < \infty$*. The latter is also used in the case of pairwise independent random variables (see Theorem 2 in [5]) and can be omitted if* $\psi_m = 0$ *for some* $m \geq 1$.
(c) For $p = 1$*, Theorem 1 does not hold. Suppose that* $\{X_k\}$ *is a stochastic sequence* $P(X_k = 1) = 1 - P(X_k = 0) = 1/2$ *constructed in the proof of Theorem 1 in [8]. Thus, if* $\{g_n\}$ *is a non-increasing sequence,* $g_n \to 0$*, then* $\psi_n \asymp g_n$*. Now, let* $\{\xi_k\}$ *be a sequence of independent random variables with* $P(\xi_k = k) = \frac{1}{2k}$, $P(\xi_k = -k) = \frac{1}{2k}$, $P(\xi_k = 0) = 1 - \frac{1}{k}$ *and independent of* X_k*. Set* $Z_k = \xi_k \cos(X_k \pi)$, $k \geq 1$ *so that* $E(e^{itZ_k}) = E(e^{it\xi_k})$*. Thus,* $EZ_k = 0, E|Z_k| = 1$*. By Proposition 3.16 on p. 82 in Vol. I, [4] and by Theorem 6.2 on p. 193 in Vol. I, [4] we have that* $\{Z_k\}$ *is* ψ*-mixing (non-stationary) with rate* $\asymp g_n$*. Let* $a_k \equiv 1$*. Now, (3) fails by the second Borel–Cantelli lemma (see [9] and p. 210 in [10]) since* $\sum_{k\geq 1} P(|Z_k| \geq k) = \sum_{k\geq 1} \frac{1}{k} = \infty$.

The following variant of the converse statement does not require strong mixing.

Proposition 1. *Let* $\{a_k\}$ *be a sequence of positive reals. Suppose* $\{X_k\}$ *is an arbitrary dependent random sequence such that* $\sup_k E|X_k| = C < \infty$ *and* $\liminf_n E|\sum_{k=1}^{n} a_k X_k| = c > 0$*. If (3) holds, then* $\sum_{k\geq 1} a_k$ *diverges.*

Set $q = |\frac{p}{p-1}|$. Theorem 1 applied with $a_k^{-1} = (E|X_k|^p)^{\frac{1}{p-1}}$ and, in case (iii) with $a_k^{-1} = E|X_k|^2 \vee (E|X_k|^p)^{\frac{1}{p-1}}$, yields

Corollary 1. *Suppose* $\{X_k\}$ *is* ψ*-mixing.*
(i) If $0 < p < 1$ *and* $\sum_{k=1}^{\infty} \|X_k\|_p^{-q}$ *converges, then*

$$\frac{\sum_{k=1}^{n} \|X_k\|_p^{-q} X_k}{\sum_{n=k}^{\infty} \|X_k\|_p^{-q}} \to_n 0, \qquad \text{a.s.} \tag{4}$$

(ii) If $1 < p \leq 2$, $\sup_n (\sum_{k=1}^{n} \|X_k\|_p^{-q})^{-1} \sum_{k=1}^{n} \|X_k\|_p^{-q} E|X_k| < \infty$, $E(X_k) = 0$ *and* $\sum_{k=1}^{\infty} \|X_k\|_p^{-q}$ *diverges, then*

$$\frac{\sum_{k=1}^{n} \|X_k\|_p^{-q} X_k}{\sum_{k=1}^{n} \|X_k\|_p^{-q}} \to_n 0, \qquad \text{a.s.} \tag{5}$$

(iii) If $p \geq 2$,

$$\sup_n \Big(\sum_{k=1}^{n} \|X_k\|_2^2 \vee \|X_k\|_p^q\Big)^{-1} \sum_{k=1}^{n} (\|X_k\|_2^2 \vee \|X_k\|_p^q)^{-1} E|X_k| < \infty,$$

$E(X_k) = 0$ *and* $\sum_{k=1}^{\infty} (\|X_k\|_2^2 \vee \|X_k\|_p^q)^{-1}$ *diverges, then*

$$\frac{\sum_{k=1}^{n} (\|X_k\|_2^2 \vee \|X_k\|_p^q)^{-1} X_k}{\sum_{k=1}^{n} (\|X_k\|_2^2 \vee \|X_k\|_p^q)^{-1}} \to_n 0, \qquad \text{a.s.} \tag{6}$$

We apply our result to the ψ-mixing Cramér model. Namely, we have sequence $\{\eta_k\}$ with $P(\eta_k = 1) = 1 - P(\eta_k = 0) = 1/\ln k$, $k \geq 3$, which is ψ-mixing. Let $\zeta_k = \eta_k \ln k$. It is easy to see that $\sigma_k^2 = \mathrm{Var}(\zeta_k) \sim \ln k$, $m_k = E(\zeta_k) = 1$ and $\sum_{k=3}^{n} \frac{1}{\sigma_k^2} \sim \frac{n}{\ln n}$. Thus, for $\{\zeta_k\}$ in the case $p = 2$, we obtain by (5) that SLLN for Cramér model independence can be replaced by ψ-mixing (see e.g., Lemma A.1 in [11]).

Lemma 1.

$$\lim_n \frac{\ln n}{n} \sum_{k=3}^{n} \eta_k = 1, \quad \text{a.s.}$$

The paper is organized as follows. In the next section, there are some auxiliary results. These results are required in the proof of Theorem 1 in the last section.

2. Auxiliary Results

The following result for $p > 1$ is in [12] and for $p = 1$ see [9] (see also Theorem 2.20 on p. 40 in [13]).

Theorem 2. *Suppose* $\{X_k\}$ *is* ψ*-mixing and* $E(X_k) = 0$, $k \in \mathbb{Z}$. *Let* $\{b_n\}$, $b_0 > 0$ *be an increasing to infinity sequence of real numbers such that for some* $p \geq 1$,
(i) $\sum_{k=1}^{\infty} b_k^{-2p} E(|X_k|^{2p}) < \infty$;
(ii) $\sum_{k=1}^{\infty} b_k^{-2} (b_k^2 - b_{k-1}^2)^{1-p} (E(X_k^2))^p < \infty$;
(iii) $\sup_n b_n^{-1} \sum_{k=1}^{n} E|X_k| < \infty$.
Then, $b_n^{-1} S_n \to 0$, $n \to \infty$, *almost surely (a.s.).*

The next result improves Lemma 2.1 slightly in [14].

Proposition 2. *Suppose* $\{X_k\}$ *is* ψ*-mixing and* $E(X_k) = 0$, $k \in \mathbb{Z}$. *Let* $b_n \in \mathbb{R}$, $b_0 > 0$, $b_n \uparrow \infty$, *and* $\sup_n b_n^{-1} \sum_{k=1}^{n} E|X_k| < \infty$, $p \in (1, 2]$, $\sum_{k=1}^{\infty} \frac{E|X_k|^p}{b_k^p} < \infty$, *then* $b_n^{-1} S_n \to 0$, $n \to \infty$, *a.s.*

Proof of Proposition 2. Set $\bar{X}_k = X_k I(|X_k| \leq b_k) - E(X_k I(|X_k| \leq b_k))$. In view of Theorem 2, we can assume $1 < p < 2$.

$$\sum_{k \geq 1} P(X_k \neq X_k I(|X_k| \leq b_k)) \leq C \sum_{k \geq 1} \frac{E|X_k|^p}{b_k^p} < \infty.$$

Further,

$$\begin{aligned} b_n^{-1} \Big|\sum_{k=1}^{n} E(X_k I(|X_k| \leq b_k))\Big| &\leq b_n^{-1} \sum_{k=1}^{n} E(|X_k| I(|X_k| > b_k)) \\ &\leq b_n^{-1} \sum_{k=1}^{n} b_k^{-p+1} E(|X_k|^p I(|X_k| > b_k)) \leq b_n^{-1} \sum_{k=1}^{n} b_k^{-p+1} E|X_k|^p \to 0. \end{aligned}$$

So that
$$\sum_{k\geq 1}\frac{E\bar{X}_k^2}{b_k^2}\leq \sum_{k\geq 1}\frac{E(X_k^2 I(|X_k|\leq b_k))}{b_k^2}\leq \sum_{k\geq 1}\frac{E|X_k|^p}{b_k^p}<\infty.$$
Now, apply Theorem 2 to $\{\bar{X}_k\}$ with $p=1$. □

By Lemma 3.6″ on p. 284 in [15] and Kronecker's lemma (see e.g., [16], p. 236) we have the following SLLN for arbitrary dependent random variables (see also [17]).

Lemma 2. *Suppose $\{X_k\}$ is a sequence of random variables, $p\in(0,1]$, $b_n\uparrow\infty$ and $\sum_{k=1}^{\infty}\frac{E|X_k|^p}{b_k^p}<\infty$. Then, $b_n^{-1}S_n\to 0$, $n\to\infty$, a.s.*

3. Proofs

Proof of Theorem 1. The key role in the proof of Theorem 1 is played by the Dini theorem (see e.g., [18], Theorem 4 on p. 127) and the Abel–Dini theorem (see e.g., [18], Theorem 1 on p. 125) (for a generalization, see Lemma 11 in [7]).

For $p\in(0,1)$ by the Dini theorem,
$$\sum_{n=1}^{\infty}\frac{a_n^pE|X_n|^p}{(\sum_{k=n}^{\infty}a_k)^p}\leq C\sum_{n=1}^{\infty}\frac{a_n}{(\sum_{k=n}^{\infty}a_k)^p}<\infty$$
since $\sum_{k=1}^{\infty}a_k<\infty$. Thus, (2) holds by Lemma 2.

Now, assume $p\in(1,2]$. By the Abel–Dini theorem,
$$\sum_{n=1}^{\infty}\frac{a_n^pE|X_n|^p}{(\sum_{k=1}^{n}a_k)^p}\leq C\sum_{n=1}^{\infty}\frac{a_n}{(\sum_{k=1}^{n}a_k)^p}<\infty$$
since $\sum_{k=1}^{\infty}a_k=\infty$. Set $b_n=\sum_{k=1}^{n}a_k$. Since $\sup_n b_n^{-1}\sum_{k=1}^{n}a_kE|X_k|<\infty$,
$$\frac{\sum_{k=1}^{n}a_kX_k}{\sum_{k=1}^{n}a_k}\to_n 0,\qquad \text{a.s.}$$
holds by Proposition 2.

In the case that $p>2$, set $b_0=0.5b_1$. By Theorem 2 and the previous point, it is enough to prove that
$$S=\sum_{n=1}^{\infty}\frac{(b_n^2-b_{n-1}^2)^{1-\frac{p}{2}}}{b_n^2}\frac{a_n^p(E(X_n^2))^{\frac{p}{2}}}{b_n^p}<\infty.$$
Let $\delta=\frac{2\epsilon}{p}$, where $\epsilon\in(0,1)$ is fixed. In view of $b_n\to\infty$, we have that there exist $C>0$ such that $a_nE(X_n^2)\leq Cb_n^{3-\delta}$, for each n. Therefore,
$$a_n^{p-1}E(X_n^2)^{\frac{p}{2}}\leq Cb_n^{\frac{3p}{2}-\epsilon}a_n^{\frac{p}{2}-1}.$$
But $(b_n^2-b_{n-1}^2)^{1-\frac{p}{2}}=(a_nb_n(2-\frac{a_n}{b_n}))^{1-\frac{p}{2}}$ so that by the Abel–Dini theorem,
$$S\leq C\sum_{n=1}^{\infty}\frac{a_n(a_nb_n)^{1-\frac{p}{2}}}{b_n^{p+2}}b_n^{\frac{3p}{2}-\epsilon}a_n^{\frac{p}{2}-1}=C\sum_{n=1}^{\infty}\frac{a_n}{b_n^{1+\epsilon}}<\infty.$$
Since $\sup_n b_n^{-1}\sum_{k=1}^{n}a_kE|X_k|<\infty$, Theorem 1 is proved. □

Proof of Proposition 1. Suppose $\sum_{k\geq 1} a_k < \infty$ and (3) holds. Choose N_1 such that $\sum_{k\geq n} a_k < \frac{c}{3C}$ for $n \geq N_1$. Next, choose $N_2 \geq N_1$ such that $E|\sum_{k=1}^{n} a_k X_k| > c/2$ for $n \geq N_2$. Now, for a fixed $N \geq N_2$, we have

$$\sum_{k=N+1}^{n} a_k X_k \to_n -\sum_{k=1}^{N} a_k X_k, \qquad \text{a.s.}$$

On the other hand, by Fatou's lemma (cf. Theorem 5.1 on p. 218, [19]),

$$c/2 < E|\sum_{k=1}^{N} a_k X_k| \leq \liminf_n E|\sum_{k=N+1}^{n} a_k X_k| < c/3.$$

Thus, $c < 0$. Contradiction. □

Funding: This research received no external funding.

Institutional Review Board Statement: Not applicable.

Data Availability Statement: Data is contained within the article.

Conflicts of Interest: The author declares no conflict of interest.

References

1. Komlós, J.; Révész, P. On the weighted averages of independent random variables. *Magyar Tud. Akad. Mat. Kutató Int. Közl.* **19**6 *9*, 583–587.
2. Révész, P. *The Laws of Large Numbers*; Academic Press: New York, NY, USA, 1968.
3. Chow, Y.S.; Teicher, H. *Probability Theory. Independence, Interchangebility, Martingales*, 3rd ed.; Springer Texts in Statistics: New Yo NY, USA, 2003.
4. Bradley, R.C. *Introduction to Strong Mixing Conditions*; Kendrick Press: Heber City, UT, USA, 2007; Volume I–III.
5. Rosalsky, A. A strong law for weighted averages of random variables and the Komlós–Révész estimation problem. *Calcut Statist. Assoc. Bull.* **1986**, *35*, 59–66. [CrossRef]
6. Cohen, G. On the Komlós–Révész estimation problem for random variables without variances. *Acta Sci. Math.* **2008**, *74*, 915–9
7. Szewczak, Z.S. On the Komlós–Révész SLLN for dependent variables. *Acta Math. Hungar.* **2018**, *156*, 47–55. [CrossRef]
8. Kesten, H.; O'Brien, G.L. Examples of mixing sequences. *Duke Math. J.* **1976**, *43*, 405–415. [CrossRef]
9. Blum, J.R.; Hanson, D.L.; Koopmans, L.H. On the Strong Law of Large Numbers for a Class of Stochastic Processes. *Z. Wa Verw. Gebiete* **1963**, *2*, 1–11. [CrossRef]
10. Petrov, V.V. *Limit Theorems of Probability Theory. Sequences of Independent Random Variables*; Oxford Studies in Probability Clarendon Pr: Oxford, UK, 1995.
11. Weber, M.J.G. Critical probabilistic characteristics of the Cramér model for primes and arithmetical properties. *Indian J. Pure Ap Math.* **2024**. [CrossRef]
12. Szewczak, Z.S. On the Wittmann strong law for mixing sequences. *Period. Math. Hungar.* **2024**, *89*, 257–264. [CrossRef]
13. Hall, P.; Heyde, C.C. *Martingale Limit Theory and Its Applications*; Academic Press: New York, NY, USA, 1980.
14. Hu, D.; Chen, P.; Sung, S.H. Strong laws of weighted sums of ψ–mixing random variables and applications in errors-in-variabl regression models. *TEST* **2017**, *26*, 600–617. [CrossRef]
15. Loève, M. On almost sure convergence. In Proceedings of the 2nd Berkeley Symposium on Mathematical Statistics and Probabili Berkeley, CA, USA, 31 July–12 August 1950; University of California Press: Berkeley, CA, USA, 1951; pp. 279–303.
16. Ash, R.B. *Probability and Measure Theory*; Academic Press: New York, NY, USA, 2000.
17. Petrov, V.V. On the order of growth and sums of dependent variables. *Theory Probab. Appl.* **1974**, *18*, 348–350. [CrossRef]
18. Knopp, K. *Infinite Sequences and Series*; Dover Publication Inc.: New York, NY, USA, 1956.
19. Gut, A. *Probability: A Graduate Course*, 2nd ed.; Springer: New York, NY, USA, 2013.

entropy

Article

Semi-Quenched Invariance Principle for the Random Lorentz Gas: Beyond the Boltzmann–Grad Limit

Bálint Tóth [1,2]

[1] Alfréd Rényi Institute of Mathematics, Reáltanoda utca 13-14, 1053 Budapest, Hungary; toth.balint@renyi.hu or balint.toth@bristol.ac.uk
[2] School of Mathematics, University of Bristol, Fry Building, Woodland Road, Bristol BS8 1UG, UK

Abstract: By synchronously coupling multiple Lorentz trajectories exploring the same environment consisting of randomly placed scatterers in $\mathbb{R}^3$, we upgrade the annealed invariance principle proved in [Lutsko, Tóth (2020)] to the quenched setting (that is, valid for almost all realizations of the environment) along sufficiently fast extractor sequences.

Keywords: Lorentz gas; invariance principle; scaling limit; coupling; almost sure convergence

MSC: 60F17; 60K35; 60K37; 60K40; 82C22; 82C31; 82C40; 82C41

Révész Pali emlékére.
Dedicated to the memory of Pál Révész.

1. Introduction

Since the late 1970s, random walks in random environment (RWRE) have been a central subject of major interest and difficulty within the probability community; see Pál Révész's classic monograph [1]. One should keep within sight, however, the original motivation of RWRE: the urge for understanding diffusion in true physical systems. An archetypal example is the random Lorentz gas, where in the three-dimensional Euclidean space $\mathbb{R}^3$, a point-like particle of mass 1 moves among infinite-mass, hard-core, spherical scatterers of radius r, placed according to a Poisson point process of density ϱ. Randomness comes with the placement of the scatterers (PPP in $\mathbb{R}^3$) and the initial direction of the velocity of the moving particle (uniform in an angular domain). Otherwise, the dynamics is fully deterministic. The question is whether in the long run the displacement of the moving particle is random-walk-like or not. In [2], we proved an invariance principle for the Lorentz trajectory, under the Boltzmann–Grad (i.e., low density) limit *and simultaneous* diffusive scaling, valid in the annealed sense. (For precise formulation, see Theorem 1 below.) The objective of this note is upgrading that result to a semi-quenched setting that is valid for almost all realizations of the environment, along sufficiently fast extractor sequences.

Let $(\Omega, \mathcal{F}, \mathbf{P})$ be a sufficiently large probability space which supports (inter alia) a Poisson Point Process (PPP) of intensity 1 on $\mathbb{R}^d$, denoted ϖ. Other, independent random elements jointly defined on $(\Omega, \mathcal{F}, \mathbf{P})$ will also be considered later. Therefore, it is best to think about $(\Omega, \mathcal{F}, \mathbf{P})$ as a product space which in one of its factors supports the PPP ϖ and on the other factor (or factors) many other random elements, independent of ϖ, to be introduced later. To keep the notation simple, we do not denote explicitly this product structure of $(\Omega, \mathcal{F}, \mathbf{P})$. However, as this note is about *quenched* laws, that is, about laws and limits conditioned on *typical* ϖ, we denote

$$\mathbf{P}_\varpi(\,\cdot\,) := \mathbf{P}(\cdot \mid \mathcal{F}_{\mathrm{PPP}}), \qquad \mathbf{E}_\varpi(\,\cdot\,) := \mathbf{E}(\cdot \mid \mathcal{F}_{\mathrm{PPP}}),$$

where $\mathcal{F}_{\mathrm{PPP}} \subset \mathcal{F}$ is the sigma algebra generated by the PPP ϖ.

Given

$$\varepsilon > 0, \qquad r = r_\varepsilon := \varepsilon^{d/(d-1)}$$

and

$$v \in S^{d-1} := \{u \in \mathbb{R}^d, |u| = 1\}$$

let

$$t \mapsto X_\varepsilon(t) \in \mathbb{R}^d$$

be the Lorentz trajectory among fixed spherical scatterers of radius r centered at the points of the rescaled PPP

$$\varpi_\varepsilon := \{\varepsilon q : q \in \varpi,\ |q| > \varepsilon^{-1} r = \varepsilon^{1/(d-1)}\}, \tag{1}$$

with initial conditions

$$X_\varepsilon(0) = 0, \qquad \dot{X}_\varepsilon(0) = v.$$

In plain words: $t \mapsto X_\varepsilon(t)$ is the trajectory of a point particle starting from the origin with velocity v, performing free flight in the complement of the scatterers and scattering elastically on them.

Notes: (1) In order to define the Lorentz trajectory, we have to disregard those points of the rescaled PPP ϖ_ε within distance r from the origin. However, this will not affect whatsoever our arguments and conclusions since, with probability 1, for ε that is sufficiently small, there are no points like this.

(2) Given ε and the initial velocity v, the trajectory $t \mapsto X_\varepsilon(t)$ is almost surely well defined for $t \in [0, \infty)$. That is, almost surely all scatterings will happen on a unique scatterer, the singular sets at the intersection of more than one scatterers will be almost surely avoided.

In order to properly (and, comparably) formulate our invariance principles, first we recall the relevant function spaces. Let

$$\mathcal{C} := \mathcal{C}([0,\infty), \mathbb{R}^d) := \{\mathfrak{z} : [0,\infty) \to \mathbb{R}^d : \mathfrak{z} \text{ continuous}, \mathfrak{z}(0) = 0\},$$

endowed with the topology of uniform convergence on compact subintervals of $[0, \infty)$, which is metrizable and makes $\mathcal{C}$ complete and separable. For details, see [3]. Further on, let

$$\mathcal{C}(\mathcal{C}) := \mathcal{C}(\mathcal{C}([0,1], \mathbb{R}^d), \mathbb{R}) := \{F : \mathcal{C} \to \mathbb{R} : F \text{ continuous}, \|F\|_\infty := \sup_{\mathfrak{z} \in \mathcal{C}} |F(\mathfrak{z})| < \infty\},$$
$$\mathcal{C}_0(\mathcal{C}) := \mathcal{C}_0(\mathcal{C}([0,1], \mathbb{R}^d), \mathbb{R}) := \{F \in \mathcal{C}(\mathcal{C}) : \forall \delta > 0, \exists K \Subset \mathcal{C} : \sup_{\mathfrak{z} \in \mathcal{C} \setminus K} |F(\mathfrak{z})| < \delta\}.$$

$(\mathcal{C}_0(\mathcal{C}), \|\cdot\|_\infty)$ is a separable Banach space. We will also denote by $t \mapsto W(t)$ a standard Brownian motion in $\mathbb{R}^d$, and recall from [3–5] criteria for the weak convergence of probability measures on $\mathcal{C}$.

In [2], the following *annealed* invariance principle is proved.

Theorem 1 ([2] Theorem 1). *Let $d = 3$, $\varepsilon \to 0$, $r_\varepsilon = \varepsilon^{d/(d-1)}$ and $T_\varepsilon \to \infty$ be such that*

$$\lim_{\varepsilon\to 0} r_\varepsilon T_\varepsilon = 0. \tag{2}$$

Let $t \mapsto X_\varepsilon(t)$ be the sequence of Lorentz trajectories among the spherical scatterers of radius r_ε centered at the points ϖ_ε cf. (1)*, and with deterministic initial velocities $v_\varepsilon \in S^{d-1}$. For any $F \in \mathcal{C}_0(\mathcal{C})$,*

$$\lim_{\varepsilon\to 0}\Big|\mathbf{E}\big(F(T_\varepsilon^{-1/2}X_\varepsilon(T_\varepsilon\cdot))\big) - \mathbf{E}\big(F(W(\cdot))\big)\Big| = 0. \tag{3}$$

Remark 1. *(On dimension.) Although some crucial elements of the proofs in [2], on which the present note is based, are worked out in full detail in dimension $d = 3$ only, we prefer to use the generic notation d for dimension with the explicit warning that in the actual results and proofs, $d = 3$ is meant. See Remark (R7) below and the paragraph "remarks on dimension" in Section 1 of [2] for comments on possible extensions to the dimensions other than $d = 3$.*

Remark 2. *Theorem 1 is an* annealed *invariance principle in the sense that on the left-hand side of* (3)*, the probability distribution of the rescaled Lorentz trajectory is provided by the random environment ϖ. The proofs in [2] rely on a genuinely annealed argument: a simultaneous realization of the PPP ϖ and the trajectory $t \mapsto X_\varepsilon(t)$.*

Remark 3. *The main result in [2] (Theorem 2 of that paper) is actually stronger, assuming*

$$\lim_{\varepsilon\to 0}(r_\varepsilon|\log\varepsilon|)^2 T_\varepsilon = 0$$

rather than (2)*. However, the* semi-quenched *invariance principle of this note, Theorem 2 below, is directly comparable to this weaker version.*

The main new result presented in this note is the following.

Theorem 2. *Let d=3, $\varepsilon \to 0$, $r_\varepsilon = \varepsilon^{d/(d-1)}$, $T_\varepsilon \to \infty$ and $\beta_\varepsilon \in (0,1]$ be such that*

$$\lim_{\varepsilon\to 0} r_\varepsilon(T_\varepsilon + \beta_\varepsilon^{-1}) = 0, \tag{4}$$

and define the solid angle domains

$$B_\varepsilon := \{u \in S^{d-1} : 2\arcsin\sqrt{(1-u\cdot e)/2} \le \beta_\varepsilon\}, \qquad e \in S^{d-1} \text{ deterministic.}$$

Let $t \mapsto X_\varepsilon(t)$ be the sequence of Lorentz trajectories among the spherical scatterers of radius r_ε centered at the points ϖ_ε cf. (1)*, and with initial velocities $v_\varepsilon \sim \mathtt{UNI}(B_\varepsilon)$ sampled independently of the PPP ϖ. For any $F \in \mathcal{C}_0(\mathcal{C})$,*

$$\lim_{\varepsilon\to 0}\mathbf{E}\Big(\Big|\mathbf{E}_\varpi\big(F(T_\varepsilon^{-1/2}X_\varepsilon(T_\varepsilon\cdot))\big) - \mathbf{E}\big(F(W(\cdot))\big)\Big|\Big) = 0.$$

Remark 4. *Theorem 2 is an invariance principle valid* in probability *with respect to the random environment ϖ. An equivalent formulation is that under the stated conditions, for any $\delta > 0$*

$$\lim_{\varepsilon\to 0}\mathbf{P}\big(\{\varpi : D_{\mathrm{LP}}\big(\mathtt{law\text{-}of}(T_\varepsilon^{-1/2}X_\varepsilon(T_\varepsilon\cdot)\,|\,\mathcal{F}_{\mathrm{PPP}}), \mathtt{law\text{-}of}(W(\cdot))\big) > \delta\}\big) = 0,$$

where $D_{\mathrm{LP}}(\cdot,\cdot)$ denotes the Lévy–Prohorov distance between probability measures on $\mathcal{C}$.

We actually prove a stronger statement from which Theorem 2 follows as a corollary. In the setting of Theorem 2, for almost all realizations of the PPP ϖ, along (precisely quantified) sufficiently fast converging subsequences $\varepsilon_n \to 0$, the invariance principle holds.

Theorem 3. *Let $d = 3$, $\varepsilon_n \to 0$, $r_n := \varepsilon_n^{d/(d-1)}$, $T_n \to \infty$ and $\beta_n \in (0,1]$ be such that*

$$\sum_n \Big(\log n\, r_n T_n + (\log n)^2 \Big(r_n \beta_n^{-1}\Big)^{(d-1)/d} \Big) < \infty, \tag{5}$$

and define the solid angle domains

$$B_n := \{u \in S^{d-1} : 2 \arcsin \sqrt{(1 - u \cdot e)/2} \leq \beta_n\}, \qquad e \in S^{d-1} \text{ deterministic}. \tag{6}$$

Let $t \mapsto X_n(t)$ be the sequence of Lorentz trajectories among the spherical scatterers of radius r_n centered at the points $\varpi_n := \varpi_{\varepsilon_n}$ cf. (1), *and with initial velocities $v_n \sim \mathtt{UNI}(B_n)$ sampled independently of the PPP ϖ. For almost all realizations of the PPP ϖ, for any $F \in C_0(\mathcal{C})$,*

$$\lim_{n\to\infty} \Big| \mathbf{E}_\varpi \big(F(T_n^{-1/2} X_n(T_n \cdot))\big) - \mathbf{E}\big(F(W(\cdot))\big) \Big| = 0.$$

Remark 5. *Theorem 2 is a corollary of Theorem 3, as under condition* (4) *from any sequence $\varepsilon_n \to 0$ a subsequence $\varepsilon_{n'}$ can be extracted that satisfies condition* (5)*. On the other hand, Theorem 3 is genuinely stronger than Theorem 2, as the former provides an explicit quantitative characterization of the sequences $\varepsilon_n \to 0$ along which the quenched (i.e., almost sure) invariance principle holds.*

Remark 6. *For a comprehensive historical survey of the invariance principle for the random Lorentz gas, we refer to the monograph [6] and to Section 1 on [2]. We just mention here that the main milestones preceding [2] are [7–10]. The new result of this note (i.e., Theorems 2 and 3) is to be compared with that in [10], where a fully quenched invariance principle is proved for the two-dimensional random Lorentz gas in the Boltzmann–Grad limit, on kinetic time scales. The weakness of our result (compared with [10]) is that the limit theorem is semi-quenched, in the sense that almost surely the invariance principle is proved along* sufficiently fast *converging sequences ε_n only. On the other hand, the strengths are twofold. ($\star$) The proof works in dimension $d = 3$ and it is "hands-on", not relying on the heavy computational details of [10] (performable only in $d = 2$). See Remark (R7) below for possible extensions to dimensions other than $d = 3$. ($\star\star$) The time-scale of validity is much longer, $T_\varepsilon = o(\varepsilon^{-d/(d-1)})$ rather than $T_\varepsilon = \mathcal{O}(1)$, as in [10].*

Remark 7. *The results of [2] are stated, and the proofs are fully spelled out for dimension $d = 3$. Therefore, the new results of this note (which rely on those of [2]) are also valid in $d = 3$ only. However, as noted in the paragraph "remarks on dimension" in [2], extension to other dimensions is possible, at the expense of more involved details due partly to recurrence (in $d = 2$) and partly to the non-uniform scattering cross section (in all dimensions other than $d = 3$). For arguments in $d = 2$, see [11,12].*

The strategy of the proof in [2] (also extended to [11,12]) is based on a *coupling* of the mechanical/Hamiltonian Lorentz trajectory within the environment consisting of randomly placed scatterers and the Markovian random flight trajectory. The coupling is realized as an *exploration* of the random environment along the trajectory of the tagged particle. This construction is *par excellence* annealed, as the environment and the trajectory of the moving particle are constructed synchronously (rather than first sampling the environment and consequently letting the particle move in the fully sampled environment). However, this exploration process can be realized synchronously with multiple (actually, many) moving particles, which, as long as they explore disjoint areas of the environment, are independent in the annealed sense (due to the Poisson character of the environment). Applying a Strong Law of Large Numbers to tests of these trajectories will provide the quenched invariance principle, valid for typical realizations of the environment. A somewhat similar exploration strategy is used in the very different context of random walks on sparse random graphs, ref. [13].

2. Construction and Quenched Coupling

2.1. Prologue to the Coupling

The proof of Theorem 3 is based on a coupling (that is, joint realization on the same enlarged probability space $(\Omega, \mathcal{F}, \mathbf{P})$) of

$$\big((\varpi, (X_j(t) : 1 \le j \le N, 0 \le t \le T)\big), \big((Y_j(t) : 1 \le j \le N, 0 \le t \le T)\big), \tag{7}$$

where we have the following:

- ϖ is the PPP of intensity ϱ in $\{x \in \mathbb{R}^d : |x| > r\}$ serving as the centers of fixed (immovable) spherical scatterers of radii r, and $(X_j(t) : 1 \le j \le N, 0 \le t \le T)$ are Newtonian Lorentz trajectories starting from $X_j(0) = 0$ with prescribed initial velocities $\dot{X}_j(0) = v_j$, and moving among the same randomly placed scatterers. Note, that the trajectories $(X_j(t) : 1 \le j \le N, 0 \le t \le T)$ are fully determined by the PPP ϖ and their initial velocities.
- $(Y_j(t) : 1 \le j \le N, 0 \le t \le T)$ are i.i.d. Markovian random flight processes (see Section 2.3) with the same initial data, $Y_j(0) = 0$, $\dot{Y}_j(0) = v_j$.

The coupling is realized so that, with high probability, the two collections of processes stay identical for a sufficiently long time T. Thus, from limit theorems valid for the Markovian processes (which follow from well-established probabilistic arguments), we can conclude the limit theorems for the mechanical/Newtonian trajectories.

The coupling can be constructed in two different but mathematically equivalent ways:

(a) Start with the i.i.d. Markovian trajectories $(Y_j(t) : 1 \le j \le N, 0 \le t \le T)$ and (conditionally on) given these construct *jointly* the environment ϖ and the Newtonian trajectories $(X_j(t) : 1 \le j \le N, 0 \le t \le T)$ exploring it *en route*. The details of this narrative are explicitly spelled out for $N = 1$ in [2]. Extension of the construction for $N > 1$ is essentially straightforward.

(b) Start with the PPP ϖ and the Lorentz processes $(X_j(t) : 1 \le j \le N, 0 \le t \le T)$ moving in this joint random environment ϖ. Then, (conditionally) given these, construct the i.i.d. Markovian flight processes $(Y_j(t) : 1 \le j \le N, 0 \le t \le T)$ by disregarding recollisions (with already seen scatterers) and compensating for the (Markovian) scattering events shadowed by the r-tubes in $\mathbb{R}^d$ swept by the past trajectories. For full details of this narrative, see Section 2.3 below.

Construction (a) is somewhat easier to narrate and perceive ([2]). Its drawback is that this construction is par-excellence annealed. The environment ϖ is explored and constructed on the way, jointly with the trajectories $(X_j(t) : 1 \le j \le N, 0 \le t \le T)$, and therefore conditioning on the environment as requested in a quenched approach is not possible (or, at least not transparent). Construction (b) of the present note starts with the environment ϖ given and therefore is suitable for the quenched arguments. Its drawback may be that the i.i.d. Markovian flight processes $(Y_j(t) : 1 \le j \le N, 0 \le t \le T)$ are constructed in a less intuitive way (see Section 2.3 below). We emphasize, however, that both constructions provide the same joint distributions of the processes in (7).

Since in all considered cases $rT \to 0$ in the limit, see (2), (4), and (5), without any loss of generality, throughout this paper we will assume

$$rT \leq 1. \tag{8}$$

2.2. *Synchronous Lorentz Trajectories*

Beside ε and $r = \varepsilon^{d/(d-1)}$ let $N \in \mathbb{N}$, and

$$v_j \in S^{d-1}, \qquad 1 \leq j \leq N.$$

Given these, we define *jointly* N synchronous Lorentz trajectories

$$t \mapsto X_j(t) \in \mathbb{R}^d, \qquad 1 \leq j \leq N,$$

among fixed spherical scatterers of radius r centered at the points of the rescaled PPP ϖ_ε cf. (1), with initial conditions

$$X_j(0) = 0, \qquad \dot{X}_j(0) = v_j, \qquad 1 \leq j \leq N.$$

(Given the parameters and the initial velocities, the trajectories $t \mapsto X_j(t)$, $1 \leq j \leq N$, are almost surely well defined for $t \in [0, \infty)$).

We will consider the càdlàg version of the velocity processes

$$V_j(t) := \dot{X}_j(t). \qquad 1 \leq j \leq N,$$

and use the notation $X := \{X_j : 1 \leq j \leq N\}$.

In order to construct the *quenched coupling* with Markovian flight processes (in the next subsection), we have to define some further variables in terms of the Lorentz processes $t \mapsto X(t)$.

First the *collision times* $\tau_{j,k}$, $1 \leq j \leq N$, $k \geq 0$:

$$\tau_{j,0} := 0, \qquad \tau_{j,k+1} := \inf\{t > \tau_{j,k} : V_j(t) \neq V_j(\tau_{j,k})\}.$$

In plain words, $\tau_{j,k}$ is the time of the k-th scattering of the Lorentz trajectory $X_j(\cdot)$. We will use the notation

$$X_{j,k} := X_j(\tau_{j,k}), \qquad V_{j,k+1} := V_j(\tau_{j,k}). \qquad X'_{j,k} := X_{j,k} + r\frac{V_{j,k} - V_{j,k+1}}{\left|V_{j,k} - V_{j,k+1}\right|}$$

That is, $X_{j,k}$ is the position of the Lorentz trajectory at the instant of its k-th collision, $V_{j,k+1}$ is its velocity right after this collision, and $X'_{j,k}$ is the position of the center of the fixed scatterer which caused this collision. Altogether, the continuous-time trajectory is written

$$X_j(t) = X_{j,k} + (t - \tau_{j,k})V_{j,k+1}, \qquad \text{for} \quad t \in [\tau_{j,k}, \tau_{j,k+1}).$$

Next, the *indicators of freshness*

$$a_{j,0} := 1, \qquad a_{j,k} := \begin{cases} 1 & \text{if} \quad \forall \delta > 0 : \min\limits_{\substack{1 \leq i \leq N \\ 0 \leq s \leq \tau_{j,k} - \delta}} \left|X_i(s) - X'_{j,k}\right| > r \\ 0 & \text{otherwise} \end{cases} \qquad (k \geq 1).$$

In plain words, $a_{j,k}$ indicates whether the j-th trajectory at its k-th collision encounters a fresh scatterer, never seen in the past by any one of the N Lorentz trajectories.
Finally, the *shadow indicators* $b_j(t,v)$, $t \in [0,\infty)$, $v \in S^{d-1}$:

$$b_j(t,v) := \begin{cases} 0 & \text{if} \quad \forall \delta > 0: \min\limits_{\substack{1 \le i \le N \\ 0 \le s \le t-\delta}} \left| X_i(s) - X_j(t) + r\dfrac{v - V_j(t)}{|v - V_j(t)|} \right| > r, \\ 1 & \text{otherwise} \end{cases}$$

In plain words, $b_j(t,v)$ indicates whether at time t a virtual scatterer (virtually) causing new velocity v would be *mechanically inconsistent* with the past of the paths.

2.3. Quenched Coupling with Independent Markovian Flight Processes

On the same probability space $(\Omega, \mathcal{F}, \mathbf{P})$ and jointly with the Lorentz trajectories X, we construct N *independent Markovian flight processes*

$$t \mapsto Y_j(t) \in \mathbb{R}^d, \qquad 1 \le j \le N,$$

with initial conditions identical to those of the Lorentz trajectories

$$Y_j(0) = 0, \qquad \dot{Y}_j(0) = v_j, \qquad 1 \le j \le N.$$

The processes $\{Y_j(\cdot)\colon 1 \le j \le N\}$ are independent, and consist of i.i.d. $\texttt{EXP}(1)$-distributed free flights with independent $\texttt{UNI}(S^{d-1})$-distributed velocities. See [2] for a detailed exposition of the Markovian flight processes. We will again consider the càdlàg version of their velocity processes

$$U_j(t) := \dot{Y}_j(t), \qquad 1 \le j \le N.$$

and use the notation $Y := \{Y_j : 1 \le j \le N\}$.

The construction of the coupling goes as follows. Assume that the probability space $(\Omega, \mathcal{F}, \mathbf{P})$, besides and independently of the PPP ϖ, supports the fully independent random variables

$$\widetilde{\xi}_{j,k} \sim \texttt{EXP}(1), \qquad \widetilde{U}_{j,k+1} \sim \texttt{UNI}(S^{d-1}), \qquad j = 1, \dots, N, \quad k \ge 1,$$

and let

$$\widetilde{\theta}_{j,k} := \sum_{l=1}^{k} \widetilde{\xi}_{j,l}, \qquad b_{j,k} := b_j(\widetilde{\theta}_{j,k}, \widetilde{U}_{j,k+1}).$$

We construct the piecewise constant càdlàg velocity processes $U_j(\cdot)$ successively on the time intervals $[\tau_{j,k}, \tau_{j,k+1})$, $k = 0, 1, \dots$:

- At $\tau_{j,k}$:
  - If $a_{j,k} = 0$, then let $U_j(\tau_{j,k}) = U_j(\tau_{j,k}^-)$.
  - If $a_{j,k} = 1$, then let $U_j(\tau_{j,k}) = V_{j,k+1}$.
- At any $\widetilde{\theta}_{j,l} \in (\tau_{j,k}, \tau_{j,k+1})$
  - If $b_{j,l} = 0$, then let $U_j(\theta_{j,l}) = U_j(\theta_{j,l}^-)$.
  - If $b_{j,l} = 1$, then let $U_j(\theta_{j,l}) = \widetilde{U}_{j,l+1}$.
- In the open subintervals of $(\tau_{j,k}, \tau_{j,k+1})$ determined by the times $\{\widetilde{\theta}_{j,l} : l \ge 1\} \cap (\tau_{j,k}, \tau_{j,k+1})$ keep the value of $U_j(t)$ constant.

It is true, and not difficult to see, that the velocity processes $\{U_j(t) : 1 \leq j \leq N\}$ constructed in this way are independent between them, and distributed as required. That is, they consist of i.i.d. $\texttt{EXP}(1)$-distributed intervals where their values are i.i.d. $\texttt{UNI}(\texttt{S}^{d-1})$. This is due to the fact that each Lorentzian scatterer is taken into account exactly once, when first explored by a Lorentz particle, and missing scatterings (due to areas shadowed by the ε-neighborhood of past trajectories) are compensated for by the auxiliary events at times $\widetilde{\theta}_{j,l}$.

Consistently with the notation introduced for the Lorentz trajectories, we write

$$\theta_{j,0} := 0, \qquad \theta_{j,k+1} := \inf\{t > \theta_{j,k} : U_j(t) \neq U_j(\theta_{j,k})\},$$

and

$$Y_{j,k} := Y_j(\theta_{j,k}), \qquad U_{j,k+1} := U_j(\theta_{j,k}), \qquad Y'_{j,k} := Y_{j,k} + r\frac{U_{j,k} - U_{j,k+1}}{\left|U_{j,k} - U_{j,k+1}\right|}.$$

That is, $Y_{j,k}$ is the position of the Markovian flight trajectory at the instant of its k-th scattering, $U_{j,k+1}$ is its velocity right after this scattering, and $Y'_{j,k}$ would be the position of the center of a spherical scatterer of radius r, which could have caused this scattering. Altogether, the continuous-time Markovian flight trajectory is written as

$$Y_j(t) = Y_{j,k} + (t - \theta_{j,k})U_{j,k+1} \qquad \text{for} \quad t \in [\theta_{j,k}, \theta_{j,k+1}).$$

Note that

$$\{\theta_{j,k} : k \geq 0\} \subseteq \{\tau_{j,k} : k \geq 0\} \cup \{\widetilde{\theta}_{j,k} : k \geq 0\}.$$

This coupling between Lorentz trajectories and Markovian flight processes has the same joint distribution as the one presented in [2]. However, it is realized in a different way. While in [2] first we constructed the Markovian flight process Y and conditionally on this we constructed the coupled Lorentz exploration process X, here we perform this in reverse order: first, we realize the N Lorentz exploration processes $X = \{X_1, \ldots, X_N\}$ and given these, we realize the N independent Markovian flight processes $Y = \{Y_1, \ldots, Y_N\}$ coupled to them.

2.4. Control of Tightness of the Coupling

We quantify the tightness of the coupling.

The relevant filtrations are

$$\begin{aligned} \mathcal{F}_t^X &:= \sigma(\{X_j(s) : 1 \leq j \leq N,\ 0 \leq s \leq t\}), \\ \mathcal{F}_t^Y &:= \sigma(\{Y_j(s) : 1 \leq j \leq N,\ 0 \leq s \leq t\}), \\ \mathcal{F}_t^{X,Y} &:= \mathcal{F}_t^X \vee \mathcal{F}_t^Y. \end{aligned}$$

Next, we define some relevant stopping times, indicating explicitly the filtration with respect to which they are adapted

$$\begin{aligned} &\sigma_1 := \min\{\tau_{j,k} : a_{j,k} = 0\} && \text{stopping time with respect to } \mathcal{F}_t^X, \\ &\sigma_2 := \min\{\theta_{j,l} : b_{j,l} = 1\} && \text{stopping time with respect to } \mathcal{F}_t^{X,Y}, \\ &\sigma_3 := \inf\{t > 0 : \min\{\left|Y_j(t) - Y'_{i,k}\right| : \theta_{i,k} < t\} < r\} && \text{stopping time with respect to } \mathcal{F}_t^Y, \\ &\sigma_4 := \min\{\theta_{i,k} : \inf\{\left|Y_j(s) - Y'_{i,k}\right| : 0 \leq s \leq \theta_{i,k}\} < r\} && \text{stopping time with respect to } \mathcal{F}_t^Y, \\ &\sigma\ := \inf\{t : X(t) \neq Y(t)\} = \min\{\sigma_1, \sigma_2\} && \text{stopping time with respect to } \mathcal{F}_t^{X,Y}. \end{aligned}$$

In plain words:

- σ_1 is the first time an already explored scatterer is re-encountered by one of the N Lorentz particles. We call it the time of the first recollision. This is a stopping time with respect to the filtration $\mathcal{F}_t^X$.
- σ_2 is the first time when in the construction of the Markovian flight processes a compensating scattering occurs. We call it the time of the first shadowed scattering. This is a stopping time with respect to the largest filtration $\mathcal{F}_t^{X,Y}$.
- σ_3 is the first time when a Markovian flight trajectory encounters a virtual scatterer which would have caused an earlier scattering event of one of the Markovian flight processes. This is a stopping time with respect to the filtration $\mathcal{F}_t^Y$.
- σ_4 is the first time a scattering of one of the Markovian flight processes happens within the r-neighborhood of the union of the past trajectories of all flight processes. (This kind of event is mechanically inconsistent.) This is a stopping time with respect to the filtration $\mathcal{F}_t^Y$.
- σ is the time of the first mismatch between the Lorentz trajectories $X(t)$ and the coupled Markovian flight trajectories $Y(t)$. This is (a priori) a stopping time with respect to the largest filtration $\mathcal{F}_t^{X,Y}$.

Although these are stopping times with respect to different filtrations, it clearly follows from the construction of the coupling that

$$\sigma_1 \mathbb{1}\{\sigma_1 < \sigma_2\} = \sigma_3 \mathbb{1}\{\sigma_3 < \sigma_4\} \qquad \text{and} \qquad \sigma_2 \mathbb{1}\{\sigma_2 < \sigma_1\} = \sigma_4 \mathbb{1}\{\sigma_4 < \sigma_3\}.$$

Hence, $\min\{\sigma_1, \sigma_2\} = \min\{\sigma_3, \sigma_4\}$ and thus, in fact

$$\sigma = \min\{\sigma_3, \sigma_4\}. \tag{9}$$

Although by definition σ is a priori adapted to the joint filtration $\mathcal{F}_t^{X,Y}$, due to the particularities of the coupling construction, according to (9), it is actually a stopping time with respect to the filtration of the Markovian flight trajectories $\mathcal{F}_t^Y$, which makes it suitable to purely probabilistic control. In what follows, we use the expression (9) as the definition of the first mismatch time σ.

Proposition 1. *There exists an absolute constant $C < \infty$ such that for any $r > 0$, $N, T < \infty$ obeying* (8), *the following bound holds*

$$\mathbf{P}(\sigma < T) \leq Cr(NT + N^2 w^{-1}), \tag{10}$$

where

$$w := 2 \min_{1 \leq i < j \leq N} \arcsin \sqrt{(1 - v_i \cdot v_j)/2} \tag{11}$$

is the minimum angle between any two of the starting velocities.

Proof. Let for $1 \leq i \leq N$, respectively, for $1 \leq i \neq j \leq N$

$$A_i := \{ \min\{ |Y_i(t) - Y_{i,k}| \, : \, 0 < \theta_{i,k} < T, \;\; t \in (0, \theta_{i,k-1}) \cup (\theta_{i,k+1}, T) \} < 2r \} \tag{12}$$

$$B_{i,j} := \{ \min\{ |Y_i(t) - Y_{j,k}| \, : \, 0 < \theta_{j,k} < T, \;\; 0 < t < T \} < 2r \} \tag{13}$$

Obviously,

$$\{\min\{\sigma_3, \sigma_4\} < T\} \subseteq \Big(\bigcup_{1\le i\le N} A_i\Big)\bigcup\Big(\bigcup_{1\le i\ne j\le N} B_{i,j}\Big). \tag{14}$$

By careful application of the Green function estimates of Section 3 in [2], we obtain the bounds

$$\mathbf{P}(A_i) \le CrT, \tag{15}$$

$$\mathbf{P}(B_{i,j}) \le Crw^{-1}, \tag{16}$$

with some universal constant $C < \infty$.

The bound (15) is explicitly stated in Corollary 1 of Lemma 4 (on page 608) of [2]. We do not repeat that proof here. When proving the bound (16), one has to take into account that the directions of the first flights of Y_i and Y_j are deterministic, v_i, respectively, v_j, and the angle between these two directions determines the probability of interference between the two trajectories during the first free flights. Otherwise, the details of the proof of (16) are very similar to those in [2] but not quite directly quotable from there. We provide these details in the Appendix A.

Finally, (10) follows from (14)–(16) by a straightforward union bound. □

3. Proof of Theorem 3

The clue to the proof is replacing averaging with respect to the random initial velocity in the quenched (typical, almost surely) environment by a strong law of large numbers applied to sufficiently many annealed sampled trajectories, which by the coupling construction are (with sufficiently high probability) identical with i.i.d. Markovian flight trajectories. The subtleties of this "replacement procedure" are detailed in the present section. The main technical ingredients are the Green function estimates (15) and (16) of Proposition A1.

Triangular Array of Processes

Let now $\varepsilon_n \to 0$, $r_n = \varepsilon_n^{d/(d-1)}$, $T_n \to \infty$, $\beta_n \in (0,1]$ be as in (5), and choose an increasing sequence N_n such that

$$(\log n)^{-1} N_n \to \infty \tag{17}$$

and the stronger summability

$$\sum_n \Big(N_n r_n T_n + N_n^2 \big(r_n \beta_n^{-1}\big)^{(d-1)/d}\Big) < \infty \tag{18}$$

still holds. (Given (5), this can be performed.)

Assume that the probability space $(\Omega, \mathcal{F}, \mathbf{P})$ supports a *triangular array* of processes

$$\{\{(X_{n,j}(\cdot), Y_{n,j}(\cdot)) : \quad 1 \le j \le N_n\} : n \ge 1\}$$

row-wise constructed as in Section 2, with parameters ε_n, r_n, β_n, and with i.i.d. initial velocities

$$v_{n,j} \sim \texttt{UNI}(B_n), \qquad 1 \le j \le N_n, \tag{19}$$

which are also independent of all other randomness in the row.

Note the following:

- The row-wise construction, and thus the joint distribution of $\{ (X_{n,j}(\cdot), Y_{n,j}(\cdot)) : 1 \leq j \leq N_n \}$ is prescribed.
- The PPP $\varpi_n := \varpi_{\varepsilon_n}$ are obtained by rescaling *the same realization* of the PPP ϖ. This makes the sequence of couplings *quenched*.
- The joint distribution of the probabilistic ingredients—a part of ϖ—in different rows is irrelevant.

Lemma 1. *Let the sequence $N_n \in \mathbb{N}$ be as in (17) and $\{ \{\Upsilon_{n,j} : 1 \leq j \leq N_n \} : n \geq 1 \}$, a jointly defined triangular array of real valued, uniformly bounded, row-wise i.i.d. zero-mean random variables:*

$$\mathbf{P}(|\Upsilon_{n,j}| \leq M) = 1, \qquad \mathbf{E}(\Upsilon_{n,j}) = 0.$$

Then,

$$\mathbf{P}\big(\lim_{n\to\infty} N_n^{-1} \sum_{j=1}^{N_n} \Upsilon_{n,j} \to 0 \big) = 1.$$

Proof. This is a triangular array version of Borel's SLLN, and a direct (and straightforward) consequence of Hoeffding's inequality and the Borel–Cantelli lemma. By Hoeffding's inequality, for any $\delta > 0$

$$\mathbf{P}\big(\pm N_n^{-1} \sum_{j=1}^{N_n} \Upsilon_{n,j} > \delta \big) \leq e^{-\delta^2 N_n/(2M^2)}.$$

Hence, due to (17) and Borel–Cantelli, for any $\delta > 0$

$$\mathbf{P}\big(\overline{\lim_{n\to\infty}} \pm N_n^{-1} \sum_{j=1}^{N_n} \Upsilon_{n,j} > \delta \big) = 0.$$

□

Proposition 2. *Almost surely, for any $F \in \mathcal{C}_0(\mathcal{C})$,*

$$\lim_{n\to\infty} \Big(N_n^{-1} \sum_{j=1}^{n} F(T_n^{-1/2} Y_{n,j}(T_n \cdot)) - \mathbf{E}\big(F(T_n^{-1/2} Y_{n,1}(T_n \cdot))\big) \Big) = 0 \tag{20}$$

$$\lim_{n\to\infty} \Big(N_n^{-1} \sum_{j=1}^{n} F(T_n^{-1/2} X_{n,j}(T_n \cdot)) - \mathbf{E}_\varpi\big(F(T_n^{-1/2} X_{n,1}(T_n \cdot))\big) \Big) = 0 \tag{21}$$

Proof. The same statement with "for any $F \in \mathcal{C}_0(\mathcal{C})$, almost surely" follows from Lemma 1, noting that the triangular array of *annealed* random variables

$$\Upsilon_{n,j} := F(T_n^{-1/2} Y_{n,j}(T_n \cdot)) - \mathbf{E}\big(F(T_n^{-1/2} Y_{n,j}(T_n \cdot))\big), \qquad 1 \leq j \leq N_n, \quad n \geq 1$$

respectively, for almost all realizations of ϖ, the triangular array of *quenched* random variables

$$\widetilde{\Upsilon}_{n,j,\varpi} := F(T_n^{-1/2} X_{n,j}(T_n \cdot)) - \mathbf{E}_\varpi\big(F(T_n^{-1/2} X_{n,j}(T_n \cdot))\big), \qquad 1 \leq j \leq N_n, \quad n \geq 1$$

meet the conditions of the lemma.

Going from "for any $F \in \mathcal{C}_0(\mathcal{C})$, almost surely" to "almost surely, for any $F \in \mathcal{C}_0(\mathcal{C})$" we rely on separability of the Banach space $(\mathcal{C}_0(\mathcal{C}), \|\cdot\|_\infty)$. □

Proposition 3. *For any $F \in \mathcal{C}_0(\mathcal{C})$,*

$$\lim_{n\to\infty} \mathbf{E}\big(F(T_n^{-1/2} Y_{n,1}(T_n \cdot))\big) = \mathbf{E}\big(W(\cdot)\big)\big). \tag{22}$$

Proof. This is Donsker's theorem. □

Proposition 4.

$$\mathbf{P}\big(\max\{n : \sigma_n < T_n\} < \infty\big) = 1. \tag{23}$$

That is, almost surely, for all but finitely many n

$$X_{n,j}(t) = Y_{n,j}(t), \quad 1 \le j \le N_n, \quad 0 \le t \le T_n. \tag{24}$$

Proof. Let

$$\alpha_n := r_n^{1/d} \beta_n^{(d-1)/d}.$$

With this choice

$$r_n \alpha_n^{-1} = (\alpha_n \beta_n^{-1})^{d-1} = (r_n \beta_n^{-1})^{(d-1)/d}$$

As in (11), denote

$$w_n := 2 \min_{1\le i<j\le N_n} \arcsin \sqrt{(1 - v_{n,i} \cdot v_{n,j})/2}$$

the minimum angle between any two of the starting velocities. Then, obviously

$$\mathbf{P}(\sigma_n < T_n) \le \mathbf{P}(w_n < \alpha_n) + \mathbf{P}(\{\sigma_n < T_n\} \cap \{w_n \ge \alpha_n\}).$$

Recall (6) and (19). For $1 \le i < j \le N_n$, we have from elementary geometry

$$\mathbf{P}\big(\arcsin \sqrt{(1 - v_{n,i} \cdot v_{n,j})/2} < \alpha_n\big) < C(\alpha_n \beta_n^{-1})^{d-1},$$

and hence by a union bound

$$\mathbf{P}(w_n < \alpha_n) \le C N_n^2 (\alpha_n \beta_n^{-1})^{d-1}.$$

On the other hand, by the stopping time bound (10) of Proposition 1,

$$\mathbf{P}(\{\sigma_n < T_n\} \cap \{w_n \ge \alpha_n\}) \le C(N_n r_n T_n + N_n^2 r_n \alpha_n^{-1}).$$

Putting these together,

$$\mathbf{P}(\sigma_n < T_n) \le C(N_n r_n T_n + N_n^2 (r_n \beta_n^{-1})^{(d-1)/d}).$$

The claim of Proposition 4 follows from Borel–Cantelli, using (18). □

Finally, putting together (21), (20) of Proposition 2, (22) of Proposition 3 and (23)/(24) of Proposition 4, we obtain that assuming (5), for almost all realizations of the PPP ϖ, for any $F \in \mathcal{C}_0(\mathcal{C})$,

$$\lim_{n\to\infty} \mathbf{E}_{\varpi}\big(F(T_n^{-1/2}X_{n,1}(T_n\cdot))\big) = \mathbf{E}\big(F(W(\cdot))\big),$$

which concludes the proof of Theorem 3.

Funding: This work was supported by the grant no. K-143468 of the Hungarian National Research, Development and Innovation Office (NKFIH).

Institutional Review Board Statement: Not applicable.

Data Availability Statement: Data is contained within the article.

Acknowledgments: I thank Pietro Caputo and Justin Salez for drawing my attention to their paper [13]. I also thank two anonymous reviewers for their thoughtful comments on presentation and advice for improvements.

Conflicts of Interest: The author declares no conflicts of interest.

Appendix A. Proof of (16)

Recall that Y_i and Y_j are two independent Markovian flight processes with deterministic initial velocities $v_i, v_j \in S^{d-1}$ closing an angle $2\arcsin\sqrt{1 - v_i \cdot v_j} > w$. Since w is the minimum of angles between any pair of $N \gg 1$ different directions in $\mathbb{R}^d$, we can assume that $0 < w < \pi/6$ and thus $\sin w > w/2$.

We break up the right-hand side of (13) as

$$B_{i,j} = B_I \cup B_{II} \cup B_{III} \cup B_{IV},$$

where

$$B_I := \{\min_{0<t<\theta_{i,1}\wedge T} |Y_i(t) - Y_{j,1}| < 2r,\ \theta_{j,1} < T\} \subseteq \{\min_{0<t<\theta_{i,1}} |Y_i(t) - Y_{j,1}| < 2r\} =: \widetilde{B}_I$$

$$B_{II} := \{\min_{\substack{0<t<\theta_{i,1}\wedge T\\ \theta_{j,1}<\theta_{j,k}<T}} \left|Y_i(t) - Y_{j,k}\right| < 2r\} \subseteq \{\min_{\substack{0<t<\theta_{i,1}\\ 2\le k<\infty}} \left|Y_i(t) - Y_{j,k}\right| < 2r\} =: \widetilde{B}_{II}$$

$$B_{III} := \{\min_{\theta_{i,1}<t<T} |Y_i(t) - Y_{j,1}| < 2r,\ \theta_{j,1} < T\} \subseteq \{\min_{\theta_{i,1}\le t<\infty} |Y_i(t) - Y_{j,1}| < 2r\} =: \widetilde{B}_{III}$$

$$B_{IV} := \{\min_{\substack{\theta_{i,1}<t<T\\ \theta_{j,1}<\theta_{j,k}<T}} \left|Y_i(t) - Y_{j,k}\right| < 2r\}$$

and bound in turn the probabilities of these events.

I: Obviously

$$\widetilde{B}_I \subseteq \{\theta_{j,1} < 4rw^{-1}\},$$

and hence, since $\theta_{j,1} \sim \mathtt{EXP}(1)$,

$$\mathbf{P}(B_I) \le \mathbf{P}(\widetilde{B}_I) \le Crw^{-1}. \tag{A1}$$

To estimate the probabilities of the events $\widetilde{B}_{II}, \widetilde{B}_{III}, \widetilde{B}_{IV}$, first note that the processes

$$t \mapsto \widetilde{Y}_i(t) := Y_i(\theta_{i,1} + t) - Y_{i,1}, \qquad t \mapsto \widetilde{Y}_j(t) := Y_j(\theta_{j,1} + t) - Y_{j,1}, \qquad t \ge 0,$$

are distributed as a Markovian process flight $t \mapsto Y(t)$, $t \geq 0$, with $\texttt{UNI}(S^{d-1})$-distributed initial velocity. They are independent between them and also independent of the random variables $\theta_{i,1}, \theta_{j,1}, Y_{i,1}, Y_{j,1}$.

We rely on the following Green function estimates explicitly stated in [2].

Proposition A1. *Let $t \mapsto \widetilde{Y}(t)$, $t > 0$ be a Markovian flight process with initial position $\widetilde{Y}(0) = 0$ and $\texttt{UNI}(S^{d-1})$-distributed initial velocity. Denote by $\widetilde{Y}_k$, $k \geq 1$, its position at the successive scattering events. Let $A \subset \mathbb{R}^d$ be open bounded. Then, the following bounds hold:*

$$\mathbf{P}(\{k > 0 : \widetilde{Y}_k \in A\} \neq \emptyset) \leq \mathbf{E}\Big(\Big|\{k > 0 : \widetilde{Y}_k \in A\}\Big|\Big) \leq \int_A \gamma(x)\, dx, \tag{A2}$$

$$\mathbf{P}(\{t > 0 : \widetilde{Y}(t) \in A\} \neq \emptyset) \leq r^{-1}\mathbf{E}\Big(\Big|\{t > 0 : \widetilde{Y}(t) \in A_r\}\Big|\Big) \leq r^{-1} \int_{A_r} \gamma(x)\, dx, \tag{A3}$$

where $\gamma : \mathbb{R}^d \to \mathbb{R}_+$,

$$\gamma(x) := C(|x|^{-d+1} + |x|^{-d+2})$$

with a suitable $C < \infty$, and $A_r := \{x \in \mathbb{R}^d : \operatorname{dist}(x, A) < r\}$.

II: Conditioning on $\theta_{i,1}$ and using (A2) we obviously obtain

$$\begin{aligned}
\mathbf{P}(\widetilde{B}_{II}) &\leq \mathbf{E}\Big(\sup_{\substack{x\in\mathbb{R}^d \\ v\in S^{d-1}}} \mathbf{P}\Big(\min_{\substack{0<t<\theta_{i,1} \\ 1\leq k<\infty}} \Big|x + tv - \widetilde{Y}_k\Big| < 2r \mid \theta_{i,1}\Big)\Big) \\
&\leq \mathbf{E}\Big(\sup_{\substack{x\in\mathbb{R}^d \\ v\in S^{d-1}}} \int_{\mathbb{R}^d} \gamma(y)\mathbb{1}\{ \min_{0<t<\theta_{i,1}} |x + vt - y| < 2r\}\, dy\Big) \\
&= \int_0^\infty e^{-s} \int_{\mathbb{R}^d} \gamma(y)\mathbb{1}\{ \min_{-s/2<t<s/2} |vt - y| < 2r\}\, dy\, ds \qquad (v \in S^{d-1}).
\end{aligned}$$

In the last step, we use the fact that the function $y \mapsto \gamma(y)$ is rotation invariant, radially decreasing, and $\theta_{i,1} \sim \texttt{EXP}(1)$. Finally, by straightforward computations

$$\mathbf{P}(B_{II}) \leq \mathbf{P}(\widetilde{B}_{II}) \leq Cr. \tag{A4}$$

III: Now we condition on $Z := Y_{i,1} - Y_{j_1}$ and use (A3) to obtain

$$\begin{aligned}
\mathbf{P}(\widetilde{B}_{III}) &= \mathbf{E}(\mathbf{P}(\min_{0<t<\infty} \Big|Z - \widetilde{Y}(t))\Big| < 2r \mid Z)) \\
&\leq r^{-1}\mathbf{E}\Big(\int_{\mathbb{R}^d} \gamma(y)\mathbb{1}\{|Z - y| < 3r\}\, dy\Big) \\
&\leq r^{-1} \int_0^\infty e^{-s} \int_{\mathbb{R}^d} \gamma(y)\mathbb{1}\{|sv - y| < 3r\}\, dy\, ds \qquad (v \in S^{d-1}).
\end{aligned}$$

In the last step, we use again the fact that the function $y \mapsto \gamma(y)$ is rotation invariant, radially decreasing, and also

$$|Z| = \big|v_i\theta_{i,1} - v_j\theta_{j,1}\big| \geq \big|\theta_{i,1} - \theta_{j,1}\big| \sim \texttt{EXP}(1).$$

Finally, by straightforward computations

$$\mathbf{P}(B_{III}) \leq \mathbf{P}(\widetilde{B}_{III}) \leq Cr. \tag{A5}$$

IV: We proceed similarly. This time, we have to use both bounds (A2) and (A3) of Proposition A1. However, noting that in dimensions $d < 5$, when estimating $\mathbf{P}(B_{IV})$, we cannot extend the integrals to the whole $\mathbb{R}^d$. In dimensions $d = 3$ and $d = 4$, we will see dependence on T in the upper bound:

$$\begin{aligned}
\mathbf{P}(B_{IV}) &\leq r^{-1} \sup_{u \in \mathbb{R}^d} \int_{\mathbb{R}^d} \int_{\mathbb{R}^d} \gamma(x) \mathbb{1}\{|x| < T\} \gamma(y) \mathbb{1}\{|y| < T\} \mathbb{1}\{|(x-u)-(y+u)| < 3r\} dx dy \\
&\leq C r^{-1-d} \sup_{u \in \mathbb{R}^d} \int_{\mathbb{R}^d} \int_{\mathbb{R}^d} \gamma(x) \mathbb{1}\{|x| < T\} \gamma(y) \mathbb{1}\{|y| < T\} \times \\
&\qquad \Big(\int_{\mathbb{R}^d} \mathbb{1}\{|x-(z+u)| < 3r\} \mathbb{1}\{|y-(z-u)| < 3r\}\, dz \Big) dx dy \\
&= C r^{-1-d} \sup_{u \in \mathbb{R}^d} \int_{\mathbb{R}^d} \Big(\int_{\mathbb{R}^d} \gamma(x) \mathbb{1}\{|x| < T\} \mathbb{1}\{|x-(z+u)| < 3r\}\, dx \Big) \times \\
&\qquad \Big(\int_{\mathbb{R}^d} \gamma(y) \mathbb{1}\{|y| < T\} \mathbb{1}\{|y-(z-u)| < 3r\}\, dy \Big)\, dz \\
&\leq C r^{-1-d} \int_{\mathbb{R}^d} \Big(\int_{\mathbb{R}^d} \gamma(x) \mathbb{1}\{|x| < T\} \mathbb{1}\{|x-z| < 3r\}\, dx \Big)^2 dz \\
&\leq C r + C r^{d-1} \big(\mathbb{1}\{d=3\} T + \mathbb{1}\{d=4\} \log T + \mathbb{1}\{d \geq 5\} \big).
\end{aligned}$$

The last step follows from straightforward computations. Finally, using (8), we obtain

$$\mathbf{P}(B_{IV}) \leq C r. \tag{A6}$$

Putting together (A1) and (A4)–(A6), we obtain (16). □

References

Révész, P. *Random Walk in Random and Non-Random Environment*, 2nd ed.; World Scientific: Singapore, 2005.

Lutsko, C.; Tóth, B. Invariance principle for the random Lorentz gas—Beyond the Boltzmann-Grad limit. *Commun. Math. Phys.* **2020**, *379*, 589–632. [CrossRef]

Whitt, W. Weak convergence of probability measures on the function space $C[0, \infty)$. *Ann. Math. Statist.* **1970**, *41*, 939–944. [CrossRef]

Billingsley, P. *Convergence of Probability Measures*; Wiley: New York, NY, USA, 1968.

Stone, C. Weak convergence of stochastic processes defined on a semi-infinite time interval. *Proc. Am. Math. Soc.* **1963**, *14*, 694–696. [CrossRef]

Spohn, H. *Large Scale Dynamics of Interacting Particles*; Springer: Berlin/Heidelberg, Germany, 1991.

Gallavotti, G. Rigorous theory of the Boltzmann equation in the Lorentz gas. *Nota Interna Univ. Roma* **1970**, *358*.

Gallavotti, G. *Statistical Mechanics. A Short Treatise*; Theoretical and Mathematical Physics Series; Springer: Berlin, Germany, 1999.

Spohn, H. The Lorentz process converges to a random flight process. *Comm. Math. Phys.* **1978**, *60*, 277–290. [CrossRef]

Boldrighini, C.; Bunimovich, L.A.; Sinai, Y.G. On the Boltzmann equation for the Lorentz gas. *J. Stat. Phys.* **1983**, *32*, 477–501.

Lutsko, C.; Tóth, B. Invariance principle for the random Wind-Tree Process. *Ann. Henri Poincaré* **2021**, *22*, 3357–3389. [CrossRef]

Lutsko, C.; Tóth, B. Diffusion of the random Lorentz process in a magnetic field. *arXiv* **2024**, arXiv:2411.03984.

Bordenave, C.; Caputo, P.; Salez, J. Random walk on sparse random digraphs. *Probab. Theory Relat. Fields* **2018**, *170*, 933–960. [CrossRef]

MDPI AG
Grosspeteranlage 5
4052 Basel
Switzerland
Tel.: +41 61 683 77 34

Entropy Editorial Office
E-mail: entropy@mdpi.com
www.mdpi.com/journal/entropy

www.ingramcontent.com/pod-product-compliance
Lightning Source LLC
Chambersburg PA
CBHW041343210926
51850CB00013B/2976
9783725845552